The Revelations of Saint Birgitta

EDITED FROM THE GARRETT MS.
PRINCETON UNIVERSITY LIBRARY
DEPOSIT 1397

EARLY ENGLISH TEXT SOCIETY

Original Series, No. 178

1929 (for 1928)

(Princeton University Library Deposit 1397)
Garrett MS. fol. 2 b

The Revelations of Saint Birgitta

EDITED FROM THE FIFTEENTH-CENTURY MS. IN
THE GARRETT COLLECTION IN THE LIBRARY OF
PRINCETON UNIVERSITY

BY

WILLIAM PATTERSON CUMMING, Ph.D.

LONDON:
PUBLISHED FOR THE EARLY ENGLISH TEXT SOCIETY
BY HUMPHREY MILFORD, OXFORD UNIVERSITY PRESS
AMEN HOUSE, E.C.
1929

KRAUS REPRINT
Millwood, N.Y.
1987

UNIVERSITY PRESS

Great Clarendon Street, Oxford OX2 6DP
United Kingdom

Oxford University Press is a department of the University of Oxford.
It furthers the University's objective of excellence in research, scholarship,
and education by publishing worldwide. Oxford is a registered trade mark of
Oxford University Press in the UK and in certain other countries

© The Early English Text Society 1929

The moral rights of the authors have been asserted

Database right Oxford University Press (maker)

First Edition published in 1929

All rights reserved. No part of this publication may be reproduced,
stored in a retrieval system, or transmitted, in any form or by any means,
without the prior permission in writing of Oxford University Press,
or as expressly permitted by law, or under terms agreed with the appropriate
reprographics rights organization. Enquiries concerning reproduction
outside the scope of the above should be sent to the Rights Department,
Oxford University Press, at the address above

You must not circulate this book in any other form
and you must impose this same condition on any acquirer

Published in the United States of America by Oxford University Press
198 Madison Avenue, New York, NY 10016, United States of America

British Library Cataloguing in Publication Data
Data available

Library of Congress Cataloging in Publication Data
Data available

Original Series, 178

ISBN 978-0-85-991914-2

TO MY PARENTS

PREFACE

I WISH to express my grateful appreciation for the invaluable advice and encouragement of Professor Gordon Hall Gerould of Princeton University throughout the editing of this manuscript. My thanks are also due to Dr. E. C. Richardson, Director of Princeton University Library, and to Mr. S. H. Leach, former Reference Librarian of Princeton University Library, who first called my attention to the Garrett manuscript. This work was originally submitted to the English Department of Princeton University in fulfilment of the partial requirement for the Doctor of Philosophy degree; certain sections of the original work have been omitted and the Introduction has been re-written.

The especial acknowledgement of the Early English Text Society, as well as of the editor, is due to Mr. Walter Roesler of New York City for his generous gift to the Society of a sum to assist in the cost of publishing this work.

W. P. C.

DAVIDSON,
    NORTH CAROLINA,
        February, 1929.

CONTENTS

	PAGE
FACSIMILE	facing Title-page
PREFACE	vii
TABLE OF ABBREVIATIONS	x

INTRODUCTION

PART I. MANUSCRIPT xi
   A. *Description of the Manuscript* xi
   B. *Date* xiii
      1. *Language* xiii
      2. *Scribes* xv
   C. *Other English Manuscripts* xvi
   D. *Text of the Garrett Manuscript* xxi

PART II. SAINT BIRGITTA xxiii
   A. *Life of Saint Birgitta* xxiii
   B. *Revelations of Saint Birgitta* xxvii
   C. *Revelations of Saint Birgitta in England in the Fifteenth Century* xxix

PART III. METHOD OF TRANSCRIPTION . . . xxxix

TEXT 1–124

NOTES 125–129

GLOSSARY 131–135

TABLE OF ABBREVIATIONS

A.S. = *Acta Sanctorum*, quotquot toto coluntur, Bruxellis & Parisiis, October, tom. iv, Birgitta.

Durantus = *Revelationes Sanctae Birgittae*, Olim a Card. Turrecremata recognitae & approbatae, & a Consaluo Duranto Episcopo Ferettrano notis illustratae, & in duos Tomos distributae. Romae, apud Ludouicum Grignanum, 1628.

Klemming = *Heliga Birgittas Uppenbarelser*, G. E. Klemming, Svenska Fornskrift-Sällskapet, vols. i-v, Stockholm, 1857-64.

S.R.S. = *Scriptores Rerum Suecicarum Medii Aevi*, vols. i-iii, edited by E. M. Fant, E. G. Geijer, I. H. Schröder, and C. Annerstedt, Upsala, 1818-76.

Westman = *Birgitta-Studier*, K. B. Westman, *Uppsala Universitets Årsskrift*, Bd. i, Upsala, 1911, pp. 1-304.

Wyld = *A History of Modern Colloquial English*, H. C. Wyld, London, 1920.

INTRODUCTION

PART I. MANUSCRIPT

A. *Description of the Manuscript*

Princeton University Library Deposit 1397, a M.E. manuscript containing translations from the revelations of Saint Birgitta, is the property of Mr. Robert Garrett, Baltimore, Maryland, U.S.A.

The manuscript has a cover of dark leather bound on boards. The dimensions of the binding are 23·7 cm. × 17·0 cm. The leather is gold tooled, with a gold line border, and with an oval-shaped medallion (on each cover) between the initials B and S. The medallions have the same design; each represents the crucifixion, with two figures standing on either side of the cross, and the sun, moon, and stars above. On the back of the binding, printed in later type, is the erroneous title, *Life of S. Brigit*.

There are four paper fly-leaves at the beginning, and six at the end, of the volume, which are probably contemporary with the binding. On the inside of the front cover are pencilled in different hands 'Revelations of St. Bridgitt', '7313', and 'R. G. Oct. 1905'.[1] The first and second fly-leaves are mutilated; the third has 'Old No. 894' in pencil. The fourth fly-leaf, recto, has the stamp of a lion rampant above 'Sir T[homas] P[hillips], Middle Hill', with '1366' written below in pencil. The fourth fly-leaf, verso, has 'Saint Brigitt' and 'Phillipps MS. 1366' in ink; the first vellum leaf also has 'Phillipps MS. 1366' in ink.

The manuscript has seventy-seven vellum leaves, 22·7 cm. × 16·5 cm.[2] The nine gatherings vary in length; the first gathering has nine leaves, the next three ten leaves, the next

---

[1] Bought by Robert Garrett in October 1905.

[2] The vellum used in the manuscript is not of very good quality. There are six holes within the text columns, and some leaves have been made by pasting together pieces of vellum.

three eight leaves, and the last two only seven leaves.¹ Most of the signatures were lost when the manuscript was bound. The remaining signatures, as well as all the catchwords, are noted in the text. The text, which usually runs over the four marginal lines that are drawn on every page, averages 17·3 cm. × 11·5 cm. The text shows the handwriting of two scribes, both of whom wrote in the cursive bookhand of the middle of the fifteenth century. The first hand runs to leaf 63a, most of which, as well as all of leaf 63b, is left vacant. The second hand begins at the top of leaf 64a and continues to the end. The chapter headings and quotations from the Vulgate are rubricated; the marginal glosses and capitals in the text of the second scribe are also frequently rubricated. The initial letters of each revelation throughout the manuscript are two lines in height and coloured in blue. The lines average thirty-one to the page.

There are no colophons or marginal notes to give a clue as to the names of the scribes or the early history of the manuscript. The manuscript is not listed in the Syon Monastery catalogue.² However, the catalogue is for the men's library, and this manuscript may have been a copy of a translation for the nuns.³ The binding is of the late sixteenth or early seventeenth century;⁴ I have been unable to identify the medal-

[1] Originally, the last gathering had eight leaves; see the note to line 123/30 of the text.
[2] Mary Bateson, *Catalogue of the Library of Syon Monastery*, Cambridge University Press, 1898, pp. 107-8, 115. Syon Monastery is the only monastery of the Birgittine order in England of which we have record. There are seven volumes of Birgitta's works listed in the catalogue, apparently all in Latin (Bateson, *op. cit.*, p. ix).
[3] It is probable that the nuns' library had a translation of the revelations. *The Myroure of Our Lady* (E.E.T.S., E.S., xix) and the *Martilogue* (*ibid.*, p. xlvi) were both Englished for the nuns; and we know that they had other books translated for them because of their inability to understand Latin (Bateson, *op. cit.*, p. ix, note 1, and p. xiv).
[4] The water-marks in the fly-leaves put an *a quo* limit to the binding of 1578. The water-mark is a double cross with two opposed C's under a crown. There is a rather complicated countermark. C. M. Briquet (*Les Filigranes*, Hiersemann, Leipzig, 1923, vol. ii, p. 493 and water marks 9320 ff.) says that the opposed C embracing the crowned cross of Lorraine originated in 1578; this mark became very common, and countermarks were used for more complete identification.

The Manuscript

lion.[1] The manuscript was finally acquired by Sir Thomas Phillipps; it was sold at the auction of part of his library in June, 1896.[2] In October, 1905, Mr. Robert Garrett, the present owner, bought the volume, and later placed it in the Princeton University Library as a loan deposit.[3]

B. Date.

1. *Language.* Both scribes write in the London dialect of the fifteenth century. The frequent use by the scribes of *her, hyr, hir,* for the third person plural possessive pronoun indicates that the manuscript was written before 1475.[4] The first scribe has a very few scattered forms in *ther*; the second scribe uses *her,* but also *their, thair,* and especially *thaire.* Both scribes use *hem,* but the second also writes *thaym, them,* and especially *thaim.* The regular use of the plural form *schulle(n)* by the second scribe points to a date some years before 1475.[5] The use of personal pronouns and verbal endings coincides in many important respects with the language of Gregory's *Chronicle.* William Gregory, who died in 1467, wrote the genuine London English of his day.[6] The similarity in

---

[1] The late date of the binding seems to preclude the possibility of the *B S* standing for Bibliotheca Syonis, nor do the seals of the monastery which I have seen bear the device (G. M. Aungier, *History and Antiquities of Syon Monastery,* 1840, plate opposite p. 106).

[2] Phillipps Sales Catalogue, 10–17 June 1896, p. 24. The description is an amusing combination of fact and misinformation:
'(No.) 141 BRIGIT. THE LYFE AND REVELATIONS OF SEYNTE BRIGITTE, *fine manuscript of the fourteenth century, written in old English* ON VELLUM, *with capitals coloured and titles rubricated, in first-rate preservation, calf* 154 pages, 4to, XIV CENT. The binding on both sides of the volume is impressed with a representation of the Crucifixion, gilt, with the initials B.S. on either side. A very valuable and probably unique manuscript.'
In the Princeton University Library copy of the catalogue, which has a list of the purchasers and the auction prices, the hand has here written 'Quaritch, 88.—.—.' in the margin.

[3] Mr. G. M. Peck of the Princeton University Library informs me that the date of accession was 12 February 1906.

[4] H. C. Wyld, *A History of Modern Colloquial English,* London, 1920, p. 327.

[5] *Ibid.,* p. 357.   [6] *Ibid.,* pp. 92–5.

xiv   *Introduction*

language extends to other forms and spellings common in the London dialect of the period. The interchange of *w* and *v*, of which there are several examples in the Garrett MS., is found in the writings of Gregory and other London writers.[1] By the middle of the fifteenth century the prefix of the past participle is chiefly confined to texts showing a Southern provincial influence. However, Gregory and the scribes of the Garrett MS. both use the past participle prefix.[2] The first scribe has a number of Northern or North-Eastern forms;[3]

---

[1] Wyld, p. 292. The Garrett MS. has the interchange of *w* for *v* in *wessell* 72/24, *woyce* 62/30, *wery* 98/4, and of *v* for *w* in *vykked* 21/25, *videw* 38/14. A few other examples of similarities in language may be noted. Gregory and the Garrett MS. have comparatively few *e*-forms for O.E. *y, i,* and these are all known to have been in use in genuine London English: Gregory has *steryd, besely, levyd* (*ibid.*, pp. 92-3); the Garrett MS. has *besyly* 68/5, *besy* 61/29, *besily* 101/18, *steryth* 3/10, *leving* 115/23, *beld* 9/10. The combination *-an* is often written *-on* not only in *londe, stonde, honde,* but also in the unlengthened combination *thonke* (*ibid.*, p. 93). The relative pronoun *who* is occasionally written *ho, hoo, hos,* showing that the *w* was not pronounced (*ibid.*, p. 95). The third person singular present ending of the verb is usually *-eth*, although the first scribe of the Garrett MS. has exceptions in *-es*, and *strenght* 14/17, *plesyt* 23/1, *hat* 30/25, and *punishet* 59/10. In the third person plural the first scribe has the Southern *-eth*, a very few endings in the more typical E.Midl. *-en*, a few *-es* endings, and no ending (cf. *ibid.*, p. 76). With the second scribe *-en* is more frequent. The present part. is regularly *yng(e), ing(e),* but the second scribe occasionally has *eng* (cf. *ibid.*, p. 76). The past part. of weak verbs is usually *-ed(e), id*; but the first scribe occasionally has no ending; *wesh* 17/36, *kepe* 26/15, *translate* 51/32, *devote* 52/8.

[2] Wyld, pp. 95, 342. All occurrences of the prefix in the Garrett MS. are given here: the first scribe, *y-joue* 4/27, *I-gote* 30/18, *I-comme* 38/25, *ishamed* 41/21 (O.E. *gesceomod*), *I-gotte* 50/25, *I-gott* 79/9, *I-yeve* 86/38, 97/31, *I-do* 92/25; the second scribe, *I-done* 121/23, *I-write* 123/4.

[3] *Awn* 36/22, *aune* 87/2, 'own'; *worching* 29/31, 'working' (H. M. Flasdieck, *Forschungen zur Frühzeit der Neuenglischen Schriftsprache,* Teil ii, *Studien zur Englischen Philologie,* Heft lxv, p. 32, ' O dringt in London erst sehr spät und spärlich ein'); *whenched* 8/24, 'quenched', *qwhik* 68/28, *whykke* 20/22, *whyke* 77/1, 'quick'; *whiter* 47/8, 'quitter', 'pus'. *At* 26/105, 48/183, 65/27, is a Northern form of 'that'. The third person singular present indicative occasionally ends in *es, -ys,* which is unusual at this time (Wyld, pp. 332-7): *spekys* 1/19, *callys* 36/19, *stondes* 10/7, *thynkes* 16/3, *betokenes* 18/3, *spekes* 64/22, *despices* 96/35. The *-es* ending for the third person plural present indicative is a Northern form of which there are no contemporary examples found in the genuine London writings (*ibid.*, p. 340); *stondes* 5/7, *sees* 7/21, *profettes* 23/14, *beholdes* 57/13,

The Manuscript

whether these were in the original translation or are due to the present scribe it is very difficult to determine. Northern forms are the exception rather than the rule, and it seems more probable that a Midland translation was copied by a scribe in or from the Northern dialect area.[1]

2. *Scribes.* The first scribe expected the manuscript to end with his *Assint laudes deo.* The heading of the last chapter (see text, 98/1-5) and the discoloration of leaf 63b, which indicates that for a time it was the end of the manuscript, show this. The second scribe, on the other hand, with his more frequent use of the pronominal *their* and *them* forms, the more pointed style in his handwriting, and the increase in flourishes,[2] has characteristics which naturally place him a few years later than the first scribe. The first scribe was probably a transcriber; the frequent omission of single words, the repetition of words and phrases, and other errors bear strong evidence for this view.[3] The second scribe may have translated directly from the Latin. He makes several corrections, and has repetition of a word once.[4] However, the second

---

abydes 62/34, *towches* 63/28. Other unusual or interesting forms which occur in the manuscript will be found in the Glossary.

[1] From the list of brethren in Syon Monastery we know that a few were from Yorkshire; and two of the three bequests of translations of the Revelations which are mentioned in contemporary wills are from Cecily, Duchess of York, and Elizabeth Sywardby of Sywardby in Yorkshire (p. xxxviii, notes 1, 2).

[2] Maunde Thompson, *Introduction to Greek and Latin Palaeography,* Oxford, 1912, p. 554.

[3] A list of passages in the first hand where words or phrases have been omitted, with the corresponding words in the Latin text, follows: *te* 16/36, *ventus* 33/22, *Deum* 36/12, *cogitauit* 39/24, *consilio* 41/2, *& Filii mei* 41/12, *non* 46/16, *Benedictum* 53/10, *quia sentiunt* 55/5, *bitumen* 58/34, *nullum* 60/9, *non* 61/4, *per* 70/31, *Deo* 73/2, *& post* 74/20, *animae* 78/15, *facere* 80/37, the preposition *of* in *Angelum Dei* 84/12, a complete clause 87/34, *me* 89/6, *veniet* 97/33. The scribe seems to have misrendered *maly*[t]*e* as *malyce* 77/28, [f]*rosses* as *throsses* 82/18, and Latin *praedicabam* as *purchesed* 91/2; his eye probably skipped from the first to the second *hauyn* .. *hauyn* 33/26-27, an error which he later rectified. I have not included the repetition of letters made when beginning a new page in the following list of words and phrases which have been repeated: 12/14, 18/9, 21/17, 21/37, 29/26, 30/29, 32/7, 44/5, 66/8, 69/31, 75/21, 80/30, 88/34, 90/1, 94/34.

[4] He repeats *I* 115/35, and makes three corrections: see 99/31, 100/27,

scribe is a much more careful writer than the first, and he may have made an unusually clean copy.

Since the date of the manuscript has to be determined entirely on internal evidence, no exact dating is possible. The first scribe wrote shortly before 1450, while the second scribe probably wrote towards the end of the third quarter of the century.

C. Other English Manuscripts

I

1. *British Museum MS. Julius F. II.* 'The Revelations of S. Bridget, princess of Nerike in Sweden', Bks. I–VII, translated into English; with the Prologue of Matthias, canon of Lincöping. The Prologue begins: 'Wondyr and marvelys are herd in owre cuntre and [*erased* or] in owre land. yt was a mervelous thinge.' A leaf is missing after f. 92, containing Bk. III, middle of ch. 20 to middle of ch. 23; Bk. IV ends at ch. 130; Bk. V includes the Prologue and the 'Expositio et Declaratio' at the end; Bk. VI ends with ch. 109; Bk. VII is complete and ends with ch. 31 on f. 246 b. It is followed immediately by the Epistola Solitarii ad Reges Domini Alphonsi, beginning 'O ȝe cler and bright kynges and wold to god' and includes the Recapitulation [ch. 7] which ends 'as it schewis breffly in all thinges before seid. And of the seyinges of al doctours and holy fadris vpon this matur diffusely and manyfold wise speking'. This is followed on f. 254 by an Epilogue beginning 'yt shewys euydently to all cristen pepil þat in þe yere fro thincarnacion of our lord ihesu crist M^{lo} CCC^o LXXII the 10° Kalend of August þat is the day aftir mary mawdeleyn blissid lady Brigid of Swecy died in the cety of Rome'. This Epilogue (part of which has been printed by G. M. Aungier, *History and Antiquities of Syon Monastery*, 1840, p. 19) gives a brief account of her death, writings, and canonization. On the last page (f. 254 b) are two Latin prayers to St. Birgitta.

Paper: ff. 254. 12" × 8½". Fifteenth century.

105/15. He writes *bys[p]renglith* as *bystrenglith* 108/32. The haplography on 102/5 may have been made either by the scribe or in the Latin.

The Manuscript

2. *British Museum MS. Claudius B. I.* 'The Revelation of sainct Bridgitte', translated into English; preceded by a life of St. Birgitta, imperfect at beginning and end (ff. 2–4), which differs from the other extant English lives. Many chapters are abbreviated throughout the text. The Revelations are imperfect at the beginning, commencing in the middle of ch. 1 (f. 5): ' of man þat I have boght with mine owen blode bot he dose noght þat as mightier þan I '. Bk. I, chs. 15 and 18 are reversed; Bk. I, end of ch. 38, chs. 39–40, and beginning of ch. 41 missing through loss of two leaves after f. 42; Bk. II, end of ch. 10 and beginning of ch. 11 are missing through loss of a leaf after f. 84; Bk. III, end of ch. 28 and beginning of ch. 29 are missing through loss of a leaf after f. 144; Bk. IV, end of ch. 16 to end of ch. 31 missing through loss of several leaves after f. 167; Bk. IV, end of ch. 111 to beginning of ch. 115 missing through loss of leaf after f. 203; end of ch. 129 and ch. 130 (where Bk. IV ended) missing through loss of leaf after f. 211; Bk. V is complete with the Prologue, except for the short introductory paragraph at the beginning of the book (beginning in the Latin 'Vidi thronum'); Bk. VI has 107 chapters which correspond to chs. 1–109 of the Latin printed edition with the omission of ch. 65, as ch. 64 includes chs. 64 and 66 of the printed edition; Bk. VII, chs. 1–29 (last chapter imperfect) correspond to chs. 1–28 of the Latin printed edition, as ch. 13 is divided into two parts; the manuscript ends in the middle of ch. 28 of the printed edition, and chs. 29–31, which are the last three chapters of Bk. VII, are missing.

Vellum: ff. 281. $13\frac{1}{4}'' \times 9''$. Gatherings of 8 leaves (first[6], II[9], V[7], VI[6], IX[9], XI[7], XXII[7], XXVIII[7], last[2]). Fifteenth century.

3. *British Museum MS. Harley 4800.* An English translation of Bk. IV and the beginning of Bk. V of the Revelations of St. Birgitta. The end of ch. 6 and the beginning of ch. 7 of Bk. IV are missing through loss of a leaf after f. 8; two gatherings (e–f) are missing after f. 38 containing chs. 40–72, which are wanting; one leaf is also missing after f. 67, containing middle of ch. 89. Begins: ' A persone appered to þe spouse semynge to her þat he was cutted about as yn maner of repref'. Ends in the middle of Bk. V, ch. 2: 'Therfor ho

þat forsaketh hys propre wyl and ys obedient to me he schal have hevyn wythoute peyne'. There are traces of several leaves having been torn out at the end. Pages from f. 1 to f. 106 are headed 'liber quartus', but from ff. 1–28 'liber primus' was originally written and cancelled in the same hand.

Paper: ff. 109. $11\frac{1}{4}'' \times 8\frac{1}{4}''$. Gatherings of 10 leaves, letters a–d, g–o (first[8], VI[9], and last[2] imperfect). Fifteenth century. Chapters numbered. Headings in black, initials in red. The name Edward South is written on f. 1, probably as a former owner. On f. 53 b is written: 'Luke vnto Mr Syr James Parson of no church and vycare of the same', and on f. 54 'I lent my mony vnto my frend as many men dothe in land I axed my mony of my frend by-cause yt was so longe. I loste my mony and my frend me thought it was great wrong. J. Bray'; both in the same seventeenth-century hand.

4. *Bodleian MS. Rawlinson C. 41.* Selections from the revelations. The manuscript is imperfect; the first leaf is numbered f. 97. There are two parts. I. The first part contains the life of the Blessed Virgin Mary, and begins in the middle of Bk. I, ch. 9: 'Shew to the how moche my son hath honourde my name, my body, & my soule. [Chapter heading follows.] Of the most excellent dignite of the holy name of this vergin mary. Cap*itulu*m primu*m*. I am gwen to hevyn'. Chapter 9 is followed by selections from different books, rather loosely translated. Each leaf is headed with the running title 'Vita b*e*ate Ma*ri*e'. Ends on f. 43 b: 'Here have I shewyd to the how much god wyche ys my sonne hath lovyd and honourd my soule & my body. Amen. Deo gra*ti*as'. II. The second part contains 'The wordis of Christ to hys spowse of the artyclys of the very trewe feyth & what be the ornamente*s* & tokyns & the wyll that a spowse ought to have to her spowse'. There are three chapters (ff. 44 a–52 a). The first revelation is Bk. I, ch. 2, and begins: 'I am maker of hevyn, of erth, of the see, and of all thyngs that be in them'. The second part ends with Bk. II, ch. 26 on f. 52 a: 'then for to covete and have a wyll allway to synne'.

Paper: ff. 91 4to. End of fifteenth century.

Bound in with the same volume is a poem written about the

end of the seventeenth century by Th. Robinson, and dedicated by him to W. Taylor, B.D., his former tutor: 'The life and Death of Mary Magdalene, or, Her Life in Sin and Death to Sin'. ff. 54-91.

5. *British Museum MS. Arundel 197.* A small volume containing mystical and religious pieces; on ff. 38 b-47 b two chapters 'drawy*nn*e out of the revelatio*un* of s*en*t Bryde'. On f. 38 b begins a treatise on active and contemplative life (Bk. VI, ch. 65): 'I finde as Y rede bi doctoris and holimennis wretinge'. This is followed on f. 46 b by a short revelation (Bk. II, ch. 16) in which God admonishes St. Birgitta to love him above all things and to eschew pride and the lusts of the flesh. It ends: 'This bethe the wordis that oure lorde speke to Sent Bryde, his owne spouse and derelynge'.

Vellum: ff. 73. $8\frac{3}{4}'' \times 5\frac{1}{4}''$. 4to. The last half of fifteenth century.

6. *Lambeth Palace Library MS. 432.* For a description of all the items in the manuscript see C. Horstmann, *Anglia*, iii, p. 319. The manuscript is a miscellaneous collection, written about the middle of the fifteenth century; it has several revelations and a prayer of Birgitta, which are scattered through the work. A revelation on ff. 36 a-36 b has the following chapter heading: 'how our lady seint marie comendith seint Jerom to þe reuelecion of seint Burgitt'. Another short revelation (ff. 36 b-7 a) continues Mary's praise of Jerome to Birgitta. A translation of Bk. I, ch. 10, is found on ff. 76 a-83 a, with the chapter heading: 'wordys of the Blessed virgyne our lady seint marye to Seint Burgitt of the incarnacion and passion of our lord Ihesu Crist'. F. 83 a-b has a translation of Bk. VI, ch. 6: 'Ihesu Crist Blamythe Seint Brygytt for vnpaciens, and techith hir Sonne to with-stonde hitt'. A prayer of Birgitta in Latin follows on ff. 83 b-84 a. The first two revelations (ff. 36 a-37 a) have been edited by C. Horstmann, *Anglia*, iii, pp. 359-60.

Paper: ff. 99. $8\frac{3}{4}'' \times 6''$. 4to. Fifteenth century.

II

The seven extant manuscripts vary greatly in size, content, and literary value. They bear no apparent relationship to

each other. Rawlinson C. 41 differs in method of translation
and in style from all the others. It expands the Latin text
and adds ideas not in the original. Arundel 197 and Lambeth
Palace Library 432 contain a few extracts from the revelations.
Claudius B. I abbreviates and omits passages in the Latin text
frequently. It differs both in style and wording from the
other manuscripts, and has many Northern forms (*kyrke, ilk,
ane, awn, wald, swylke*). Harley 4800 has only the fourth book
and part of the fifth book; the translation is a poor one.
Julius F. 2, which has a translation of the first seven books of
the revelations, is the most complete of the manuscripts. The
forms are slightly later than those of the Garrett MS.; it uses
seis, them, ther, shall, where the Garrett MS. has *seyth, hem, her,
schullen.* There is a tendency in Julius F. 2, as in Harley
4800, to abbreviate by the excision of words or phrases; the
method of abbreviation is not as pronounced as that of
Claudius B. I, which omits long sections or paragraphs.
Julius F. 2 is the fullest of the manuscripts, and for this
reason ranks next in interest to the Garrett MS., a collection
of the revelations which, in care of translation and in literary
style, stands apart from all the others. The Garrett MS.
has passages of excellent prose and gives evidence of care in
the selection of the revelations; the other manuscripts vary
from businesslike translations to mere rough jottings which
show the general content of the work. It is only natural that
straightforward translations from the Latin, even when entirely
independent, should have frequent similarities; the translators
of most of the manuscripts, when they follow the Latin at all,
hold as nearly as possible to the Latin order in the sentence,
and frequently use the Latin word in translation. The indi-
vidual words, phrases, and methods of translations continually
differ. The chapter headings of each of the manuscripts
differ from each other, as well as from the standard Latin text.
The Syon Monastery Library, because of its great resources,
was a 'lending library',[1] and may have sent its copies of the
revelations to the other libraries to be transcribed.[2] Since

[1] Bateson, *Catalogue of the Library of Syon Monastery*, Cambridge, 1898, p. x.
[2] Latin MSS. in English Libraries are fairly numerous: Harley 612

The Manuscripts xxi

there was apparently no English translation of the revelations in the library,[1] this may account for separate translations by those who wished to have the revelations Englished.

D. *The Text of the Garrett MS.*

The Garrett MS. is the logical choice for an edition under the circumstances. There is no question of the earliest text, since the manuscripts are independent. For practical purposes, Julius F. II and Claudius B. I are both too long to edit. Hundreds of chapters in the full text are occasional, repetitive, and uninteresting. The Garrett MS. is a selection of the best revelations,[2] and has by far the most studied and interesting prose. The translation was probably made from a manuscript in the library of Syon Monastery which, in turn, was derived from the original Latin manuscript at Vadstena. A manuscript which was carefully transcribed from this original in Sweden for the English chapter is still extant.[3]

The sequence of chapters in the Garrett MS. is independent of the order which is followed in the Latin manuscripts. A

(transcribed for Syon Monastery in 1427 from the original in Vadstena), St. John (Cambr.) 69, Merton (Oxf.) 215, Bodley 346, Bodley 169, Royal 7. C. IX, Canon. (Bodl.) 475, Sloane 982, Magd. Coll. (Oxf.) 77, Trinity Coll. (Camb.) 0. 9. 28, Brit. Mus. 982, Arundel 66, Royal 13. E.X., Royal 8. B.X., Royal 11. A.I., Vespasian E. VII. Emmanuel Coll. (Cambr.) II. 2. 17 and III. 3. 8. Some of the manuscripts have only short extracts from the revelations.

[1] There are seven Latin MSS. listed (Bateson, *op. cit.*, p. xiii). The nuns had a library distinct from the monastery library.

[2] It contains, for example, Bk. VIII, ch. 48, one of the most powerful of Birgitta's revelations, which is in no other extant English manuscript.

[3] British Museum MS. Harley 612 can be identified as M. 64 of the Syon Monastery Library (Mary Bateson, *op. cit.*, p. 107). The manuscript is a huge volume of 1,202 columns which contains fourteen books of the revelations (including prologues, &c.), attestations, various lives, and other matters. At the end one Peter, notary public of Lincöping, Sweden, certifies that the book is an accurate transcription from the true original, made at the request of John Hartman 'pro parte Roberti Belle et Thome Sterinton, Professorum in Monasterio de Syone'. Dated May 1427.

The arrival of the brothers and the cause for their mission is noted in the *Diarium Wazstenense* for 18 April 1427 (E. M. Fant, *Scriptores Rerum Suecicarum*, tom. i, p. 146) : 'In die Parasceves venerunt de Anglia duo fratres ordinis nostri petentes & reportantes raciones super aliquis chapter from the second book follows one from the fourth ; a chapter from the sixth book precedes one from the first. Chapters relating to the same general subject-matter are often placed together ; this grouping, however, is not systematically carried out. Some of these groups are gathered together from two or three different books, while others are connected by position and subject-matter in the Latin also. The chapters included in 100/20-117/23 (Bk. II, ch. 28 ; Bk. IV, ch. 9, Bk. VI, ch. 52) deal with humility and its opposite, pride. In Bk. VIII, ch. 48 (63/14-87/4) and Bk. VIII, ch. 56 (87/5-97/32), the translator has brought together two visions of judgement on unjust rulers. Bk. II, chs. 24-7 (19. 12/13-25/13), Bk. IV, ch. 7-9 (43/7-53/6), and Bk. I, chs. 50-9 (53/7-59/34) are groups of chapters with a common theme in the Latin ; the translator has recognized and preserved their unity. The revelations which have been selected are those which deal with general subjects. Birgitta wrote many of her revelations for particular persons, and these naturally have a local application which would not be suitable in a translation for English readers.

The translation follows the Latin closely. Occasional passages which are awkward and unidiomatic are so because of this strict adherence to the Latin order. The sentences are sometimes long and involved. But in general both scribes write with a directness and simplicity which admirably bring out the pictorial qualities of the revelations. Neither scribe adds anything to the original. The omissions of phrases, which are made occasionally by the first scribe are probably accidental.

punctis regule.' On 30 September 1428 Robert Belle was appointed confessor-general of Syon Monastery on the death of Thomas Fishbourne, the first confessor-general. At that time John Hartman was a lay brother ; Thomas Sterinton is not mentioned. (G. J. Aungier, *History and Antiquities of Syon Monastery*, 1840, pp. 51-2.)

PART II. SAINT BIRGITTA

A. The Life of Saint Birgitta[1]

In the year 1302 or 1303[2] Birgitta[3] was born at Finstad, a town a few miles from Upsala in the province of Upland. Her father was Birger, the lagman or governor of Upland. Birgitta began to have visions at the age of seven;[4] in these visions an angel, the Blessed Virgin Mary, or Christ, usually appeared and talked to her. When she was 10 years of age she heard a sermon on the passion of Christ. That night Christ appeared to her as if he had just been crucified, and said, 'Thus am I tortured'. Birgitta, thinking that the wounds were fresh, asked, 'O Lord, who has done this to Thee?' Christ replied, 'Whoever despises Me and spurns My love does this to Me'. From that day on, the passion of Christ affected her so much that she seldom could think of it without tears.[5] It is a constantly recurring theme in her revelations.

---

[1] The main authorities for the life of Birgitta are the *Vita Sanctae Birgittae* (edited in S.R.S. iii, pp. 185-206, by C. M. Annerstedt), which was written within four months after her death by her two confessors, Peter, prior of Alvastra, and Peter Olafson, the first confessor of Vadstena ; and the later *Vita Sanctae Birgittae* (A.S., pp. 485-93), by Birger, archbishop of Upsala. The *Vita Abbreviata*, published in the first printed edition of her revelations, and also printed in Durantus's edition, uses the revelations themselves as a chief source. C. M. Annerstedt (S.R.S. iii, pp. 186-88) has a full list and critical discussion of the *Vitae*. Klemming (v, pp. 244-58) gives a list of manuscript lives and printed biographies up to 1884. The best modern critical biographies are by Fr. Hammerich, *Den hellige Birgitta og Kirken i Norden*, Copenhagen, 1863 ; Comtesse de Flavigny, *Sainte Brigitte*, Paris, 1892; and K. Krogh-Tonnung, *Die heilige Birgitta*, *Sammlung illustrierter Heiligenleben*, Band v, Kempten und München, 1907.

[2] The earliest authorities differ (S.R.S. iii, p. 189, note *k*).

[3] Birgitta is her correct name, and not Brigitte, Brigida, or Bridget. Birgitta is probably from Brighitta (cf. A. Noreen, *Altschwedische Grammatik*, § 339. 2), borrowed from Irish ⰁⱃⰋⰃⰋⰕ (Brighid), which is from ⰁⱃⰋⰃ (brigh), virtue, strength, an extension of ⰁⱃⰋ, which has the same sense. Cf. Fr. Stark, *Sitzungsber. d. Kais. Akad. v. Wissenschaften*, Phil.-hist. Classe, Wien, lix. 2. 196-7, 1868.

[4] S.R.S. iii, p. 190.

[5] Durantus, ii, p. 476 (*Vita Abbreviata*).

xxiv *Introduction*

At thirteen years of age her father, much against her wishes,[1] married her to the eighteen-year-old Ulf Gudmarson, a youth of noble family and fine personal character. They lived together continently for a year,[2] and Birgitta was especially fervent in her prayers and ascetic devotions. Ulf eventually became the lagman of the province of Nericia,[3] and Birgitta bore him four sons and four daughters.[4] St. Catherine, who later accompanied her mother on many of her journeys, was the most famous of her children.[5] During this period of Birgitta's life, the learned Matthias, canon of the cathedral of Lincöping, was her father confessor and constant adviser.[6] Ulf, her husband, died in 1344, after they had lived for some years in continence and pious study.[7]

A few days [8] after her husband had died, Christ appeared to Birgitta and told her that he had chosen her to be his bride.[9] From this time on Birgitta's life was changed; she turned over the management of her estate to others and devoted herself to a religious life. She greatly increased her self-discipline; she fasted often, dressed poorly, and underwent severe penances. In 1346 she received a revelation bidding her to go to Rome.[10] But it was no easy undertaking to leave her affairs

[1] S.R.S. iii, p. 225, *De Processu Canonizationis Birgittae*, depositio Katerinae filiae Birgittae, super quarto articulo.
[2] S.R.S. iii, pp. 191, 225. Their continency was probably due as much to their youth as to piety, which is the reason given by her biographers.
[3] The title 'Princess' of Nericia or Sweden was often given to Birgitta. C. M. Annerstedt has shown conclusively that she had no real claim to the title (S.R.S. iii, p. 188, notes c, d, e).
[4] S.R.S. iii, p. 209, *Chronicon de Genere et Nepotibus Sanctae Birgittae*, auctore Margareta Clausdotter, abbatissa Vadstenensi.
[5] Durantus, ii, pp. 530-58, *Vitae Divae Catherinae*.
[6] S.R.S. iii, pp. 191-2.   [7] S.R.S. iii, p. 193.
[8] A.S., p. 404, no. 151. Some of the early accounts say that it was a year or two after Ulf's death, but the weight of evidence seems to be that Christ chose her to be 'sponsa mea et canale meum' within a few days.
[9] S.R.S. iii, p. 194, note *k*. This revelation forms the first chapter of the Garrett MS.
[10] *Revelationes Extravagantes*, ch. 8: 'Christus loquitur Sponsae existenti in Monasterio Aluastri, dicens: Vade Romam, & manebis ibi, donec videas Papam, & Imperatorem, & illis loqueris ex parte mea verba, quae tibi dicturus sum. Venit igitur Sponsa Christi Romam, anno aetatis suae xxxxii, & mansit ibi iuxta diuinum praeceptum xv annis, antequam veniret Papa, videlicet Vrbanus V & Imperator Carolus Boemus. Quibus

Saint Birgitta xxv

and arrange for her children ; two or three years elapsed before her journey began.[1] With a small retinue, including her two confessors, Peter, prior of Alvastra, and Peter Olafson, first confessor of the Vadstena monastery, she finally left Sweden, never more to return alive. On the way to Rome Peter of Alvastra began to teach her the use of Latin. However, she continued to write down her revelations in Swedish, and her confessors translated them into Latin.[2]

Long before leaving Sweden Birgitta had shown a fearless nature in her denunciations of the king and his court.[3] During the years of her stay in Rome she waged ceaseless war against the widespread corruptions in the Church. She unhesitatingly condemned the prelates, forced the abbots to improve the standard of living at their monasteries, and frequently sent letters of advice or denunciation to the pope himself.[4]

She was especially anxious that the papal seat, which had long been at Avignon, should be re-established at Rome. But the popes did not wish to leave the quiet of Avignon for the turmoil of a rebellious city. It was not until 1367 that Urban V brought the long absent court back to Rome. The conditions prevalent in Rome at that time were unendurable to the pope, and he decided to abandon Rome in 1370. This aroused in Birgitta great anger and grief ; she warned him, upon penalty of God's severe displeasure and punishment, not to leave Rome.[5] This revelation was delivered to him by

obtulit Reuelationes pro reformatione Ecclesiae, & Regulam.' Birgitta did not see Urban V until 1367, over twenty years later ; see A.S., p. 444, nos. 317-18, for an attempt to explain this chronological discrepancy.

[1] S.R.S. iii, p. 202, notes *m, n, o*.
[2] A.S., p. 406, ch. xi.
[3] In *Revelationes Extravagantes*, chs. 74 and 77, Birgitta flays Magnus Erikson, the king of Sweden, and his court for their worldliness ; she also visited and rebuked the king personally. Book VIII, called *Liber Celestis Imperatoris ad Reges*, has denunciatory revelations which were sent to many kings and queens. Although the revelations seemed to have but little effect on their lives, Birgitta must have instilled a wholesome fear in the hearts of those to whom she wrote, for she was received with the greatest consideration and respect wherever she went.
[4] See 5/20-6/12 of the text for an outspoken statement concerning the condition of the Church.
[5] Bk. IV, ch. 33.

Alphonso,[1] one of Birgitta's devoted friends, but did not change the pope's decision. He left the city, and died the same year, in less than a month after returning to Avignon.

Another desire of Birgitta was to have her Order, the Order of St. Saviour or the Birgittine Order, officially approved. She firmly believed that she had received and had written down the rules of the Order exactly as they were given to her by the Mother of God. This Order, the founding of which is Birgitta's chief religious accomplishment, was to consist of sixty sisters and twenty-five monks. The monks and nuns were to live in separate houses, communicating with the church; the nuns' choir was to be placed above in such a position as to enable them to listen to the offices of the monks in the lower choir. The monastery was so arranged that the monks and nuns could not see each other, even at confession. Severe, chaste, and abstemious living were strictly prescribed.[2] After many years of command and entreaty by Birgitta, the Order was approved by Urban in 1370.[3] The monastery at Vadstena had been in existence for some time,[4] and after this date the Order rapidly expanded.[5]

In 1372, in obedience to the divine command,[6] Birgitta went to Jerusalem.[7] While in Palestine she had many visions revealing to her incidents in the life of Christ and the Blessed Virgin Mary; these revelations form the major part of Bk. VII. Birgitta returned to Rome the same year, very much enfeebled. On 23 July 1373, surrounded by a group of her

[1] Alphonso the hermit, formerly bishop of Jaën, wrote the *Prologus* of Book VIII and edited Birgitta's revelations in 1377.

[2] Durantus, ii, pp. 351-70, *Regula Sancti Salvatoris*.

[3] A.S., p. 445, no. 322.

[4] S.R.S. i, pp. 1-224, *Diarium Wazstenense ab anno 1344 ad annum 1545*, edited by E. M. Fant.

[5] The monastery of Syon House, of the Birgittine Order, was founded by Henry V in the manor of Isleworth, in Middlesex, in 1414-16. It became one of the richest monasteries in England. See William Dugdale, *Monasticon Anglicanum*, London, 1830, pp. 540-4; G. J. Aungier, *History and Antiquities of Syon Monastery*, London, 1840; J. H. Blunt, the preface to *The Myroure of Oure Ladye*, E.E.T.S., E.S. xix, pp. xi-xix.

[6] Bk. VII, ch. 1.

[7] On the death of her son Charles at Naples see note on 117/37-118/1 of the text.

followers, she died. Her bones were carried to Vadstena,[1] where they may still be seen.[2]

Her two confessors, and Catherine, her daughter, soon returned to Rome to inaugurate the proceedings for her canonization. Gregory XI appointed a commission to investigate the life and writings of Birgitta. The commission was headed by Cardinal Johannes de Turrecremata, who made a very careful study of the revelations. After some delay the canonization, performed by Boniface IX, took place with great pomp on 8 October 1391. On account of the great schism which had split the Church at that time, the validity of the canonization was questioned. The bull of canonization of Birgitta and her Order were confirmed by John XXIII in 1414; and after the schism had ceased, Martin V, after another investigation, signed a confirmation in 1419.[3]

B. *The Revelations of St. Birgitta*[4]

The works of many mystics show careful revision and study. Their writings are the result of a conscious reconstruction, caused either by the advice of a confessor or produced out of their own theological knowledge. Birgitta, on the other hand, immediately after beholding a vision, wrote down the revelation, or dictated it to an amanuensis if she were too ill to write it herself. She wrote in Swedish, and one of her confessors translated the revelation into Latin. This translation was then read to her that no word might be omitted or changed. The original was often destroyed, but Peter of Alvastra wrote the Latin in a book which developed into the *Revelationes Celestes*.[5]

It is this lack of supplementation and literary revision which differentiates Birgitta's visions from others of their type.[6] Her revelations were usually the result of some particular situation

[1] Durantus, ii, p. 480; A.S., p. 462, no. 389.
[2] Sven Gronberger, *St. Bridget of Sweden, American Catholic Quarterly Review*, vol. xlii, 1917, p. 145.
[3] A.S., pp. 409-18, chs. xii-xiv.
[4] Birgitta's revelations reach a total of over 650.
[5] Klemming (iv, pp. 177-85) has edited the only two fragments of Birgitta's handwriting which have been preserved.
[6] In the *Sermo Angelicus* and the fifth book of the revelations (*Liber Questionum*) there is evidence of a re-ordering of the material.

or occasion. A friend would inquire about the condition of a dead relative ; shortly afterward, Birgitta would not only have a revelation which showed the condition of the soul of the dead person, but could also inform the anxious relative what alms or prayers would shorten the stay of the deceased in purgatory or alleviate his sufferings while there.[1] Or if the wickedness of a king or the worldliness of a prelate needed correction, Birgitta would receive a revelation in which Christ or the Mother of God denounced his sin in no uncertain words. After such a vision had been revealed and written down, a copy of it was made and immediately sent to the inquiring friend or offending sinner.[2] The lack of revision in the revelations shows itself in repetitions, useless elaboration, and frequent lack of cohesion and unity of thought.

If the revelations show lack of conscious literary style, they are strong in imaginative versatility. Birgitta had an unusually active imagination, and her descriptions of hell and purgatory, of Christ's crucifixion, and of incidents in the life of the Blessed Virgin Mary, stand out vividly. She prefers concrete representations to abstract theological discussions. She does not propound universal dogmas, as does Hildegard of Bingen ; her visions are not rationally and consciously constructed as are those of Elizabeth of Schönau.[3] However, her fifth book (*Liber Questionum*) could (with very little rearrangement) be turned into a popular theological tract. These defects, however, do not obscure the positive literary qualities which the revelations possess. Through her visions Birgitta exercised a remarkable authority over the laity as well as over the kings and prelates of her time. The drastic strength of her warnings and the profuse wealth of images which her visions contain explain the popularity which they have enjoyed. The revelations are given a high place in Swedish literature of the Middle Ages by literary historians of the present day.

[1] See note on 116/27.
[2] S.R.S. iii, pp. 196-7.
[3] Westman (pp. 151-259) compares Birgitta with the other mystics of her time. See also the letter of Westman, reprinted in Notes, p. 125.

C. The Revelations of St. Birgitta in England in the Fifteenth Century

Birgitta died in Rome, 23 July 1373. Even before her death, Latin copies of the revelations found their way into England and aroused great interest in Oxford and London.[1] Bale writes in his *Scriptorum Illustrium Maioris Brytanniae*: 'Huius Dianae tenebrosa somnia, seu, ut ipsi uocant, Revelationes, in scholis Oxoniensibus & in cathedris publicis, magistraliter exposuerunt magni sua aetate doctores, Thomas Stubbes Dominicanus, Ricardus Lauynham Carmelita, & adhuc alii eius generis multi, circa Domini 1370, ut talibus muliercularum delirationibus sole clariorem Dei veritatem sophistae obnubilarent.'[2]

With the marriage of Philippa, daughter of Henry IV, to Eric XIII of Sweden in 1406, the knowledge of St. Birgitta became more general in England. Henry V decided to establish a foundation of the Birgittine Order, and on 22 February 1415 laid the corner-stone of Syon Monastery in the presence of Richard Clifford, Bishop of London. The new monastery, which at the time of the dissolution ranked eighth in wealth in England, had an uninterrupted career of prosperity for a hundred and twenty years. Bequests of books to the library were frequent and generous, as the still existing catalogue

[1] Pits (John Pits, *De Illustribus Angliae Scriptoribus*, Paris, 1616, p. 512) enumerating the works of Thomas Stubbes, a Dominican, who he says died in 1373, mentions: *In revelationes S. Brigidae, Librum vnum* [beginning] *Beata & venerabilis Domina*. Recording the works of Richard Lavenham (d. 1381), confessor to Richard II and Professor of Theology at Oxford, Pits (*ibid.*, pp. 532-5) lists: *Determinationes notabiles Oxoniae & Londoni publice lectas pro libro revelationum S. Birgittae, Libros septem*, [beginning] *Stupor & mirabilia audita sunt*. But *Stupor & mirabilia audita sunt* is the beginning of the Prologue to the revelations written by Matthias, father confessor to St. Birgitta, and it may be that these 'notable public lectures in seven books' are merely seven books of the revelations with the usual Prologue. The volume attributed to Lavenham in the Bodleian (Bodl. MS. 169), which I have examined, has nothing but the Prologue and the first four books of the revelations.

[2] John Bale, *Scriptorum Illustrium maioris Brytannię*, Basileae, 1557, *Pars Posterior*, p. 188. Bale confuses St. Birgitta with St. Bridget of Ireland.

shows.[1] One of the most famous donors to the library was Thomas Gascoigne, Vice-Chancellor (1434–9) and Chancellor (1442–5) of Oxford, who seems to have taken an especial interest in Syon Monastery. He wrote a life of St. Birgitta, which he translated into English for the sisters and monks of Syon.[2] In his *Dictionarium Theologicum*, Gascoigne records examples of miracles performed by St. Birgitta at Oxford, where a man ' possessed of an evil spirit' was saved by prayers to the saint from onlookers.[3]

[1] M. Bateson, *Catalogue of the Library of Syon Monastery*, Cambridge, 1898, Appendix I.

[2] There are three English prose lives of St. Birgitta extant, none of which seems to be that written by Gascoigne. One is *The Life of St. Bridget*, printed by Pynson in 1516 (ed. J. H. Blunt, E.E.T.S., E.S. xix, pp. xlvii–lix). Pynson's *Life* is usually ascribed to Thomas Gascoigne (*ibid.*, p. ix); but the miracle which Gascoigne says he included ('quam historiam scripsi latius in vita ejusdem Sanctae Brigittae' : see next note) is not found in the printed *Life*. The revelations in Claudius B.I, are preceded by a life of Birgitta, imperfect at the beginning and end (ff. 2–4), which differs from and is fuller than the printed *Life*. The revelations in Julius F. II are followed on the last leaf of the manuscript (f. 254) by a description of Birgitta's writings and the circumstances of her death.

[3] 'Sicut nuper novi Oxoniae, circa annum Domini m°cccc°l°, et circa annum Domini m°cccc°lij°, quando hominibus orantibus ad Sanctam Brigittam viduam quondam, et principissam Sueciae, novi virum graviter mentaliter vexatum horrore et timore per Sathanam immisso, quem novi tunc subito liberatum ab illa magna vexatione mentali, beata Brigitta sibi in mentali visione aut specie fulgente apparenti et cum verbis mentalibus eum consolante. Item, novi tunc Oxoniae quendam magistrum Ricardum Tenant, qui horribiliter et saepissime vexatus est, possessus a maligno spiritu vel a malignis spiritibus, quia semper longo tempore clamavit, "Ego sum dampnatus! et sententia est data. Ite, maledicta, in ignem aeternum!" "Nullus est Deus nisi dyabolus!" et hoc saepissime dixit publice coram pluribus, et me dicente sibi, "In nomine Jesu Xti, dicatis, Jesu Xte. Deus et homo! miserere mei!" Ipse michi saepe respondebat dicens, "Non possum hoc dicere"; et tunc, clausis labiis suis, similiter statim iterum verba praedicta horribiliter clamavit, dicens, "Ego sum dampnatus, ego sum dampnatus, non est Deus nisi dyabolus!" et circumstantibus diversis hominibus, et ex motione unius ad sanctam Brigittam sponsam Xti orantibus, praedictus magister Ricardus Tenant liberatus fuit de manibus daemonum, et dixit saepe, "O Domine Jesu Xte, miserere mei". "Ego", inquit, "fui male vexatas"; et postea saepe osculatus est ymaginem Xti Jesu crucifixi pro nobis; et postea saepe, me audiente, "Sancta Brigitta, ora pro nobis"; et receptis sacramentis ecclesiae infra biduum post suam liberationem mortuus est, in die Veneris et in vigilia

Saint Birgitta   xxxi

Hoccleve (*Regement of Princes*, E.E.T.S., E.S. lxii, p. 194) has a paraphrase of Revelations, Bk. IV, ch. 105, in which St. Birgitta advises the kings of France and England to obtain peace by an alliance of marriage. In Arundel MS. 66 (f. 291), a beautifully ornamented manuscript for the use of Henry VII, are *Visiones de Regibus Angliae et Franciae*, which are extracts from the revelations in Latin.

The blind and deaf poet John Audelay, chaplain in the monastery of Haghmon(d), which lay four miles north-east of Shrewsbury, in Shropshire, wrote a *Salutacio Sancte Brigitte*. It is found in the only extant copy of Audelay's poems, Douce 302 (Bodl.), and was written shortly after 1426. The poem, which has not been printed, is on ff. 25 a (col. 1)–26 a (col. 2).[1]

[A Salutation to St. Birgitta.]

Hic incipit salutacio Sanctę Birgittę virginis & quomodo dominus Ihesus Christus apparuit illi corporaliter & dedit illi suam benedictionem suam.   quoþ Awdelay.

1 Hayle! maydyn & wyfe. hayle! wedow brygytt.
  Hayle! þu chese to be chast & kepe charyte,
  Hayle! þu special spouse, kyndle to þe knyt;
  Hayle! he consentyd to þe same by concel of the
    To be relegyous.
  Hayle! fore þe loue of Ihesus Crist
  ȝe foresake ȝour fleschele lust ;
  þer-fore be ȝe boþ eblest
    In þe name of swete Ihesus.

Pentecostis Oxoniae sepultus in ecclesia sanctissimae Mariae semper virginis ; quam historiam scripsi latius in vita ejusdem Sanctae Brigittae, quam vitam ego transtuli de Latino in Anglicum sororibus et monialibus de ordine Sancti Salvatoris in monasterio Syon, Londiniensis dioceseos. Haec ergo mulier, sancta sponsa Xti Brigitta, magnam fecit confusionem in domo principis tenebrarum.'—J. E. Thorold Rogers, *Loci e Libro Veritatum*, 1881, pp. 139-40.

[1] J. E. Wülfing, *Der Dichter John Audelay und sein Werk*, Anglia, xviii, 1896, pp. 175–217, gives a description of the contents of the manuscript. J. K. Rasmussen, *Die Sprache John Audelay's*, Bonn, 1914, has a study of the Salopian dialect of the manuscript. On f. 22b (col. 2) of the manuscript is a short colophon, dated 1426, which tells us all we know about the life of John Audelay. Since the *Salutacio Sancte Brigitte* is written only a few pages later, it was composed not long after 1426.

l. 3. *knyt*: Ulf Gudmarson, her husband.

10 Haile! þe moder of god to þe con apere.
　Haile! he told þe of his passion & of his spetus payne.
　Hayle! ȝe wepit fore wo to-geder when ȝe were,
　Hayle! fore his dolful deþ þat so was eslayne,
　Oure lade to þe gan say:
　Hayle! blessed bregit, let be þe chere
　& þonke my sun fore his deþ dere
　Þat has eȝeuen þe powere
　To be wyfe, wedow, ond may.

19 Haile! seche a kyndle coupil can no mon here kyn.
　Hayle! ȝe fore-soke reches & ryal aray.
　Hayle! ȝe hopid hile in ȝour hert þen.
　Hay[le]! al þe worchip of þis word wol sone wynd away
　With-in a lytil stownd.
　Haile! þis wordle honour
　Hit fallis & fadis as a flour
　To-day is fresche in his colour
　To-morrow he gyrdis to grownd.

28 Hayle! ȝe be-toke ȝour tresouur to þe trinete
　Fore he is truste & trew with-out treynyng.
　Hayle! he dissayuyd no soule with no sotelte.
　Hayle! fayþfully þat ȝe fond at ȝour endyng,
　Þe soþe fore to say.
　Hayle! oþer tresoure haue we noȝt
　Out of þis word when we be broȝt
　Bot good word, wil, dede, & þoȝt,
　When we schuld wynd away.

37 Hayle! with þese iiij feyþfully ȝe [b]oȝt ȝoue heuen blis,
　With good word, will, dede, & þoȝt, To obey godis bidyng.
　Hayle! with þe werkis of merce ȝe geten ȝou mede, I wis.
　Haile! ȝe fore-soken flesschele lust, þe fend, false couetyng,
　Þat were ȝour iij enmys.
　Haile! þai sett yn al her sotelte
　Houe mons soule þai mow distre
　With pride, lechory, & glotonye
　& cursid couetyse.

l. 11. *spetus*: despitous, cruel.
l. 22. MS. *hay*.
l. 29. *treynyng*: training, deceit.
l. 37. MS. *hoȝt*.
l. 38. This line is incorrectly divided in the manuscript; a new line begins with *To obey* in the manuscript.

Saint Birgitta

46 Haile! blessid bregid fore þi benyngnete,
Haile! þe perles prince to þe con apere.
Haile! he grownded þe in [g]race in þi vergenete,
Hayle! specially he speke with þe oft in þi prayere
Hayle! to þe pope þe send
Fore to grawnt þe his special [g]race
& to al þat vesid þi holy place
To assoyle ham of here trespas
Þat here mysdedis wol amend.   fol. 25 b.

55 Haile! he bed þe bild a plas o relygion.
Haile! blessid bregid, fore fro][one place
Haile! to pope Urban, to Rome, þu shalt goon,
Þat is my veker in erþ to grawnt þe his grace
To have þe same perdon
Þat is in pet[e]rs cherche at Rome:
To al þe pilgrems þat to þe cum,
Þat vesid þe in Cristis name,
To have playn remyssion.

64 Haile! he said: if þat pope wil grawnt þe no grace
With-out mone or mede be-cause of couetys,
Haile! þe fader of heuen schal preuelege þi place
Haile! & schal conferme þi bul, þat above him is.
Þat schal he, y know.
Haile! my moder my sele schall be;
My witnes, al þe sayntis of heuen on hye;
My blessyng, þe hole gost I be-take to þe.
Þe pope schal lout ful low.

73 Haile! to þat perles prelat, to þe pope, when þu come,
Haile! þu mendist þi mesage in a meke manere.
Haile! faypfulli þat fader ful reverenly at Rome,
Haile! he welcumd þe worþele with a wonder chere
Into þat hole place.
Haile! he said with myld steuen:
Welcum be ȝe fro þe kyng of heuen
Now blessid be þai þat in þe leuen,
Þat ever þu borne was.

82 Haile! meruelus maide ful of mekenes,
Haile! hele þe hole gostis lyȝt þe with-in.
Haile! god haþ grouned þe gracfulli in his goodnes

l. 51. MS. crace.   l. 55. MS. o : of.   l. 60. MS. petrs.

c

Haile! to be sauer of soulis & seser of syn
Be his ordenans.
Haile! i grawnt to al remyssion
Þat chryue hem clene with contrichon
& wil do here satisfaccion;
I reles here penans.

91 Haile! to al þat worþely veset yn þe hole place.
Haile! þat sechen þi socor schal have saluacion,
Haile! fore sake of þat sofren þat þe to me send had
Haile! in reuerenc of þat lord I grawnt hem remyssion
Of al here trespace.
Haile! to þi pilgrems perpetualy
Þat worchipen þi place graciously
With prayers, siluer, gold, lond of fe,
I grawnt ham þis special grace.

100 Now gramarce, gracious fader, of your blessyng I ȝou pray;
Mi blessid suster bregit, my blessyng ȝif I þe.
Here I grawnt þe þis grace specialy I say,
With-outen mone or mede I make hit to þe fre,
Þis special perdon.
To al þe pilgrems fer & nere
Þat veset yn þi place in good manere
To here gostele fader I grawnt pouere
To asoyle ham everchon.

109 Haile! to þat pereles priynce, bregit, fore me pray,
Þat haþ groundid þe in grace & is þi [g]ouernoure.
Haile! my blessid doȝter, þi blessidnes hit may
At þe day of my deþ my soule þen socour
& ȝif me wil & wit
Mi misdedis here to amend
Out of þis word or þat I wynd.
To þe trenite I þe recommend;
Fare wel, blessid breget.

118 Þus þe pope preueleged here place & haloud hit to Christis entent.
Anon hure hole husbond a couennt to him con take,
& Bregit mad here of maydyns anoþer blest couent
Þat fore-soke here fleschle lust for Ihesu Cristis sake
In þe name of þe trenete.

l. 110. MS. *couernoure*.

Saint Birgitta

Per þai disceuerd hem to.
Hure husbond to his bredern con go,
& to hure susteres heo whent him fro
To leue in chastite.

127 Haile! þus þis perles prelet fro þe passid away
When he with his benyngnete had ȝeuen þe his blessyng.
Haile! at þe day of our deþ þat settis no day,
Haile! þen, blessid Bregit, our soulis to blis bryng
& graunt vs þi special grace
In erþ, þat we mowe werchip þe.
After in heuen we may þe se
In [i]oi & blis perpetualy
With-in þat blisful place.

136 Beside þe chene soþly seuen myle fro Lundun,—
Our gracious kyng Herre þe V. wes founder of þat place,—
Haile! he let preuelege þat hole place & callid hit Bregit Sion.
Þe pope conferme þerto his bul þroȝ his special grace
In þe worchip of S. Bregit,
To al here pilgrems on Lammesday
& also Mydlentyn Sunday;
Þis perdon to last fore ȝeuer & ay.
God graunt vs a pert of hit!

144 Mekil is al Ynglan, I hold, to pray for kyng Herre,
Þat so worþele our worchip in eueroche place,
Boþ in Fraunce & in Breten & in Normandy,
Þat oure faders had lost before he get aȝayn be grace;
& more-ouer speciali
To make soche a house of relegioun,
& to preueleche þerto þat gracious perdon,—
Al Ynglond to haue remyssioune.
Now Crist on his soule haue merce.

fol. 26 a.

153 Was neuer a holeer order preueleged in no plas
Fore to red al þe rollis of relegyown.
Fore þai schal neuer schew chappe ny fygure of face;
Ne with-out lycence or leue speche speke þai non,
Bot [þ]e warden be present.
Noþer fader ne moder ne no mon leuyng
Schal speke to hom no erþle þyng
With-out þer warden be þer hereng
& know boþ here entent.

l. 134. MS. oi.   l. 157. MS. he.

Introduction

162 Redle þei rysun with gret reuerens oneþtes out of hure rest,
Devoutele with deuocion here seruys to syng & say,
& crucefyen here caren & slen here fleschele lust
With priue prayers & penans þe priynce of heuen to pay.
Deuotle day & niȝt
Þai prayn to god specialy
Fore al þat þai here leuyng be
In masse, in matyns, in memore,
To þat lord of myȝt.

171 Fore hit fars noȝt be gotele goodis as doþ be temperal;
Þe men þat han pert þer of so lasse is vche dole.
Bot he þat delis gostle goodis hit is so spiritual
Þat vche mon þat haþ his pert haþ fulle þe hole.
Ensampil chul ȝe se:
Alse mone men as may here a mas,
Vche mon his perte hole he has.
& ȝet þe masse is neuer þe lasce,
Bo[t] so more of dyngnete.

180 Pray we to god specialy to saue þat spiritual plas,
Þat þai obey obedyens þat þay be bound to.
Fore þai may þroȝ here precious prayoure purches her our grace,
Have we neuer in þis word wroȝt so muche wo,
Þai han þat pouere.
Fore al þat here wele done
Crist wil graunt hem here bone.
Þai wot neuer hou sone
He hers here prayere.

189 Crist þat was crucefid on cros & cround with þorne
& ched his blesful blod fore oure syns sake
Let neuer þis worþ lond, lord, be forelorne.
Bot puttis doune here pouere þat werris wil awake
& sese al males.
Fore ȝong kyng Herre now we pray,
Þat Crist him kepe boþ niȝt & day
& let neuer traytor him betray,
& send vs rest & pes.

198 Al þat redis reuerenly þis remyssioune
Prays to blisful Bregit, þat merceful may,

l. 162. oneþtes: uneaths, not easily.
l. 164. caren: carrion, the fleshly nature of man.   l. 179. MS. Bo.

Saint Birgitta

Fore hem þat med þis mater with dewocion,
Þat is boþ blynd & def, þe synful Audelay.
I pray ȝoue specialy,
Fore I mad þis with good entent
In þe reuer[en]s of þis vergyn verement,
Heo graunt ȝoue grace þat beþ present
To haue ioy & blis perpetualy.
                                                Amen.

The *O's of St. Bridget* or *Fifteen O's* are fifteen orisons on the Passion of Christ, attributed to St. Birgitta, which became very popular in England. Each prayer begins with *O Jesu* or a similar invocation.[1] At the time of the Reformation, these *Fifteen O's* were fiercely denounced as 'papistical superstitions'.[2] There is a short poem in Sloane MS. 3548, a fifteenth-century paper commonplace-book, which possibly refers to the orisons. It is written on a blank leaf in a word-list of Latin synonyms, and may have been copied from a manuscript containing the *Fifteen O's*, to which it served as the introduction.

l. 204. MS. *reuers*.

[1] There are several copies of a translation of the *Fifteen O's* printed by Caxton which are extant: *O Jhesu, endeles swetnes of louyng soules*, etc. 4°. [Westminster] W. Caxton. [1491.] Of this book there is a modern reproduction : *The Fifteen O's and other Prayers*, Reproduced in Photo-lithography by Stephen Ayling, Griffith and Farran, 1869. A discussion of the Bristol fragment (at the Baptist College) of Caxton's edition is found in Henry Bradshaw's *Collected Papers*, Cambridge University Press, Cambridge, 1889, pp. 341-4. At Blair's College, Aberdeen, is a copy of *The XV Oos in Englysshe with other prayers.* 16°. R. Coplåde, 1529. The *Hore beate marie virginis*, according to the Salisbury use, 1531, has the Latin *Quindecem Orationes* with an English heading: Thys be the .xv. oos the whych to (i. e., the) vyrgyn saint brigitta was wointe (i. e., wonte) to say dayly before the holy roode in saint paules church at Rome / who so sayth thys a hole yere he schall delyuer .xv. soules oute of purgatory of hys next kynred : and conuerte other .xv. synners to good lyf & other .xv. ryghtuose men of hys kynrede shall perseuer in good lyf. And what he desireth of god he sal haue yt yf it be to the saluacion of hys soule.

[2] *Certain Sermons or Homilies* (by T. Cranmer?), 1547, ch. v, *Of Good Works* : And briefly to pass over the vngodly & counterfete religions, let vs reherse some other kindes of papistical superstitions and abuses, as of beades, of lady psalters and rosaries, of .xv. Oos . . . which were so esteemed & abused to þe great preiuduce of Gods glorye and commaundementes, that they were made most high & most holy thinges, whereby to attaine to the eternal life, or remission of synne.

Sloane 3548, f. 118, b.

> A holy wooman that hight seynt Bryde
> Couetid to knowe the woundys wyde
> Of Ihesu Cryste, howe fell thei woor,
> And often prayed hem therfor.
> Ihesu, that all goodnes be-gan,
> Apperid and bad this whoman than:
> Saye every daye vppon thi knees
> XV pater nosters and XV aues
> Vnto a ȝere fulli endid bee;
> So many woundis had I for thee
> Wherefore I graunte wyth memory
> XV soules out of purgatorye
> And XV men that have dissesse
> Of there old synne I am relesse,
> Iff thei thise XV Orysyuns say
> Or ellis XV pater nosters day be day.
> More-over my body in fourme of brede
> They shall receyve or thei be dede,
> Whiche shall there saluacion bee.
> In the blisse of heven therfor saye wee
> This orysyuns with goode ententt
> To Ihesu Cryste omnipotent,
> That of this worlde when we shall misse
> He vs induce vnto his blis. Amen.

The revelations of St. Birgitta, translated into English, are mentioned in several fifteenth-century wills. The earliest occurrence is in the will of Elizabeth Sywardby proved in 1468: De libro compilato in lingua Anglica de Revelationibus Sanctae Brigidae, inferius legato, lxvjs. viijd.[1] In 1481 Margaret Purdawnce of Norwich left 'to the Nunnery of Thetford, an English book of St. Bridget'.[2] Of especial interest is the bequest of Cecily, Duchess of York, to her daughter Anne de la Pole in 1495: 'Also I geve to my daughter Anne, priores of Sion, a boke of Bonaventure and Hilton in the same in Englishe, and a boke of the Revelations of Saint Burgitte.'[3]

---

[1] *Testamenta Eboracensia*, Surtees Society, vol. iii, p. 163.
[2] *Norfolk and Norwich Arch. Soc.*, vol. iv, p. 385.
[3] *Wills from the Doctors' Commons*, ed. J. G. Nichols and John Bruce, Camden Society, 1863, p. 8.

Saint Birgitta xxxix

There are seven extant manuscripts containing translations of the revelations, which are discussed in another part of the Introduction.

PART III. METHOD OF TRANSCRIPTION

The manuscript has been followed as closely as possible and I have amended the text only in cases of obvious error. The reading from the Latin text, where this is at all necessary, has been given also.

I have modernized the punctuation, as that of the manuscript is confusing. Where in-to, to-for, ther-for, neuer-the-less, a-boue, o-lyue, in-stede, for-getting, over-come, be-hold, I-nogh, I-write, &c. are separated in the manuscript, they have been hyphenated in the text. Proper names, and among divine names God and Jesus Christ, have been uniformly capitalized; where nouns have capitals in the manuscript they remain; elsewhere, capitalization at the beginning of the sentence has been normalized. Ff in the manuscript has been normalized to F or f according to the general rules of capitalization. The crossed ll, th, and bl, the m- and n- macron, and the r- and d- flourish, which are used without meaning through-out the manuscript, are not preserved except where an expansion is obviously intended by the scribe. With a few exceptions, the first scribe does not differentiate between þ and y; in the text, y has been changed to þ when it stands for th. Where the first scribe has written y^e and y^u, I have normalized to þe and þu. All abbreviations are expanded.

THE REVELATIONS OF SAINT BIRGITTA

Owr[1] lorde Ihesu Cryst tellyth seynte Birgitte why he chesyth hyr to be hys spovse, and how as a spowse she awyth to aray hyr and be redy to hym.

fol. 1 a
Revelations,
Book I,
Chap. 2[5].

I am maker of heuen and erth and see and of all thynges
5 that bene in hem. I am on wyth the fader and the holy goste, nott as goddys of stones or of[2] golde, as some tyme was seyde, ne mony goddys, as then was wende; bott on God, fader and sone & holy goste, iij in persones and on in substance, maker of all thynges and made of none, vnchangeble and almyghty
10 lestyng with-out begynnyng & wyth-out ende. I am he that was borne of the vyrgyne, notte leuyng the godhed bott knytting itt to the manhode, þat I shuld be in on person þe verry sonne of God and the sonne of the virgyne. I am he that honge one the crosse and dyede and was beryed, þe godhed abydynge vn-
15 hurte. For þough[3] the manhode and body whych I, sonne, alone toke wer dede, yett ine[4] þe godhede in whych I was oo God wyth þe fader and þe holy goste I lyuede all way. I am also þe same þat roose frome deth and styede in-to heuyn that nowe spekys wyth þe wyth my spiryte. I haue chosse & take
20 the to me to be my spowse for to shewe the my privey concelles, for so itt lykyth me. And also thow arte myne be all maner of ryght, when in the deth of thyne hossebond thowe yeuyste þi wylle jne to myn hondes, and also after hys deth whan thowe thoughteste and praydeste how þow myght be-com
25 poor for me and for me for-sake all thynges. And ther-for of ryght þow arte myne and for so mych cheryte me byhouyth to orden for the; ther-for I take the to my spowse and to myn

---

[1] *The chapter headings are rubricated throughout, and the initial letter of each of the revelations is in blue.*

[2] MS. of *inserted above line. All insertions and corrections are in the same hand, unless otherwise stated.*

[3] MS. of *cancelled after* þough.

[4] MS. ine *marked through as if for cancellation.*

[5] *The corresponding chapters in the complete Latin text of the Revelations are given in the side-notes at the beginning of each chapter in the text.*

B

owne propur delyte, sych as semyth goode to haue with a
chaste sowle.

To the spovse þer-for it longyth to be redye when hyr spowse
wyll make hys weddyng, that she be semely arayde and clene.
Then arte thow well made clene, yf thy thowght be al-way
a-bowte þi synnes; how I clensed the frome the synne of
Adam yne þy baptym & howe often I | haue suffered the and
supportede the when þow haste fallen into synne. The spovse
also owyth to haue tokenes of hyr spovse on hyr breste; that
ys, to[1] take kepe of the benefettez and werkys that I haue
done for the; that is to sey, how nobley I made the, yeuyng
the body and sovle, and howe nobley I haue endewede the,
yeuynge the helth and temperall goodes, and how swetely
I bowght the ayeyne when I dyed for the and restorede the
thyn herytage, yf thu wyll haue ytt. The spovse owyth also
to do the wyll of hyr spovse. What is my wyll, bott that þow
wyll love me above all thynges and to wyll non other thynge
bott me? I haue made all thynge for man, and all hem soiette
to hym; bott he louyth all þynges saue me, and hatyth ryght
nott bott me. I bowght hym ayeyne hys herytage that he
lost. Bot he is so alyende & turned from reson that he
desyryth mor thys transytorye wyrshyp that is botte as froth
of the see, which sodenly rysyth vppe as a mounte and as sone
fallyth down to noȝt, than everlastynge wyrshyppe wher-in is
endeles goode.

Bot thow, my spowse, yf thu desyr no thing bott me, yf thu
dyspyse all þynges for me, nott only thy chyldren & kynne, bot
eke wyrshypes and rechesse, I shall yeve the moste precyos
and swettyste rewarde; nott gold and syluer, bot my-selfe, to
be thy spowse & endeles mede, that am kynge of blysse. And
yf þow be ashamed to be poor and dyspysed, be-hold that I thy
God goo to-for the, whome seruauntez & frendes for-soke in
erthe; for I sowght notte ertheljr frendes, botte heuynly.
And yf thow fere and drede the byrthen of labor and sykenes,
consyder how grevowse it is to brenne in the fyr whych thu
haddeste deseruede, yf þow hadde offended a temperall lorde as
thow hath offendede me. For thowgh I love the wyth all my
herte, yett I shall nott do ayenest ryghtwysnesse in þe leste

---

[1] MS. to *inserted above line*.

poynte, bott that as thu has trespased in all thy membres so that in all þu do satysfaccion. Neuer-the-lesse yett for a good wyll and purpose to amend, I chaunge ryghtwysnesse into mercy, | foryeuyng grevouse tormentez for a lytell amende- mente. Ther-fore take to the gladely a lyttell labor, that þow mayst þe sonner be made clene and come to grete rewarde. For it is semely that the spowse labor wyth hyr spovse tyll she be werye, that she may afterwarde the mor [1] sourely and trystely take hyr reste wyth hym.

Owr lorde Ihesu Cryste steryth Saynte Birgitt not to be a-ferde of hys spekynge wyth hyr, techyng hyr the dyfference of the good spirite and the euyll.

I am maker of all thynges and ayane-byer : why dredyst þow of my wordes and why thowghteste thu of what spyrite they wer, of the goode or of the evyll? Tell me what founde thu in my wordes þat thyne owne conscyence told the noght to be do? Or bade y the any thynge ayanes reson?

The spouse seynte Byrgitte answerde : No thynge, lorde, bot all þat thu sayde ar trewe, and y erred euyll.

Then seyde our lorde: I bade thee iij thynges of whych thu mayste knowe a goode spyrite. Fyrste, I bade the wyrshyp thy God that made the and yaue the all þat þou haste ; and þys thyn owne reson techyth the, to wyrshyp hym above·all thynges. Seconde, I bade the kepe and holde the ryght fayth ; that is, to be-leve that nothynge ys doo nor may be doo withoute God. The iij, I bade the lofe resonable temperance and continence of all þynges ; for the world ys made for mane that he shulde vse it to hys nede.

So also be iij contrarie to these. Thu may knowe the vnclene spirite for he steryth the to seke thyn own wyrshyp and praysyng and to be prowde of the yiftes þat God hath yeue the ; and he steryth the to intemperance of all thy membres and of all other þynges, and to þese he inflawmeth þy herte. He dysseyuyth also some tyme vnder colowr of goode ; and ther-for I haue bode the dyscusse thy conscyence and to open it to spirituell wyssemen. Þer-fore dowte the notte bot that the good spiritte of God ys than with the whan thu desyryste no

---
[1] MS. mor *inserted above line.*

fol. 2 b þing¹ | bot God, and of him thu art all inflamed. For that
may I alone do and it is inpossible the fende to negh vn-to the.
Ne he may nott neght to any euyll man, botte he be sufferede
of me, oþer for hys synnes or for some preuey doo[m]² knowe
to me. For the fende ys my creatur as all other thynges be ; 5
and of me he was well made, bot be hys own malysse he is
evyll, and therfor I am lorde ouer hym. And therfore they
that sey that they that serue me of grete deuocion wax madde
or hath a fende in hem, they putt a-pon me a wronge blame.
For they make me lyke to a manne that hadde a chaste wyffe 10
well tristyng in hyr hosbounde, and he putt hyr to a vowterer.
Sych on shulde y be, yf I sufferede a ryghtfull mane that hade
a lovyng herte to me to be take to the fende. Bot for I am
trusty & trew, the fende shall neuer haue lordeshippe in noo
sowle that deuotely seruyth me. For þough my fryndes seme 15
some tyme as madde, yett that is nott for passyon of the fende,
ne for they serue me of fervente deuocyon, bot for defaute of
her brayn or for some other priuey cause whych is to hem cause
of mor mekenes. It may also be some tyme that þe fende
takyth power of me opon the bodyes of goodemen to her 20
encrese of mede, and he that derkyth his conscience ; but in þe
sowles of hem that hath fayth and delyte in me may he³ neuer
haue lordeshyp nor power.

Revela- Her our lorde Ihesu Cryst enformyth saynt Birgytt how
tions,
Book I, the worlde stondeth anenste hym in all states and degrees 25
Chap. 41. under lykenes of v men, wher comforth and helpe ys by-hote
to the goode and herde sentence y-ʒoue a-yeynes the euyll.

I am maker of all thynges. I am gote of the fader to-for
Lucifer. And I am vndepartable in the fader and the fader in
me, and oo spirite in both. Ther-for ther ys oo God, fader, 30
sonne and holy goste, and nott iij goddes. I am he that by-
hight to Abraham⁴ endeles herytage, and by Moyses brought
my peple out of Egypte. I am also the same that spake in the
profettes. The fader sente me in-to the vyrgyns wombe, nott
dysseueryng hym fro me, bot abydyng vnseperably with me, 35

¹ a ij.   ² MS. doon ; Latin iudicium.
³ MS. he inserted above line.   ⁴ MS. ra abbreviation written above final m.

The Revelations of Saint Birgitta 5

that manne whych was goo frome God shuld be my cherite turne
aȝeyn | to God.   fol. 3 a
Bot now to-fore yow, my heuynly Courte, þough ye see &
knowe all thinges in me, ȝett for knowlege and instruccion of
5 thys my spouse that is presente and may nott perceyve
spirituell thynges, I compleyne me apon these v men that
stondes to-fore me, that they offende me ine mony wyse. For
as some tyme by the name of Israel I vnderstonde all the men
ine the worlde, so now by these v men I vnderstonde all the
10 men ine þe worlde. The fyrst man is the gouernour of the
chyrch and hys clerkys. The ij is wykedde lay peple. The iij,
Ieweys. The iiij, paynems. The v, my frendys. Bot oute of
the Iewes I excepte all the Iewes that ar pryueley crysten men
and serue me priualy in clene charite and ryght feyth and per-
15 fyte werke. And oute of the paynems I excepte all thoo þat
wolde gladely goo by the way of my commaundementes yf they
wyst how. And yf they wer enformyd and in dede they doo what
they kan or may, these shall in no wyse be demed wyth hem.

Bot now I compleyne on þe, thow hedde of my chyrch, that
20 syttest[1] in my sete, whych I take to Peter & hys successours
to sytte ine iij fold dygnite and auctoryte. Fyrst, that they
shuld haue power to bynde and lowse sowles from synne.
Secunde, that they shulde opyn heuyn to heme that doth pennance. Thryde, that they shulde sparr heuyn to wyked and
25 cursede and dyspyse[r]s.[2] But thu that owest to vnbynd
sowles and presente hem to me, thu arte verely a sleer of
soules. For I ordenyd Peter to be a shypperde and a keper of
my shepe ; bot thu arte a dysperpeler and a reicetter of hem.
For thu arte wors and mor envyouse then Lucyfer. For he
30 hadde envye to me and desyride to flee non bot me, that he
myght be lorde in stede of me. Bot thu arte so mych wors
and mor envyouse then he, that thu nott only fleest me, puttyng
me frome the be thyn wyll & werkes, bot also thu sleste soules
by thin euyll ensample. I bowght sowles with my blode and
35 toke hem to the as to a trewe frende. Bot thu takeste hem
ayayne to the enmy from whom | I bowgh[t][3] hem. Thu art fol. 3 b
mor vnryghtwosse then Pylate, that demed non to deth bott

---

[1] MS. syttsest.   [2] MS. dyspyses : Latin, contemnentibus.
[3] MS. bowgh.

me. Bot thu not only demest me as lorde of non ne worthy
any goode, bot also thu demeste innocent soules, and lattes
gylty goo vnpunyshed. Thu arte more enmy than Iudas, for
he solde non bot me. Bot thu selleste notte me allone bot eke
the sowle of my chosen for thy sowle wynnyng and vayne
name. Thu arte mor abhomynable then þe Iewes, for they
crucyfiede bot my body; bot thu crucyfyes & punyshyth þe
sowles of my chosen, to whom thy malyce and trespace is
bitterer then any swerde. And therfor, for thu art lyke to
Lucyfer in envye, more vnryghtfull than Pylate, mor enmy
than Iudas, and mor abhominable then the Iewes, therfor
worthely I compleyne a-pon the.

To the ij man, that is, to the lewed peple, our lorde sayde
thus: I haue made all thynges for thi profett, and thu haste
consented in me & I in the. Thow hast yeuen thy fayth to
me and by-hight with thin oth to serue me, bot now art
gone from me as a man not knowyng hys God. Thu counteste
my wordes bot lesynges and my werkes bot vanite ; thow seyst
that my wyll and commawndementes ar ou[er]¹ herde ; thu
haste broke the fayth that thu by-highest me and forsake my
name ; thu haste dysseuerede the fro the novmbre of my
sayntes, and thu art comen to the novmbre of fendes and made
her felaw. Þe semyth that none ys worthy to haue praysyng
and wyrshyp bott thu alone. All my wyll and all that thow
art hold to do to me is herde to the, and all that pleysyth the
is esy. Therfor worthely I compleyne apon the. For thu
haste broke þi feyth that þu yaue me in thy baptim ; and seth
mor-ouer for my charite which I shewed the in worde & dede,
thow blameste me as a lyer. And for my passion thu sayste
I am a fowle.

To the iij, that is, to the Iewes, our lorde seyde thus: I
bygan my cherite with yow and chose yow be my peple.
I bowght yow oute of thraldam and yafe yow my lawe and
ledde yow into the londe that I by-hight your faderes. | I sente
yow profettes to yowr comforth, and after I chesse me a vyrgyn
of yow, of whom I toke manhod. Bott now I compleyn me
apon yow now that ȝe wyll nott belefe, saying that Cryst come
not ȝett, bot he ² ys to come.

¹ MS. ou herde; *Latin* nimis grauia.   ² MS. the.

The Revelations of Saint Birgitta 7

To the iiij, that is, to the hethen, our lorde sayde thus: I haue made the and bought the as well as a cristenne man, and done all godenesse for the. Bot thu art as a wode man, for thu wott not wheþer thow gost. Thu wyrshipis creators for
5 thy maker and fals for throwth, and bowes thy kne to-for that is lesse worthy than thu. And þer-for I compleyn apon the.

To the v our lorde seyde thus: Come ner, my frynde. Then anon our lorde seyde vnto hys heuynly courte: my louyd fryndes, I haue on frynde by whom I vnderstonde mony. He
10 is as a man closede amonge shrewes & prisonde full herde. Yf he sey treugth, they stoppe his mowth. Yf he do good, þey put a sper in his breste. Loo, my fryndes and all my sayntes, how longe shall I suffer all þese folke and sych contempte of hem?

15 Seynt Iohn þe Baptyst vnswerd: Thu, lorde, art as a myrrour moste clene; for in the as in a myrrour we see and know all thynges. With-out any worde or spech thu arte incomparable swettenes wher-in all goodenes sauoreth to vs. Thu art as a swerde most sharpe that demeste in euynesse.

20 Than vnswerde our lorde to hym: forsoth, my frynde, thu sayth trew. For in me all my chosen sees all good and all ryghtwysnesse; and so doth wykked spirites also, þough it be not non lyght bot in her conscience. As yf a man that had lernede lettruer wer putt in prison, þough he wer in derkenes and
25 myght nott see, yett he cowde the thynges he lorned to-for; ryght so feendes, þough they see nott in ryghtwysnesse in lyght of my clernesse, yett they know as they see in her conscyence. I am also as a thyng that partyth a thyng in too, for so do I to ych as he desyrith.

30 After this our lord seyde to saynt Peter: thow art founder of fayth and of my church; sey þu in the heryng of all my hevenly courte what ryghtwysnes wyl that be doo of these v men.

Seynte Peter aunswerd, | and seyde: praysyng and wyrshuppe fol. 4 b
35 be to the, lorde, for thy cherite that thow doste with thin erth. Blessedde be thu of all thy heuenly cowrte, for thu makys vs see & know in the all thynges that ar doo and shal be do. For in the we see and knowe all thynges. Thys is verray ryghtwosnesse, that the fyrst man that syttes in thy sete and hath

werkes of Lucifer leese with repreve þat sete wher-in he pre-
sumyth to sette, & be made pertener in peyne with Lucifer.
Of the ij, ryghtwyssenesse ys that, for he hath gone from thy[1]
fayth, he descende to helle with hys hed downwarde and hys
fete upwarde; for he hath despysede the that shulde be his 5
hede, and loved him-selfe. Of the iij, ryghtwysnes is that he
see nott thy face, bot that he be punysshed after hys malice &
couetyse; for they that ar in mysbyleue deserue not to see thy
syght. Of the iiij, rych[t]wysnes[2] is that, as madde man, he be
closed and putt in derke plase. Of the v, ryghtwysnes ys that 10
helpe be sente to hym.

Thes thynges herde, our lorde aunswerde and seyde : I swer
by God the fader, whose voyce Iohn Baptyste herde in Iordan,
I swere by the body þat Iohn Baptyst see & towched in Iordan,
I swer by that spirite that in Iordan apperid in lykenesse of a 15
coluer, that I shal do ryghtwosnes vppon these v men.

After this our lorde seyde to the fyrst man of the v, that is,
to the clergye: the swerde of my cruelte shal enter in-to thy
body. And it shal be-gyn to enter at the ouer-parte of thyn
hede, and so myghtyly it shal be smytten in that it shal never 20
be drawe out. Thi seete shal be throwe dovn as a ston most
heuy that abydyth nott tyl it come to the loweste depnes of
hell. Thyn fyngurs, that is to sey thyn assissours, shal brinne
in fyr and brymston that neuer shall be whenched. Thyn
armes, þat ys to say, thy vycares, whych-owe to be strechede 25
out to þe profette of sowles and now ar streched oute to the
profyte & wyrship of the world, shal be dampnede with the
payne that Dauid spekyth of, sayinge: 'Fiant filij eius orphani'
& 'vxor eius vidua & alieni accipiant substanciam eius': that
is, 'hys|chyldren mote be faderlesse and hys wyf a wydow, & 30
alyenes motte take hys wyrshyp and goodes'. What is his
wyfe bot hys sowle, whych shall be for-sake from the blysse of
heuyn and made wydow from God. Hys sonnes, that is to
say, hys vertues that he semede to haue and my simple peple
that was vnder hem, shall be departed frome hem. And her 35
worthynes and goodes shall passe to other & þey for her worthynesse shall enherett endeles confucion. And then shall the

---

[1] Y written over original a.   [2] MS. ryghwynes.

The Revelations of Saint Birgitta

aray of her hedes be drownede in the fylth of hell, from whense they shall never a-ryse. Bot as they ascendede above other here by wyrshyp and pride, so shall the[y]¹ be drowned byneth other in hell so depe þat it shall be inpossible to hem
5 euer to a-ryse. Her membres and soiettes, that is to sey her followers and her clerkes and fawtoures, shall be kytt of and descended from hem as a wall that is dystroyde, wher no stone is lefte vppon other, ne wher morter clevyth to the stones. For mercy shall no[t]² come apon hem, for my cherite shall nott
10 make hem hote. Ne they shall nott be beld in endeless beldyng, dwellyng in heuyn, bott with her hedes shall be tourmented with-oute ende, departed from all goode.

To the ij man, that is, to the lay peple, I sey: for thow wyll nott hold the fayth that thu haste by-hote me ne haue cherite
15 to me, I shall sende to þe a beste þat shal come oute of a sharpe rennyng flode, and swalow the ine ; & as a rennyng flode goth away downwarde, so shall that best lede the dovn in-to the iner partyes of hell. And as þu may nott goo vpp ayeine a myghty & hasty rennyng flode, so shal þu neuer mowe rysse
20 from þe pytte of hell.

To the iij man, that is, the Iewe, I sey : for thow, Iew, wyll nott now by-leve þat I am comen, þer-for when I comme to þe ij doome, þu shall nott see in my blysse, bot in thy conscience, and preve that all þat I seyde was trewe. And than shall thu
25 haue peyne, as þu hast deserued.

To the iiij man, þat is, the paynem, I sey: for thu takest no kepe to byleve ne wyll nott know the ryght feyth, þer-for thy derkenes shall shyne vn-to þe, and thy herte shal be lyghtned, that þu shall know that my domes ar trew ; & yett shall þu
30 nott come to endelesse lyght.

To the v man, þat is, Goddes seruauntes, I sey: iij thynges shall I do vn-to the. Fyrst, I shall ³ | fyll the with-inne wyth fol. 5 b myne hete. Secund, I shall make thi mouth herder and stabler than any stone, so þat stones cast the shall turne agayn.
35 Thryd, I shall arme the with myn armour, þat noo sperr shall noye the, bot all thyng shall melte to-fore the as wex ayeneste the fyr. Therfor be comforted and stonde manfully. For as

¹ MS. the ; *Latin* hi.   ² MS. non ; *Latin* neque.
³ MS. shall/shall.

a knyght that in a battell he hopeth to hafe help of hys lorde fyghtyth as longe as only lycour ys in hym, soo stounde þu sourely and fyght. For thy lorde God shall yeve þe helpe, whom noon may with-stounde ; and for þu haste bott a lytell and a small noumbre, I shall wyrshyp þe & encrese the.

Loo, my frendes, these þinges ye see and know in me, & thus stondes þe worlde to-for me. These wordes that I haue now seyde shall be fullfylled, and they shall neuer enter my kyngdom as longe as I am kynge bot yf they amende hem, for heuyn shall be yeuyn to noon bote to hem that meke hem-selfe and do pennans.

Then aunswerde all the courte of heuyn : praysyng be to the lorde God that art with-owte begynnyng & wyth-owten ende. Amen.

Revelations, Book IV, Chap. 37. Owr lorde Ihesu Cryste tellyth saynte Birgitt of herde sentence of ryghtwesnesse that he wyll doo ayainste all mankynde botte yf they amende hem.

The sonne of God askyth of saynte Birgitte and sayth: doughter, how stondeth the worlde now?

She vnswerde : it stondes as an open sake to whom all rynne, and as a man reynyng nott rekkyng whatt folow after.

Then seyde our lorde : ther-for ryghtwosnes is þat I go with my plowgh apon all the erth and worlde, both heethen and crysten. I shall neuer spar olde nor yong, poor ne rych. Bott ych shall be demed after ryghtwysnesse and ych shall dye in hys synne ; and her howse shall be lefte wythout dwellers ; and yet shall I nott make an ende of the worlde.

Seynt Birgitte sayde : o lorde, be dyspleased [not][1] þough I speke. Send some of thy frendes to warne hem and monysh hem to-for of her perell.

Our lorde aunswerde : it is writen that the rych man in fol. 6 a hell, despayring of his own helth, asked | that on myght be sente to warne his brethern that they peryshed nott on þe same wyse. And it was aunswerde to him, 'that shall nott be, for they haue Moysen and the prophettes, of whom they may be tawght'. So sey I to the. They haue the gospell & saynges of profettes ; they haue ensamples and wordes of

[1] *Latin* ne (inquit) indigneris.

doctors; they have reson and vnderstondyng. Vse they these
and they shall be sauyd. For yf I sende the, thow mȧy nott
crye so lowde to be herde; and yf I sende my frendes, they ar
bott few; and yf they crye, vnneth they shall be herde.
5 Neuer-the-lesse I shall sende my frendes to sych as me lykyth,
and they shall make redy a way to God.

Owr lorde Ihesu Cryste techyth seynte Birgitt the Revela-
dyfference be-twyx good deth and euyll deth, and how tions, Book IV,
goddes seruantes owe nott to be hevy þowht they be¹ in Chap. 40.
10 this lyf.

The sonne of God spekyth to seynte Birgitte thus: dowghter,
drede the nott; thys woman that is seke shall nott dye, for
hyr werke plese me. And whan the same woman was dede,
the sonne of God seyde ayayne to seynte Birgitte: loo,
15 dowghter, it is trewe that I seyde, thys woman is not dede,
for hyr blysse is grete. For the departyng of body and sowle
of ryghtfull men is bott a slepe, for they awake in endelesse
lyfe. Bot that is veraly to be called deth when þe sowle,
departede from the body, lyuyth in deth euerlastyng. Þer is
20 mony that takyth noo kepe of thynges to come desyris to dye
in cristen deth. Bot what is cristen deth, bot for to dye as I
dyed, innocentely, wyllfully, and pacyentely? Am I therfor
to be dispicede, for my deth was dyspisable and herde? Or ar
my chosen therfor foules, for they sufferede dyspysable tor-
25 mentez? Or come it of fortune, or was it wrought be the
course of planettes & of sterris? Nay, bot þer-for I and my
chosen sufferede herde passyon to showe in worde and in
exsample that the way to heuyn is herd, and that it shulde
besyly be hadde in mynde how mych nede the wyked haue to
30 be clensede seth the innocentes & chosen sufferede so sharpe
thynges. Therfore wete þu̇ well | that he dyth dispysabley and fol. 6 b
evyll that lyuyng dissolutly dyeth in wyll to synne, and while
he that forth goyng in the worlde desyrith to lyffe longer and
can not thanke God; bot he that lovyth God with all hys herte
35 and is trowbled innocentely with dyspysable deth or grevede
with longer sekeness, he lyves and dyeth blessedly. For a

¹ *Space for another word follows in* MS.

sharpe deth lassyth synne and payne for syn, & morith the rewarde in blysse.

Loo, I brynge too men to thy mynde that after mannes dome dyede in bytter & dyspisable deth, whych, bott they had gott such deth of my grete mercy, shuld neuer haue bene sauede. Bott for God punysheth nott twyse hem þat ar contrite in herte, þer-for they come to the crovne of endeles rewarde. Ther-for the frendys of God owe nott to be hevy, þough they haue her temperall tribulacion or þough they dye by bitter deth. For it is moste blessede to sorowe her for a tyme and to be trowblede in the world, that he come not to more grevouse purga[to]rie¹ wher is no fleyng ne tyme of laboring.

Revela- **Of the tribulacion and sorow that our lady sufferede &**
tions, **of the fruyte of² owr lordys wordys. And of iij howses**
Book II, **þat Cryst and mannys sowle owe to haue to-geder.**
Chap. 24.

Oure blessede lady spekyth to seynte Birgitt and seyth : lyke as ther wer a grete hoste of men, & one þat hadde a grete and a heuy byrthn one hys bak and on hys armys and his eyne full of teres wente forth by hem, and lokede yf eny of hem wolde haue pitee on hym and help hym of hys byrthen, ryght so was I ; for frome the byrth of my sonne vn-to hys deth I was full of tribulacion. I bare a ryght grete byrthen on my bakke, for I entendede contynually to the labour of Goddes seruice, and I suffered pacyently all that euer come vn-to me. In my armes I bar most heuy byrthene, for I sufferde tribulacion & soro of herte mor than euer dyde any creatur. I hadde myn eyne full of teres when I byheld in the members of my sonne þe place of nayles, & hys passyon þat wa[s]³ to come, and when I see fullfylled in him all that I had herde to-fore
fol. 7 a profyciede of profettes. But now I loke vn-to all þat | ar in the worlde, [l]este⁴ y myght fynde any þat hadde pyte & compassyon on me and wolde thynke on my sorow. And y fonde bot fewe that thenke on my sorowe and tribulacion. Þerfore, thu my dowghter, of I be foryette and lytell sett by, yett foryette þu nott me, bot see my sorow and folow yt as mych as þu may. Be-holde my sorow and teres and be sory ; for the

---

¹ MS. purgarie ; *Latin* purgatorium.   ² MS. of of.
³ MS. wat ; *Latin* passionem eius futuram.   ⁴ MS. beste ; *Latin* si forte.

The Revelations of Saint Birgitta

frendys of God ar bot fewe. And now stonde stabley, for, loo, my sonne comyth vn-to the.

Then come our lorde Ihesu Cryst and sayde: I that speke with the am thy God and thy lorde. My wordes ar as flowres of a goode tre; for lyke as all flowres, þough þei come oute of on rote of oo tre yett þei come not all to effecte of fruyte, so my wordes are as flowres comyng oute of the rote of godly cheryte, whych, þought þei be receyuede of mony, yett they bryng not forth fruyte in all ne wax nott ripe in all. For some take hem and kape hem for a tyme, and after caste hem owte, for they ar vnkynde to my[1] spiritte. Bot some take hem and holde hem, for they ar full of cheryte and in hem þey wyrke fruyte of devocion.

Therfor, þu my spouse, for thow art mine of godely ryght, it byhoueth[2] vs to haue iij howses. In the fyrste awe to be sych necessares as enteryth in-to þe body, as mete or drynke. In the ij awe to be clothes to helen the body with-oute. And in the iij, necessarie Instrumentez that longeth to þe profette of howsholde.

In the firste howse awe to be iij thynges: brede, drynk, and sowlle. In þe ij, other iij thinges; that is, lynen cloth, wollen cloth, and cloth of sylke that is made of the worke of wormes. In þe iij, oþer iij thynges; first, Instrumentes and vessells þat shall be fylled wyth lycour; secunde, quyk Instrumentes as horse, assys, and oþer; the iij, Instrumentez artyficiall, be whych quyke thynges ar mevyde.

Merke how in the fyrst howse awe to be brede of god wyll, drinke of godly premeditacion, and sowlle of goddely wysdom.

Revelations, Book II, Chap. 25.

I that speke with the am maker of all thynges and made of none. To-fore me no thynge was, ne after me eny thing may be; for y was and am all way. I am also þat lorde whos power none may wythstonde, and of me is all power & lorde-shyp. I speke to the as a man spekyth to hys wyfe. My wyfe, vs moste haue iij howses. In one moste be brede and

---

[1] MS. my *inserted above line before* to.
[2] *Marg. gloss.*: Nota de tribus domibus.

drynk and sowle. Bot thu may aske what meneth thys brede, whether y mene the brede that is in the auter. For-soth þat is brede to-for tho wordes; 'Hoc est enim corpus meum'. Bot tho wordes seyde of the preste, 'It is nott brede bot my blessede body that I toke of the virgyn and was crucifiede on the crosse', thys brede mene nott I here ; bot the brede þat vs muste gader into one howse is a good and a clene wyll. Bodely brede, yf it be clene and pure, it profetyth to ij thynges. Fyrst, it comforteth and yifes strenght to all the vaynes and senowes of the body. Secounde, it gadereth to it all inwarde fylth, and þer-with it goth owte fro man, and so man is clensede. Ryʒt so a clene wyll. Fyrst, it comforteth ; for yf a man wyll nothyng but that god wyll, ne laboryth no thynge bot to the wyrshyp of God, and desyryth wyth all his herte to be owte of the worlde and to be wyth God, this wyll comforthyth a man in God and encresyth the wyrshyp of God and makes the worlde vyle and fowle. It strenght pacyence and makyth stronge the hope of gettyng of blysse, so myche that he takyth & sufferyth gladly all that fallyth to hym. Seconde, a good wyll drawyth oute all fylth that noyse the sowle, as pryde, covetyse, and lecherye. Bot when the fylth of pryde or of any oþer synne comyth into the mynde, than it goth away yf a man thynke thus: pryde is veyne, for it is not semly hym to be praysed þat takes yiftes ; bot þe yeuer is to be praysed. Couetyse ys vayne, for all erthely thynge shall be lefte, and lechery ys bot stynke. Þer-for I wyll nott ther-of ; bot I wyll folowe the wyll of my God, whos rewarde shall neuer haue ende, nor hys goodes waxe not olde.

The drynke that vs muste haue in our howses ys godly thynkyng to-for in all thys that ar to be doo. Bodely drynke is veyleable in ij wise. Fyrst, it maketh goode dygestyon. For who euer purpose to do any goode dedes, yf he byholde in him-selfe & bysely caste in hys | mynde, or he do owght, what wyrshyp shall come to God þer-of, what avayle to hys neghtburr, and what profette to hys sowle, and that he wyll nott doo bot he perseyve some godely profett in hys werke, than the werke shall haue good processe & goode ende as a good dygestyon. Than, yf any vndiscrecion happen to come in doynge of that werke, it shall sone be perceyved, and then, yf

owgh⌊t⌋¹ be wronge, it may lyghtly be amendede, and hys werke shall be ryght & resonable edyficacion in the syght of man. For he that hath not ² godely thynkynge to-fore in hys worke neþer sekyth profette of sowle ne the wyrshippe of God.
5 Then of his werke hafe processe for a tyme, yette in the ende it shall turne to noght, bot yf the entente be corrected and amendett. Secunde, drynke quenchyth thyrste. What is wers thirste þan synne of wykede desyr and of yr? Bot and a man thynk to-fore what profette comyth thereof, how
10 wrechidly it is endede, and what reward if it be with-stounde, anon be the grace of God thilke wyked thyrste is quenched, and the hetee of godely charite and of good desyr comyth to the sowle, and gladnes ryseth in him that he dyde notte þe thinges that come in hys mynde. And he sekyth occasion how
15 he may from thensforth flee thoo thynges that he shuld haue be deceyuyde with, hadde nott thynkyng to-for haue holpe. And he shall be the more besy after to be-war of sych thynges. Thys, my spowse, is the drynke that we awe to gader into owr celar.
20 Thirde ; ther muste be sowle þat doth twoo thynges. Fyrst, it makyth better sauer in the mouþe, and it is more conueniente to the body than yf brede wer alon. Secunnde, it makyth the body more delycate and the blode better than brede and drynke onely. Ryght so doth gostely sowlle. What is
25 this sowlle bot godely wysdom ? For who that euer haue a gode wyll, and wyll ryght noght botte tho thynges that longe to God, yf he haue also goddely thynkyng to- | fore, doynge no fol. 8 b thynge but yf he knowe fyrst that it is to the wyrshyp of God, to hym wysdom sauoreth ryght well. But now myght thu
30 aske what is this godely wisdame, for ther ar mony so sympell that can nott her pater noster and vneth that ryght. Other ar of grete letruer and depe connyng. Is that godely wysdome ? Naye. For godely wysdom is nott onely in letturis, bot in herte and in goode lyvyng. Who euer he be that thenkyth
35 bysely the way vn-to deth and the qualite of the selfe, deth and the dome after deth, he is wyse. And who caste from hym þe vanyte of the worlde and all superflew thynges, and is contente wyth hys onely necessaries, and trauelyth in the love of

¹ MS. owgh. ² MS not *inserted above line.*

God as mych as he may, he hath sowle of wysdome, by whych
the brede of gode wyll and drynke of godely forthynkyng
sauouryth mych the better. For when a man thynkes on hys
deth, and how naked he shall be frome all thynges in hys
deth, and when he perceyuyth the dredefull dome of God, wher 5
no thyng ys hydde, no thynge left vnpunished, and when he
thenkyth also the unstablenesse and vanyte of the worlde,
Ioythe he not than, and sauour[i]th¹ it nott swetely in
hys herte that he hath loste hys wyll to Gode, and ab-
stenede hym frome synne? Is not than hys body com- 10
fortede and hys blode bettered? That is to say, all sekeness of
sowle as slewth and dissolucion of maners is dryve away, and
the blode of goodely cherite is fresh. For he sees it is mor
resonable to loue thoo thynges that ar euerlastynge than thoo
thynges that ar faylynge. Ther-fore goodely wysdome is not 15
onely in lettrur, bot in goode werke. For ther ar mony ryght-
wysse after the worlde and to here own desyris, bot they ar all
vnwyse to the commaundementes of God & to hys wyll and to
refreynynge of her flesh. And they ar not wyse, bot vnwyse
and blynde; for they know and conne tho thyngis that shall 20
fol. 9a vayle and ar profytable; bot ryght | a lytell whyle and they
dyspyce euerlastynge thynges. Other þer be tha[t]² ar vnwyse
to the delytes of the worlde and to the wyrshyp ther-of. And
they ar wyse to be-holde thoo thynges that longyth to God and
ar feruente in his seruice; and thes ar verely wyse, for the 25
byddyng of God and hys wyll is sauourye vn-to hem. Thes ar
verely lyghtned & hath her eyne open, for they loke alwaye
how they myght come to verrye lyfe and lyght. Bot the other
goth in derkenes; and it semeth to hem more delectable to be
in derkenes then to seke the way by whych they may come to 30
lyght.

Ther-fore, my spowse, gadre we in-too owre howses these
thre; that is to say, goode wyll, goodely forthynkynge, and
goodely wysdome. For these thynges be wher-with vs muste
make merye. Bot þofe I speke onely to the, yette I mene by 35
[the]³ all my chosen in the world; for the sowle of a ryghtwosse
man is my spowse, and I am hys maker and hys ayayne-byer.

¹ MS. sauourrth.   ² MS. thar; Latin alij sunt insipientes.
³ Latin in te.

The Revelations of Saint Birgitta 17

Merke how seynte Laurence folowed the pacyence and passyon of our lorde Ihesu Cryst in lyfe & deth. And how in the secunde howse muste be lynnen cloth of pece and pacyence, and wollen cloth of dedes of mercy, and sylken
5 of abstenance from euyll.

Revelations, Book II, Chap. 26.

Owre lady saynte Marie spekyth to seynte Byrgitte and seyth: festne to þe roch of the passyon of my sonne as seynte Laurance festned it to hym. For he thought thus in hys mynde: my God is my lorde, and I am his seruante to the same. Lorde Ihesu
10 was nakede and scorned; how myght it þer-fore be semely that I that am his seruante be with-owte sorow and tribulacion? And ther-for, when he was streynede oute apon the coles, and when his grese molte and ranne in-to the fyre, and fyre enflawmede all the membres of his body, he loked upp to heuyn with his
15 eyn and seyde: 'Blessede be þu, my god and my maker, Ihesu Criste. I know that I haue not well lyved in my days, and þat I haue do lytell to thy wyrshyp. Ther-for thy mercye ys moste, | fol. 9 b I pray the do with me after thy mercy.' And wyth thys worde, the sowle departed from the body. Loo, my doughter, he that
20 loved my sonne so mych and suffered such paynes for hys wyrshyp, ʒett he lett[1] him-selfe vnworthy to gett hevyn. How then ar they worthy that lyven after her own wyll? Ther-for by-holde the passyon of my sonne and hys sayntes; for they sufferede nott so grete thynges wyth-owte cause, but for to yif oþer
25 ensample of lyvynge, & for to showe how streyte a rekenyng my sonne shall aske of synne, that wyll notte that the leste synne be with-owte amendement.

Then spake the son of God to hys spowse, seynte Birgitte, and seyde: I told the to-for what muste be in our howsys.
30 And a-monge other I seyde that ther muste be iij maner of clothyng: fyrst, lynen cloth that growyth of the erth; seconde, cloth of woll, or of lether that is made of bestes; and þe iij, cloth of sylke that is made of wormes.

Lynen cloth hath ij goodes: fyrst, it is softe and esy to the
35 bare bodye; secunde, it lesyth nott hys coloure, bot the ofter it is wesh, the clenner it is. Wollen also hath ij goodes: fyrst, it heleth fro nakednes; secunde, it makyth hote aʒaynes

[1] *Latin* dixit.

C

colde. Syulke also hath ij godes : fyrst, it semyth ryght feyr
and delycate ; secunde, it is ryght der to bye.
The lynnen that is able to the naked body betokenes peese
and a-corde. That awe a deuoute sowle to haue to God that he
haue peese with hys lorde, wyllyng ryght noght nor in other 5
wyse þan he wyll, nott offendyng him by synne. For be-twix
God and the sowle is no pese, bot if synne be sesed, and wordely
and fleschly desyre refrened. He oweth also to haue peese with
hys neghtborr, doyng hym no herme, bot helpyng [1] hym yf he
haue wher-of, and suffrynge hym yf he trespas aȝaynes him. 10

fol. 10 a For what distrow- | [2] bleth the sowle more wrechedly than all
way to desyr synne and neuer to be full þer-of, all way to
couett and neuer reste? And what prykketh the sowle mor
bitterly than to be wroth ayanste hys neghtbor and to haue
envye at his goodes and welth? Ther-fore the sowle must 15
haue peese vn-to God and to hys neghtborr; for ther may no
thyng be more restefull than to seese fro syn and nott to be
besy abowte the worlde. Ther is also no thynge so lyght þan
to Ioy of the good of his neghtbor and to wyll to him as himselfe.
Thys lynnen cloth aweth to be to the naked body; for to the 20
herte wher in God wyll reste peese from synne muste cleue
moste nyghe and moste principally amongest all other vertues.
For thys is the vertue that bryngyth God in-to the herte and
holdeth hym when he ys browght ine. This peese springyth
owt of the erth as lynnen; for verry peese and pacyence 25
spryngyth of beholdynge of a mannes own frelte. For if a man
that comyth of the erth beholde hys owne feblenesse, how sone
he is wrothe and hevye yf he be offendede, hurte, or dyssesed,
yf he thenke thus, he awe nott to do to a-nother that he may
nott ber hymselfe, thenkyng in him-selfe thus : as I am frele, 30
so is my neghtborr ; and yf I wyll nott suffer such thynges, no
mor may he. For then peese lesyth nott hys colowr, that is to
sey, hys stablenesse. But it is the mor stable and sadde ; for
the beholdynge in hym-selfe of his neghtborrs freelte maketh a
man gladely to suffer all disese that cometh. And yf it happe 35
that peese be fowled in any wyse be vnpacyence, than the
ofter and the sonner it be wesshed be pennance, the whitter it

fol. 10 b is anenste God ; and the more it is trowbled and | ofter weshed,

---

[1] MS. helpyng helpyng. [2] bleth the *catch word*.

the gladder and redyer it is to ber and suffer. For it Ioys in
hope of rewarde that itt hopeth is to come to it for peese ; and
ther-for it is the besyly war that it fall nott by vnpacyence.
 The secunde cloth that is of wolle or of lethur betokeneth
5 the werkes of mercy. This clothyng is made of skynnys of
dede bestes, which ar my seyntes þat ar symple as bestes.
With her skynnes oweth the sowle to be clothede ; that is, it
oweth to folow & to[1] do the werkes of her mercye. These
werkes doth ij thynges. Fyrst, they hylle the nakednes &
10 shame fastefullnesse of the synffull sowle, and clense it that it
apper nott fowle in my syght. Seconnde, they defende the
sowle aȝaynes cold, which coldenesse is bott hardenes of the
sowle vn-to my love. Ayaynste this colde, the werkes of
mercye ar veyleable that cloth the sowle so that it is not
15 disessed with cold. For by thes werkes God vysetyth the sowle,
that it nygh alway ner & ner vn-to God.
 The thrid clothyng, that is, of sylke, that is made of wormes
and semeth ryght dere to buye, betokeneth pur abstynence.
For þat is fayr both in syght of God and angelles and men.
20 Thys is der to bye, for it semyth herde to man to refreyne hys
mowth from mych spech and vayne, and to refreyne the desyre
of hys flesh from superfluite and his delices. It semyth eke
harde to go & doo ayanste his will ; bott þof it is herde, ȝit it
is prophetable in all wyse and feyr. Ther-for, thow my spowse,
25 by whom I vnderstonde all trew cristen men, gadre we in-to
owr secunde howse peese to God & to owr neghtborr, werkes of
mercye be compassyon and helpyng of wreches, & abstinence
frome euyll desyris and lustes. For this cloth of abstynence,
as it is derrer than other, so it is fayrer than other ; so much,
30 that with-owte that, non other vertue semeth feyr. And this
abstinence muste be drawe frome wormes ; þat is to sey, oft-
thynkyng of hys trespasse aȝeneste | his God, and of my meke- fol. 11 a
nes and abstinence, that was made lyke a worme for the loffe
of man. For yf man bethinke him in hys herte how mych and
35 often he hath synned aȝenste me, and what amendes he hath
made, he shall fynde ine him-selfe that he is nott sufficiente to
make amendes with none abstinence nor labor of þat he hath
offended me. If he take kepe eke of my payne and of my

[1] MS. to *inserted above line.*

sayntes, why and in what wyse we sufferede, he shall verely
vnderstonde that seth I asked so grete streteness of my-selfe
and of my sayntes that obeyed vn-to me, how mych nor strayte
vengeance shall I aske of heme that obey me nott. Ther-for
a good sowlle muste gladly take abstynence apon hym, and to 5
haue mynde on his synnes, how evell they be þat as wormes
gnowe þe sowle ; and so of fowle wormes he shall geder preciose
sylke, that is pur abstynence in all hys membres. Wher-of
God shall Ioy, and all the company of heuyn ; and he that
gaderith it shall deserue þer-fore endelesse blysse, whych, 10
hadde þat not holpe, shuld haue hadde euerlastyng woo and
weylynge.

Revela- **Of the Instrumentes of the thirde howse, that ar good**
tions, **thoughtes, verteus, maneres, & verry confession. And of**
Book II,
Chap. 27. **the sperrynge of all thre howses.** 15

The sonne of God spekyth to hys spowse and sayth : I told
the to-for, that in our thride howse muste be iij maner of
instrumentes. Fyrst, sych as liquour is kepte in. Secunde,
instrumentes that londe is tylled wyth, as ploghe & haroo and
axes and such other, wher-with þinges ar made ayeine when they 20
ar broke. Thride, quyke Instrumentes, as assys and horses and
other lyke, by whome both whykke thynges and dede ar
caryede.

In the fyrst howse that licour ar jne muste be ij maner of
Instrumentes : oon, wher-in ar kepe thyne lycowres, & swete, 25
fol. 11 b as oyle, water, & wyne, | and such other ; anoþer, to kepe in
bitter and thykke liquores, as mustarde, meele, and such other.
For-soth, these lycoures betoken thoughtes of the sowle, goode
and euyll. For a good thought is as swete oyle and dilectable
wyne, and an evyll thought is a bytter mustarde, for it maketh 30
the sowle bytter and troblesse. And as a man nedeth other
whyle thyke lycoures, for þof they profett nott mych to þe sus-
tenance of the body, yett they profette to purgynge and helynge
of the body and brayne, right so ar euyll thoughtes ; for þof they
hele nott nor make not the sowle fatt as oyle of goode 35
thoughtes, yett they profett to purgynge of the sowle, as
mustarde doth to purgynge of the brayne. For bot yf evyll
thowghtes come other whyle amonge, els man shulde be an

The Revelations of Saint Birgitta 21

angell, and no man ; and he shulde wene to haue all of himselfe. Ther-fore, that man vnderstonde the freltee that he hath of him-selfe, and the strenghth that he hath of me, it is nedefull that he be other while, be suffrance of my grete mercye,
5 temptede with evyll thoughtes ; to which thoughtes, if man consente nott, they ar purgacion of hys sowle and kepynge of hys verteus. And þof they be as mustarde, bitter to bere, ʒett they hele the sowle full mych, and gyde it vn-to endelesse lyffe and helth, which may not be had with-owte bytternes.
10 Ther-fore the vessells of the sowle, wher goode thoughtes shall be putt, muste besily be made redy, and contynually clene. For it is profitable that euyll thowghtes come other whyle for prefe and more merette ; and ther-fore the sowle must besyly labor that it consent nott to hem, ne delyte notte in hem. For
15 elles the swettenes and encrese of the sowle shal be powred owte, and the bytternes only shall abyde.

Ine[1] the secunde howse muste be also ij maner of Instrumentes ; fyrst, owtwarde Instrumentes wher-with the londe is made redy to be sowe, & thornes and wedes turned
20 upp by the rote, as[2] | plow and harow ; secunde, profitable fol. 12a Instrumentes to þat that is necessarie both wyth-in and with-owte, as axes and such other. The Instrumentez that londe is tylled with betokenen the wyttys of man, which ar ordend to the profette of hys neghtbor, as a plowe for the londe. For
25 vykked men ar as londe or erth, for they thenke alway apon erthely thynges. They ar baron and drye fro compunccion and soroe for her synnes, for they sette her synne at noght. They ar elke colde from the lofe of God, for they seke ryght noght bot þer own wyll. They ar elke hevy to do goode dedes,
30 for they ar swyfte and redy to the wyrship of the worlde. Þer-for a goode man oweth to tyll hem by owtworde wyttes, as a goode man tyllyth his londe with þe plowgh. Fyrst, he oweth to tyll hem with his mowth, spekyng to hem sych þynges as is profytable to the sowle, & enformynge hem to the way of lyfe ;
35 affter-warde, in doyng þe goode that he may, that his neght-borr be enformed with wordes and stired wyth werkes to do goode. And then-after, he tylleth hys neghtborr[3] to be fruyte-

---

[1] MS. Ine In.   [2] MS. as/as.
[3] MS. hys neghtborr hys neghtborr.

full with all hys oþer membres, þat is to sey, wyth symple eyn, that he beholde nott vayn and vnchaste thynges, þat his varray neghtborr may lerne to kepe sobreness in all his membres. He muste also tylle with hys erres, that he here no vanton thynges, and with hys feete and hondes, þat he be redy to all goode werkes. To such erth thus tylled, I God shall ȝeue the rayne of my grace be labor of the tyll man, and so he laboryth shall Ioy of the fruyte of the londe that was drie, when it begynnyth to borione. The Instrumentes that ar necessarie to make thin[g]es¹ with-in-forth, as axes and sych other, betokenen discrete entente & goodely discussynge of his werke. For what euer a | man doo, he awe nott to do itt for wyrship and praysyng of man, bot for the love of God to endeles rewarde. Perfor a man oweth to examyn hys deyly dedes bysely, for what entente and for what rewarde he doth hem ; and if he fynde in hys werke any pride, that he kitte it anon away with the axe of descrecion. That as he tylleth hys neghtborr outwarde, whych is as it war with-owte þe howse, that is to sey, oute of the companye of my fryndes be evyll dedes, ryght so he fruyte to himselfe inwarde be the lofe of God. For lyke as þe werke of a tylle man that hath none Instrumentes wher-with to reperell hys tooles when thay ar blonte or broke is sone turnede to noght, ryght so bot yf a man examyn hys werkes with wyse dyscrecion, how he shall eese hem yf they be trauelowse, and how he may reperell hem yf they be broke, he shall not brynge hem to perfeccion. Therefor a man aweth nott only to labor effectualy outwarde, bott also bysely to loke onwarde, how and for what entent he laboryth.

In the thirde howse must be quyke Instrumentes, that caryth both quyk and deth, as horse, asses, and other bestes. These Instrumentes ar verray confession ; for it caryth and moveth both quyke and deth. What betokeneth the quyke bott the sowle that is made of my godhed and lyveth withowten ende ? For by verray confession it neghyth euery day mor and more to God. For ryght as a beste, þe ofter and better it is fedde & norysshede, is stronger to ber and farrer to see ; ryȝt so confessyon, þe ofter and the more diligentely it is made, as well of the leste as of the moste, so mych mor it fortheryth

¹ MS. thinkes.

þe sowle. & so mych it plesyt God, þat it bryngyth þe sowle evyn to the herte of God. And what betokeneth the dede þat confession caryeth and meveth, bot goode werkes that ar slayn be dedely synne. | For the selfe goode dedes that a man hath
5 doo dyeth when he doth dedely synne, and ar dede anenste God. For no goode dede may please God, bot if synne be fyrst correctede and amendett other in perfyte wyll or dede. For stynkynge thynges and swete thynges may not wele acorde to gadre in one vessell. Bot yf any man slee hys goode dedes by
10 dedely synnes and after-warde make verray and trew confessyon of the synnes that he hath doo, with wyll to amende and to be-whar frome thens forth, than anon be that confession and vertue of mekenes, hys goode dedes takyth lyfe ayayne that war slayne a-fore, and profettes hym to endeles helth.
15 Bot and he dye wyth-oute confessyon, than hys goode dedes, that neþer may in all wyse be dede and torne to noght, neþer for that dedely synne deserue euerlastyng lyffe, shall profett him to suffre mor esy payne, or elles to helth of other, so that he dyde the goode dedes with goode entente and too Goddys
20 wyrship. For and he dyde hem for wordely wyrshyp and for hys own wordely profette, then they dye with him þat dyde hem; for he hath receyved hys mede of the worlde þat he labored for.

Ther-for, my spowse, by whom I vnderstonde all my frendes, gader we in-to our howses thoo thynges wher-with goode wyll
25 gostely be delytede wyth an holy sowle.

Fyrst, into our fyrst howse brede of clene wyll, wyllyng no thyng bot that God wyll. Secunde, drynke of goodely thynkyng to-for,[1] doyng nothyng bot it be thought to the wyrship of God. Thirde, sowle of goodely wysdome, thinkyng all way
30 what is to come, and how thynges ar to be gouerned that ar nowe.

Gadre we in-to our secunde howse peese from synne vn-to God and | peese from stryfe to our neghtborr. Secunde, werkes of mercye with which we be profitable to our neghtborr in dede.
35 Thirde, perfyte abstynence, refrenynge thoo thynges that myght trowble peese.

And gadre we in-to our [2] howse goode & resonable thoughtes to array our howse with-ine. Secunde, well rewled and tem-

---

[1] Latin praemeditationis.   [2] Latin tertia omitted.

peratte wyttes to shyne to our frendis wyth-owte. Thride, trew confessyon, wher-by, þof we be seke, we may lyf ayayne.

Bot þof we haue howses, we may nott kepe þat is gadered in hem bott yf they haue doores ; ne the doores may nott honge wyth-owte hynges, ne be shytte with-oute lokkes. Þer-for, that our thynges gadered may be safe, þer moste be sette a door on our house; þat is to say, syker hope that it be broke with none aduersite. And this hope must haue too hyngges, that man noþer dyspeyr to gette blysse, ne presumpte to skape payne ; bot in all dysese he truste all way ine the mercy of God, hopynge in better amendement. The loke of the door must be godely charite, wher-with þe dor moste be sperrede, that the enmye come nott ine. For what avaylyth it to haue a dor with-owte a lokke, & what hope is it to haue hope with-owte cheryte ? For if a man hope to haue endeles blysse, and hope also in þe mercye of God, & yett dredyth nott God nor loue him, he hath a door with-owte loke, by which hys dedely enmy may come ine and slee when he wyll. Bot right hope is þat he that hopyth do þe goode that he may, wyth-oute which he may nott gete heuyn, if he cowth and myght do good and wolde nott. Bot if eny vnderstonde þat he hath do amysse & not doo the goode þat he myght, yett yf he haue a good wyll to doo the goode that he maye, and also that he may nott, latt hym hope sycurly that he may negh vn-to God by that goode wyll and goodely cherite ; that as a loke hath mony wardes wyth-in that þe enmye open it notte, ryght so in the lofe of God and of goodely charite | muste be a maner besynes, that God be nott offendede; a love-drede [1] that God goo not from hym ; a brennyng feruour, how God may be loved ; a diligence, how to folow him ; a sorow, that he may nott do as mych as he wolde and as he vnderstondeth that he is bonde ; and a mekenes, by whych he holdeth notte all that he doth ine regarde of hys synne. With thes wardes the lokke muste be strenghthed, that the fende oppen nott the lokke of cheryte and sende in hys love. Þe keye to open and sparr oweth to be only desyr of God acordyng wyth gudely cherite and wyth godely werke, so that man wyll ryght nott haue bot God, þough he myght ; & that for hys moste grete cheryte, thys desyre

[1] *Latin* sit charitiuus timor.

speryth God in the sowle and the sowle in God, for þer is bot o wyll of hem both. Thys key owe no man to haue bote the husbonde and the wyfe alone; þat ys, God and the sowle: that as often as God wyll enter and delyte hym in goodes and verteus of the sowle, he hafe fre entre be the kay of stable desyre; and as often as the sowle wyll entre to the herte of God, it may frely, for it desiryth ryght nogh bot God. Thys kay is kepte be wakernesse of the sowle and be mekenes, wher-by it arecheth all the gode that it hath vn-to God. This key is kepte eke be the power of God, and cherite, that þe sowle be notte deceved of the fende. Loo, my spouse, what cherite and love of God is to mannes sowle. Stonde þer-for seurely, and do my wyll.[1]

Our lorde Ihesu Crist techyth seynt Birgitt howe actyfe lyf and contemplatyf owe to be kepte be ensample of Marie and Martha; & fyrst, of contemplatyf lyff.

Revelations, Book VI, first part of Chap. 65.

The sonne of God seyth: Birgitt, ther ar ij lyffes þat ar lykened to Marye and Martha; which lyfes, what man or woman will folow he muste fyrst make clene confessyon of all hys synnes, takyng to him verray contricion for hem, hauyng wyll neuer to synne mor. The fyrst lyfe, as the lorde beryth wyttenes, Marie chese; and it ledeth to contemplacion of heuenly thinges; and this is þe best parte and days Iournay to euerlastyng helth. Þerfor euery man and woman that desyrith to take and holde þe lyff of Marie, it is I-now to him to haue ij thinges that ar necessarie to the body: þat is, clothing with-owte vanyte or shewyng of pryde, and mete and drinke in scarsenes and not ine superfluyte. He muste eke haue cherite with-oute any evell delectacion, and resonable fastyng after the ordynaunce of holy chyrch. And in his fastyng he muste take kepe þat he be nott seeke of vnresonable abstynence, leste be sych sekenes hys prayers or prechyng or other goode dedes þer-by be lessede, by whych he myght profett both to his neghtbor and to him-selfe. He muste also besily examyn him-selfe, that be his fastynge he be neþer made dull or hasty to the rygour of ryghtwisnes or slow to the werkes of pytee, for to punyshe hem that ar rebell, and to make vnfeythfull men soiett vn-to the yoke of fayth. It is nede as

fol. 14 b

---

[1] MS. & e; *Latin ends with* fac voluntatem meam.

well to haue bodely str[e]ngth [1] as gostely. Ther-for eny that is seke or feble, that wolde rather to my wyrshyp faste than etee, he shall haue as grete rewarde for his goode wyll as he that fasteth resonabley of cherite. And on the same wyse he that etyth for holy obydience, wyllyng rather faste than ete, shall haue þe same medee as he þat fasteth.

Secunde, Marie oweth nott to Ioye of the wyrship of the werlde ne of the prosperyte þer-of; ne he owght noght to sorowe of the aduersyte þer-of, bott in that he oweth to Ioy þat wyked men ar made deuoute and at lovers of the worlde ar made louers of God, and that godemen profett in godenesse and, by laboring in the seruice of God, ar made more deuote. Of this also oweth he þat is Marie to sorow: that synneres fall into wers, and that God is nott lovede of hys creator, & that Goddis commaundementes ar dispised and nott kepe.

Thirde, Marie oweth not to be idelle no mor then Martha; bot after he hath take his nedefull slepe, he aweth to aryse, and with inworde attendaunce of herte thanke God that of hys cherite and love made all thinges of noght; and of that ylke cherite, takyng a body of man-kynde, he made all thynges aȝayne; shewyng by his passyon and deth his love vn-to man, more þan þe which myght noon bee. Marie muste eke thanke God for all tho þat ar sauede; and for all tho that ar in purgatorie, and for hem that ar in the worlde, prayinge God mekely that he suffeur hem nott to be temptede ouer her strenghthes. Marie muste also be discrete in prayer, & ordinate in the praysynge of God; for yf he haue the necessaries of his lyvyng with-oute bysenes, he oweth to make þe longer prayeres. And if he wax tediouse in praying, and temptaciones grow apon him, then he may labor with his hondes some honeste and profitable werke, oþer to his owne profette if he have nede, or ells to the profette of other. And yf he be werye and tediouse both in prayer and in labor, than he may haue some honeste occupacion, or here wordes of other edificacion with all saddenes, and with-oute dissolucion and vanyte, till the body and sowle be made mor able and quyke to the seruyce of God. If he that is Marie be sych that he haue nott bodely sustynaunce bott of hys own labour, then he muste make his prayer the

[1] MS. strongth.

shorter for sych nedefull werk ; and that same labour shall be
profetyng and encresyng of prayer. If Marie kan nott wyrke,
or may nott, then be he nott ashamed nor hevy to begge, bot
rather Ioyfull ; for then he foloweth me, the sonne | of God ; fol. 15 b
5 for I made my-selfe poor that man shulde be made rych. And
yf he that is Marie be soiett to obedyence, lyf he after the
obedyence of hys prelate, and the crowne of rewarde shall be
dowble the mor þan he war in hys own lyberte.

Forte, Marie aweth nott to be couetouse, no mor than was
10 Martha. Bott he oweth to be ryght large ; for Martha ȝeuyth
temperall goodes for God, so oweth Marie to yiffe spirituell
goodes. And ther-for, yf Marie haue lovede God enterly in
hys herte, be he[1] warr of that worde that mony haue in her
mowth, saynge : ' It is I-noght to me, if I may helpe myn
15 own sowle. What is it to me the werkes of my neghthborrs ?'
Or thus : 'I be goode ; what longeth it to me how other men
lyff ?' O dowghter, they that say and thinke such wordes, if
they see her frende trowblett or vnhonestely tretede, they
shulde renne vn-to the deth to delyuer her frende frome tribu-
20 lacion. So muste Marie do ; he oweth to sorow that hys God
is offendede, and that hys brother, hys neghtborr, is hurte ; or
if eny fall in-to synne, Marie oweth to laborr as mych as he
maye þat he be delyuered,—neuer-the-leesse, with discrecion.
And yf for that Marie be pursewed, he muste seke a-nother
25 place mor sewr. For I my-selfe that am God bad so sayng :
'Si vos persecuti fuerint in vna civitate fugite in aliam '; that
is, yf they persewe yow in one cite, fleth into oþer. And so
dide Pawle, for he was necessarie anoþer tyme ; and ther-for he
was latte dovn by the wall in a lepe.

30 Ther-fore, that Marie be large and pytefull, fyve thinges ar
nedefull to hir : first, an howse þat gestes shall slepe ine ;
secunde, clothes to cloth þe | naked ; thirde, mete to fede the fol. 16 a
hungery ; forte, fyr to make the colde hote and warme ; fyfft,
medecyn for the seke.

35 The howse of Marie is his herte, whos wyked gestes ar all
the thinges that come to him and troble his herte : as wrethe,
hevenes, s[l]awth,[2] couetyse, pride, and mony other, whych
enter ine by the v wyttes. Ther-for all þese vyces, when they

---

[1] MS. he *inserted above line.*   [2] MS. shawth.

come, they owe to lye as gestes þat slepe in reste. For lyke as an hosteler receyvyth gestes both good & badde with pacyence, so oweth Marye to suffer all thinges for God by the vertue of pacyence, and nott consente to synne nor delyte in hit, bot remeve hit fro his herte as mych as he may by litell and litell by the helpe of grace of God; and yf he may nott remeve hem and putt hem a-way, suffer he hem pacyentely aȝeynst his wyll, as gestes knowyng certenly that they shall prophett him to more rewarde, and in no wyse to dampnacion.

Secunde, Marie oweth to haue clothes too cloth hys gestes: that is, mekenes, inwarde and owtwarde, and compassion of herte in diseese of eyn cristen. And if Marie be dispisede of men, renne he then anon to hys mynde, thinkyng how I, God, was dispisede, repreved, & suffered it pacyentely; how I was demed, and spak nott; how I was scourgett and crownede with thornes, and gurched nott. Marie muste also take hede that he shew no tokennes of wreth or vnpacyence to hem þat repreve him or dispise him; bott he oweth to blesse hem that persewe him, that they þat se it may blesse God, whom Marie foloweth; and God him-selfe shall yif blessyng for cursynge. Marie eke muste be-war that he nother bakbyte nor repreve hem that hevy him or troble him. For it is dampnable to bakkebyte and to here a bakbyter and to repreve his neghtbour wyth impacyence; and therfor, that Marye may haue perfytely the gyfte of mekenes, he muste study to monysh and to warne hem of hur perelles þat bakbite other, exhortynge hem with cheryte in worde and exsample to verrey mekenes. Also the cloth of Marye oweth to be compassyon; for if he see his eyn cristen syn, he ogh to haue compassion of hem, & to prey to God to haue mercy apon hem. And yf he sees hys neghtborr suffer wronge or harmes or repreves, he owght to be sorye þer-of, and to helpe him with hys prayeres and oþer helpe and besinesse. Yee, aneneste þe grete men off the worde; for verrey compassion sekyth nott that longyth to him-selfe, bott to evyn cristen. Bot yf Marie be sych þat is nott herde aneneste princesse & grete men and at the goynge oute of his cell profyteth nott, than pray he to God besily for hem þat ar disesede; and God, be-holder of the herte, shall for the cherite of him þat prayeth turne the hertes of men to peese of him

that is disesed. And other he shall be delyuered of his tribulacion, or ells God shall gyf him pacyence, so that his rewarde in heuyn shall be dowbled. Þer-for such a cloth of mekenes or of compassyon oweth to be in Maries herte; for þer is noo thynge
5 that drawes God so in-too a sowle as mekenes and compassyon of his euyn cristen.

Thirde, Marie muste [haue][1] mete and drinke for gestes. For grevouse gestes ar logett in the herte of Marie, whan the herte is rauyshed oute of it-self and hath appetite to see delec-
10 table thinges in erth & to haue temperall thinges; when the ere disiryth to her his own wyrship; when the flesh sekyth to delite in fleshely thinges; when the spirite pretendeth excusacion of frelte and lyghting of synne; when | þer comyth fol. 17 a tedyousnes to do gode and for-yettynge of thinges that ar to
15 come; when goode dedes ar counted money and evyll few and for-yett. Aʒayne such gestes Marie hath nede of consell, that he dissimule nott ne begynne nott to slepe. Ther-for Marie, herted with feyth, must arise strongely and vnswer thus vn-to these gestes: 'I wyll hafe no thyng of temperall thinges, save
20 onely necessarie sustinaunce of my body. I wyll not spende the beste howr or tyme, bot to Goddes wyrship. Ne I wyll take hede of feyre or fowle, ne what is profettable or vnprofetable to the flesh, ne what is sauorye or vnsauorye to the taste, saue onely the plesaunce of God and profett of the sowlle; for
25 me lyst not lyff on howr, bot to the wyrship of God.' Sych a wyll is mete[2] to gestes that comen, and such vnswer qwenchyth inordinate delytes.

Ferte, Marie muste haue fyr 'to make her gestes hote & warme, and yif hem lyght. This fyr is the hete of the holy
30 goste; for it is impossible any man to forsake his own wyll or carnall affeccion of his frendes or love of rich, bot be þe worching inspiracion and hete of the holy goste. Nor ne Marie himselfe, be he neuer so perfyte, may nott begynne ne contynue ony good lyfe with-out swetenes and informacion of the same
35 holy goste. Ther-fore that Marie shine and lyghten to the gestes that comen first, he must thenke thus: God made me for that skyll that I shulde wyrship him, love him, and drede him above all thinges; and he was boor of a virgyn to tech the

---

[1] *Latin* habeat.   [2] MS. mete meete.

way to heuyn, which I shulde folowe with mekenes. And after, with his deth, he opened heuyn, þat be desyring and comyng I shulde haste me theder. Marie muste eke examyn all his werkes and thoughtes & desires, & how he hath offended God, and how pa[cyentely God suffered man, and how in mony wyse God callyth man to him. For such thowghtes and other lyke ar the gestes of Marie, which ar all in derkenes ; bot yf they be lyʒtenede with the fyr of the holy goste, whych fyr comyth to the herte when Marie thenkyth it is resonable to serue God, and when he wolde rather¹ suffre all payne than wyttyngly provoke God vn-to wreth, be whose goodenes his sowle is made and bowght aʒayne with hys blessed blode. The herte eke hath lyght of this goode fir, when reson thenkyth and discerneth by what entent ych geste, þat is ych thowghte, comyth, when the herte examyneth yf the thowght goo vn-to euerlastynge Ioy or to transitorie Ioy ; yf it lefe no thowght vndiscussed, none vnpunyshed, none with-owten drede. Þer-for, that this fyr may be gote, and kepte when it is I-gote, it nedeth that Marie beer to-geder drye wode, by whych this fir may be noryshed : that is, that he take kepe bisely of the styrringes of the flesh, that the flesh begynne not to wax wanton ; and that he putt to all diligence, that the werkes of pitee and deuoute prayer be morede and encresede, in which the holy goste delyteth. Bot soffraynly it is to wytt & see þat wher fire is kyndelede in a close vessell and hat no vsshe, the fyr is sone quenchede and the vessell waxeth colde. And ryght so it is with Marie ; for if Marie desyr to lyf for not elles bot to do Goddes wyrship, then it is nedefull to him that his mouth be opened and the flaume of hys cherite go² owte. Than is þe mouth openede, when by spekyng in feruent cherite he geteth spirituall | sonnes vn-to God.

But Marie muste take hede besily that he open the mowth of hys prechinge when they that be goode may be made more feruente, and they that be wykked may be amendede, wher rych[t]wosnes³ may be morede and evell costome do away. For my apostell Paule wolde some tyme haue spoke ; bot he was forbede by my spirite, and þer-fore in acceptable tyme he

---

¹ MS. rather *inserted above line.* ² MS. go goo.
³ MS. rychwosnes.

The Revelations of Saint Birgitta 31

was stylle, and in tyme conuenient he spake; and some tyme he vsede softe wordes, and some tyme sharpe; and all hys wordes and dedes was to the worship of God and to comforth of the feyth. But if Marie may nott prech, and hath wyll &
5 kunnyng to prech, that he muste do as a fox that goyng abowte seketh mony places with his feete; and where he fyndyth places beste and moste able, þer he makyth a denne to reste jne. So Marie muste with wordes, exsamples, and prayers assay the hertes of mony; and when he fyndeth hertes more able to
10 receyve the worde of God, ther muste he terye and abyde, monyshing and styrringe what he may. Marye must also labour that a conuenient yshew be yeve vn-to his flame of fyr; for the mor that the flawme is, þe mor¹ ar lyghtned and enflawmed þer-of. The flawme hath than a conuenient yshew,
15 wher Marie noþer dredeth reprefe or shame, ne sekyth his own praysyng, when he dredeth neþer contrariose thinges, nor delytes in welth and prosperyte. And than it is mor acceptable to God þat Marie do his gode dedis in open than in prevey, to that extent þat they þat se hem may prayce and wyrship God.
20 Also Marie owe to yif owte ij flawmes, on in prevey, anoþer in open: that is, to haue dowble mekenes; þe fyrst in þe herte, inwarde, the oþer, owtwarde. The fyrst is that Marye thenke fol. 18 b him-selfe vnworthy and vnprofetable to all godenes, and that he prefer notte ne exalte him-selfe in his owen conceyte to-fore
25 ony creatur; and that he desyr nott to be see nor praysed, bot that he flee all pride and hyghnes, desiringe God above all thinges and folowyng his wordes. Yf Marye sende owte such a flame in his dedes, then shall his herte be lyghtened with cherite, & all contrariose thinges þat come to him shall be ouer-
30 come and esely sufferde. The secunde flame muste be in opyn; for yf verrey mekenes be in the herte, it oweth to aper in clothyng and to be herde of the mowth and to be fullfylled in dede. Verray mekenes is in clothing when Marie chesyth rather cloth of lesse price, of which he may haue hete and
35 profette, than cloth of more valeve, wher-of he myght haue pride and owtwarde shewyng. For cloth þat is litele worth and is calledde of men vile and abiecte is verely feyr anenste God, for it prouoketh mekenes. Bot that cloth that is bowght with

¹ *Latin* plures.

grete price & is called fayr is fowle anenste God ; for it beryth a-way þe fayrenes of angells, þat is, mekenes. Neuer-þe-lesse if Marie be compelled be any resonable cause to have better clothinge than he wolde, be nott trowbled ther-for ; for by that [his]¹ mede shall be morede.

Also Marie oweth to haue mekenes in mowth, spekyng meke wordes² ; fleyng vayne wordes and such as sterris to lawghing ; beynge war of mych spech ; nott vsyng sotell nor gay wordes ; nor prefessyng hys own wyll or wordes to-fore the wytte and felynges of hem that ar better. And if Marie be praysed for ony good dede, be he nott lyft vp þer-by in pride, bot aunswer he thus : 'laus sit deo qui dedit omnia' ; that is, praysing be to God that yove all goodenes. For what am I bot powder be-for the face of wynde ; or what goode comyth of me, erth³ with-out water ? & if he be reprevede, be nott he hevy bott vnswer he thus : 'It is worthi ; for I haue so often offended in the syght of God and not done pennaunce for which I am worthie | gretter tormentes. Þer-fore praye for me that by suffraunce of temperall reprcues, I may escape euer-lastyng.' If Marie be prouoked to wreth to ony mysgouernance of his evyn cristen, he muste be wysely war of vndiscrete aunswer ; for pride is ofte-tyme associate to wreth, and þer-for it is an holsom consell, that when wreth and pride come, þat he holde to-geder hys lippus so longe tyme tyll þe wyll may eske halpe of God of suffraunce and pacience ; and tyl he may be avysed what & how it is to a⁴ vnswer ; or til he may over-come him-selfe. For then wrath is quenched in the herte, and man may aunswer wysely to hem that ar vnwyse.

Know þu also þat the devell hath grete envye at Marie ; and þer-fore if he may nott lett him be brekyng of Goddes commaundementes, þan he sterith him to be lyghtly meved with grete wreth, or els to dissolucion of vayne myrth, or els to dissolute and gamefull wordes. Þer-fore Marie muste aske helpe of God þat all his spekyng and wyrkynge be gouernede of God and dressed vn-to Gode. Also Marie muste haue mekenes in his dede, þat he doo ryght noght by-cawse of erthely praysyng ; þat he attempte nothinge of nowe ; þat he be ryght noght ashamed

---

¹ MS. he ; *Latin* eius.
² MS. wordes wordes.
³ *Preceded in Latin by* qui sum.
⁴ a *inserted above line before* vnswer.

of mekenes; that he flee synglarte in his werkes; that he
wyrship all; and þat in all thinges [he] holde¹ him-selfe vnworthy. Also Marie oweth rather to sytte with the poor þan
with þe rich ; rather to obey than to be abeyde; rather to kepe
5 silence than to speke ; rather to be alon solytarie þen be conn-
staunte amonge the grete of the world or amonge his wordely
frindes. Marie must hate his own wyll and euer haue mynde
on his deth ; Marie oweth nott to be idle, ne no gurcher, ne
foryettfull of þe rightwyssnes of God and of his own affecciones.
10 Marie must be feruent to confession, besy in his temptaciones,
desiring | to lyffe for ryght nott ells bott for þat the worshipe of fol. 19 b
God and helth of sowles be encresede and morede.

Þer-for if Marie þat is thus disposede as I haue now seyde be
chose by Martha, and obeying for the love of God takyth the
15 gouernance of mony sowles, ther shal be yeve to him dowble
crown of rewarde, as I shew the be a lykenes. Ther was
a certeyn lorde of grete power that hadde a shippe chargede
with precouse marchaundyse, and seyde vn-to hys seruantes:
'Goth to sych ane havyn, and ther shall be grete wynnyng to
20 me, and gloriose fruyte. Yf the wynde arise ayaynste yow,
travelleth manfully and be nott werry ; for your rewarde shall
be grete.' Then the seruantes sayled forth. And the [wind]²
wex myghty, and tempestes arosse, and the shipp wasse grevously bete. Wherfor the gouernor of the shippe waxe wery,
25 and all they dispeyrede of her lyfe. And then they acordede
to-geder to come to sych ane hauyn as³ þe wynde wold blow
hem to, & nott to þat hauyn³ that þe lord assygned hem. When
one of the seruantes that wasse mor trew than oþer herde this,
he weylede & of feruente love and [z]ele⁴ þat he had to his
30 lorde, he toke violently þe gouernall of þe shippe, & with grete
strenghthes he browght þe shippe vn-to the hauen desired of
the lorde. Ther-fore thys man þat thus manfully browght the
shipe to þe hauen is to be rewarded with mor singler rewarde
then oþer.

35 In lyke wyse is it of a goode prelate þat for love of God and

¹ MS. be holde ; *Latin* reputet se.
² *Latin* ventus.
³ MS. as ... hauyn *inserted in margin.*
⁴ MS. yele ; *Latin* zelo. *Due to a scribe copying* zele *as* yele.

helth of sowles takyth charge of gouernaunce, nott rekkyng of
worshipe, for he shall haue dowble rewarde : fyrst, for he shall
be partener of all the goode dedes of hem þat he hath browght
to þe hauyn; secunde, for his Ioy & blisse shall be morede
with-outen ende. And so shall it be ayayne warde of hem that
fol. 20 a desir worshippes & prelacies;[1] | for they that shall be partener
of all peynes and synnes of hem that they haue take to gouerne.
Secunde, for þer confucion shall be with-owten ende. For the
prelates þat desyr wyrshippes ar mor lyke to strompettes than to
prelates. For they disseyve sowles with her evell wordes and
exsamples; and thay ar vnworthy to be calde oþer Marie or
Martha, bot they amende hem with pennaunce. Fyft, Marie
oweth to yeve his gestes medecyn: þat is, glad and comforth
hem with Goddis wordis. For to all thynges that euer be-fall
hym, wheder they be Ioyfull or hevy, he oweth to say : 'thus
I wyll; what euer God wyll, I do; and to hys wyll I am redy
to obey, þough I shulde goo to hell'. For such a wyll is
medecyn ayenste euyll thynges that fall to þe herte, and þis
wyll is delite in tribulacion and a good temperer in prosperyte.
Bot for Marie hath mony enmys, þer-for he muste make contynually confession. For as longe as he bydeth in synne &
myght be shryfe and is necligent and takyth no kepe þer-of,
than is he rather to be called apostata a-for God þan Marie.

Revela- **Of the dedes of actyf lyfe þat is vnderstonde be Martha.**
tions,
Book VI, **Cap. xj.**
Chap. 65,
completed. Know þu also þat þough the parte of Marie be beste, ȝett þe
parte of Martha is not euyll, bot prayseable and well plesinge
to God. Þer-for I shall tell the how Martha oweth to be
gouerned. For he oweth to have v goode thinges as well as
Marie. Fyrst, the ryght fayth of Goddys church. Secunde, to
know the commaundementes of the godhed & the conseles of
the trowth of the gospell; and thes oweth he perfitely to kepe
in herte and werke. Thirde, he oweth to kepe his tonge from
evyll wordes þat is aȝayn God and his neghtbor, and his honde
from all vnhoneste and vnlefull wyrkyng, and hys herte fro
ouer-mych couetyse & delyte. He oweth also to be contente of
goodes þat God hath yeve him, and not to desyr superflew

---
[1] for they þat, *catchword half cut off.*

thing*es*. Foourth, he oweth to fullfyll þe dedes of mercye resonably and mekely, þa*t* | for truste of thoo dedes he offende in no thing. Fyfte, he oweth to love God above all thinge and mor than himselfe. So dyde Martha, for he yafe Ioyfully him-
5 selfe, folowyng my word*es* and werk*es*; and aft*er* she yave all hyr godd*es* for my love. And therfor she lothed temp*er*all thyng*es*, and sowght heuynly thing*es*, and suffered heuenly thing*es* pacyentely, and toke kepe and cur of other as of hyrselfe. And therfor she thought all way on my cherite and
10 passyon; and she was gladde in tribulac*i*ones and loved all as a moder. The same Martha also folowed me euery daye, desyryng nothyng bot to her word*es* of lyffe. She had compassyon on hem þ*a*t wer in sorow; she comforted the seke; she neþ*er* cursed nor sayd evyll to ony. Bot she dissimiled the
15 frowardnesse of hyr neghtborr, and prayed [1] for all. Þ*er*-for euery man þ*a*t desyrith cherite in actyf lyffe oweth to folow Martha in love of hys neghtbor, to brynge him to heuyn, bot nott in favoryng and norishyng his vyces and synnes. He oweth also to fle hys own p*r*aysyng, pryde, and dowblenesse.
20 Eke wreth or envye oweth he nott to kepe.

But marke well that Martha, praying for hyr brother Lazar when he was dede, come fyrst to me. Bott hyr brother was not raysed anon, tyll Marie come aft*er*, whe*n* she was called. And then for both systeres her brother was arered fro deth to lyfe.
25 So in sp*iri*tu*e*ll lyf he þ*a*t p*er*fytely desyrith to be Marie muste fyrst be Martha, laboryng bodely to my wyrship. And he oweth fyrst to conne wi*th*-stonde [2] þe desyris of the flesh and the temptac*i*on of the fende and after-warde he may wyth dilib*er*ac*i*on ascende up to the degre of Marie. For he that is
30 nott p*r*eued and tempted, and he that hath not oue*r*comen þe styrryng*es* of hys flesh, how may he contynually entende and cleve to heuynly thing*es*? Who is þe dede brother of Marie and Martha, bott an vnp*er*fyte werk? | For ofte sythes a good werke is doo wyth an vndyscrete entente and wyth an vnavysed
35 herte, and þ*er*-fore it goth dolly and slawly forth. Bot þat the wyrkyng of gode dedes be acceptable to me, it muste be arered and quykened by Martha and Marie; that is, when the neghtbor is clerely loved for God & to God, and God allon is desyrid

[1] MS. p[ra *abbre.*]rayed. [2] *Latin* scire debet prius resistere.

above all things. And than euery good werke of man is
plesing vn-to God. Þer-fore I seyde in the gospell that Marie
chese the beste parte; for than is the parte of Martha good,
when he soroweth for the synnes of his evyn crysten; & then
is þe parte of Martha better, when he laboryth that men abyde
in goode lyvyng wysely and honestely, and that only for the
love of God.

Bot the parte of Marie is beste when he beholdeth onely
heuenly thinges and the lucre of sowles. And the lorde enter-
eth in-to the howse of Martha and Marie when þe herte is
fullfylled with gode affecciones; and pesed from the noyse of
wordely thinges; and thenkyth [God][1] as all way presente;
and nott onely hath mynde and meditacion in his love, bot
laboreth þer-ine day and nyght.

Revela- Our lorde Ihesu Criste telleth seynt Birgitt of his blessed
tions, incarnacion; & how man offendeth God & brekyth þat he
Book I,
Chap. 1. behyght in hys baptem; & mercy to hem þat amendeth
hem; and of herde dome to heme þat amende not; & how
swetely he callys douowte sowles to hys blysse. Cap. xij.

I am maker of heuyn and erth, one in godhed with the fader
and the holy goste. I am he þat spake to profettes & patriarkes,
& whom they abode; for whos desyr and after myn awn by-
heste I toke a body with-oute synne or luste, entering þe
madenes wombe as the sonne shynyng thorow a cler ston.
For as the sonne enteryng the glasse hurtyth it not, so þe
madened of the virgine bode incorrupte and vnsowled in
fol. 21 b takynge of my man-hod. For so [2] toke I a body þat I lest nott
the godhed; nor I was not the lasse in godhed wyth the Fadre
and the holy goste, all thynges gouernyng and fullfyllyng,
thowgh I wer in my manhode in the virgyns wombe. For as
bryghtnes is neuer departed from fyr, so my godhede was neuer
departed from my manhode; not in deth, forþer-mor. I wold
suffer my body that was moste clene frome synne to be crucified
for þe synnes of all mankynde, and to be all-to rente fro þe
soole of þe foote vn-to the toppe of the hedde. This same body
is also now euery day offered on the awter, that man shuld love
me so mych the mor, as he had my benefettes often in mynde.

[1] *Latin* Deum.   [2] c ij.

Bot now I am all for-ʒett, dispised, and sett att noght. And as a kynge caste owte of his own kyngdom, ine whose place a wykked thefe is chose and wyrshiped, I wold my kyngdome hulde be in man. & of him I awght of ryght to be kynge and
5 lorde, for I made and bowght him; bot now he hath broke and defowled the feyth þat he behyght me in baptym; he hath broke and dispised my lawes that I yaue him; he louyth his own wyll, and liste not to here me; & mor-ouer he enhanseth the wyked thefe, the fende, above me & to him hath yove hys
10 feyth which is verely a thefe. For he robbyth to him the sowle of man þat I bought with my blode be suggestyon off wyll and fals byhestes; ʒett he robbyth nott as he wer myghteer than I, while I am so myghty þat I may do all thinges with on worde, and so ryghtfull þat I shuld nott do þe leste thinges
15 ayanste ryghtwosnes, þof all saynte prayed me. Bot man that is yove to fredome, wylfully leuying my commaundementez, consenteth to the fende; and þer-for it is ryghtfull that man have experyence of hys tyrauntrie. | For the fende of me was made goode, bot throw hys own evyll wyll he fell and is as my
20 seruante to the vengeance of the wyked. Bot þough I be now thus dispised, yett I am so mercyfull that who euer aske my mercy and worthely meke him-selfe, I foryeve them that they haue trespaced, & I shall delyuer hem fro the wyked thefe. And they þat abyde in my offence and dispite, I shall vysett
25 apon them my ryghtwosnesse. So that all that her it shall tremell and wake for fere. And they þat fele it shall say: allas! þat euer we war borne and conceyved. Allas! þat euer we prouoked the lorde of maieste to wreth.

Bot þo[u]¹, my dowghter, whom I haue chose, and wyth
30 whom I speke with my spirite, love þu me with all thyne herte, nought as thy sonne, thy dowghter, thy fader, thy moder, or other frendes, bot mor than any-thing in the werld. For I that made the spared none of my membres to putt hem to torment for the; and yett I love thy sowle cheritably, that
35 rather than I shuld fayle itt, I shuld be crucyfyed aʒayne, yf it wer possible. Folow thu my mekenes; for I, kyng of blysse and angells, was clad in pour and vyle clothes, and I stode naked at a pyller and herde with myn eres all repreves &

¹ MS. of; *Latin* Tu autem filia mea.

scornes. I putt also my wyll to-for thy will, for my modor, thy lady, wold neuer other thing than I wold fro the begynnyng of hur lyf vn-to the ende. If þu do thus, than shall thy herte be wyth my herte, and it shall be enflaumed wyth my love, as a drie stykke is lyghtly enflaumede with fyr. So thy sowle shall be fullfylled of me, & I shall be in the; so that all temperall thinges shall be bitter vn-to the, and all fleshely luste as venum. Thu shall reste in the armes of my godhed, wher is no luste of the flesh bot Ioy and dilectac[i]on [1] of sprite, with fol. 22 b which a sowle delyted is full of joy with-|in and with-owte. And itt desyryth or thinkyth no-thinge bott the Ioy that it hath. Love me þer-fore onlye, and thu shalt haue all thinges that þu wylt plentevously. Is itt nott wryte that the oyle of the videw fayled nott tyll Good yaue rayne apon the erthe. after the worde of the prophete? I am a trew and a verray profette. Yf þu yif fayth to my wordes and full-fyll hem, Oyle, Ioy, and gladenes shall neuer fayle the wyth-outen ende.

Revelations, Book I, Chap. 57. Oure lorde Ihesu Cryst telleth seynte Birgitt of the synne & of vnclennes of cristen peple; and how they may haue mercye yf thay wyll amende; and elles how herde they shall be punyshede. Cap. xiij.

The sonne of God spekyth vn-to hys spowse and sayth: Crysten men do now vn-to me as some tyme dyde the Iewes. The Iewes keste me owte of the tempull and hadd fulle wyll to slee me. Bot for my tyme was [not][2] yett I-comme, I wente owte of her hondes. So do now cristen men with me. They caste me owte of her temple of her sowles, which aught to be my temple, and gladely thay wold slee me yf they myght. I am in her mouth as roten as stynkyng flesh, and I seme to hem as a man spekyng lesynges, and they reke ryght not of me. They turne hur bak to me, & I shall turne my bakke to hem. For in her mouth is no thyng bott couetyse, and in þer flesh no thinge bot luste and lecherye. In ther heryng onely pride pleseth hem, and in her syght þe dilectable thinges of the worlde. My passion and my cherite is to hem abhominable, and my lyf is grevouse to hem. Ther-for I shall do as doth that

---

[1] MS. dilectacon.   [2] Latin non dum.

beste that hath mony dennys, when he is persewed of hunteres
in one denne, he fleth to a noþer, so shall I do; for crysten
men persewe me with her evyll dedes, and caste me owte of the
denne of her hertes. Þer-for I wyll enter in-to þe hethen, in
5 whos mowth I am now bytter & saffren; & I shall be in her | fol. 23 a
mowth swetter than hony. Neuerlesse I am yett so mercyfull
þat who euer aske foryevenesse and say, 'lorde, I knowlege that
I haue grevously synned and fayne wold mende me by thy
grace; haue mercy apon me for thy bitter passyon'; I shall
10 gladely receyve hym to mercye. Bot thay þat abyde in her
evyll, I shall come vn-to hem as a gyaunte that hath three
thinges: dredefullnesse, strenghth, and sharpenes. So shall
I come to cristen men so dredefull þat they shall nott der sterr
ayaynste me her leste fynger. I shall come so stronge þat
15 thay shall be as a g[n]att[1] to-for me and I shall come to hem
so sharpe that they shall feele woo here in thys lyffe and woo
with-outen ende. Amen.

Owr lorde[2] tellyth seynte Birgitt by exsample that noo Revela-
thing plesyth God so mych as he be loved above al thinges. tions, Book VI,
20 The moder of God spekyth to the spowse of Cryste seynte Chap. 50.
Birgitt and seyth: no-thing plesyth God so mych as þat man
love him above all oþer thynges. Loo, I shall telle the by ensample of a hethen woman that knewe ryght not of cristen
fayth; bot she[3] thus by hyr-selfe: 'I knew', she sayth, 'of
25 what mater I am, and wher-of I come in-to the wombe of my
moder. I byleve also that it is impossible me to haue body,
Ioyntes, and bowelles and wyttes, bot if some had yeve it me.
And þer-for ther is some creator and maker that made me so
fayr a person of mankynde, and wolde nott make me fowle as
30 wormes and serpentes. Ther-for it semeth to me that þough
I had mony husbondes, if they all cleped me, I shulde rather
go att one callyng of my maker than at the callyng of hem all.
I haue also mony sonnes and dowghteres, yett if I see hem
haue mete in her hondes and I know þat my maker hungred,
35 for-soth I wolde take a-way the mete fro my childrens hondes

[1] MS. gatt; *Latin* culex.
[2] *The chapter heading is incorrect, since only* 'the moder of God spekyth
to the spowse'.
[3] *Latin* cogitauit *omitted*.

and gladely yeve it to my maker. I haue also mony pos-[1]|sessions which I dispose at myn owen wyll. Yett if I knew the wyll of my maker, I wolde full fayne leve myn own wyll and dispose hem to hys wyrship.'

But see, dowghter, what God dide with this hethen woman. For-soth, he sende to hyr hys frende, that enformede hir in the holy fayth. And God him-selfe visett hir herte, as þu mayst well vnderstonde be þe womans wordes, for when þat man of God preched to hir þat þer was one God with-outen begynnyng & ende which is maker of all thinges, she aunswerde : ' It is well to be beleved, þat he þat made me and all thinges hath no maker above him. And it is well lyke to be trew þat his lyffe is euer-lastyng þat myght yif me lyf.'

When this woman herde that the same maker toke mankyn[d]e[2] of a virgyne and preched with hys own mowth, she aunswerde : 'It is well to be-leve of God all vertues werkes. Bot thu, frende of God, tell me what be tho wordes that come of my maker? For I wyll leve my own wyll and obey till him after all the wordes of hys.'

Then, the frende of God prechinge to hir of the passion, crosse, and resurreccion of him, she aunswerde wyth wepynge eyn and seyde : ' Blessed be that God that so pacyentely shewed hys cherite in erth that he had vn-to vs in heuen. Þer-for if I haue loved him fyrste, for he made me, now I am mych mor bounde to love him, for he shewed me the ryght way and bought me with hys holy blode. I am also bounde to serue him with all my myghtes and all my membres, for he bowght me with all hys membres. And forther-mor, I am bounde to put fro me all myn own will & desyr þat I had to-for to my godes, possession, children, kynne, & frendes, and only to desyr my maker in his blysse & in that lyf that neuer hath ende.'

Then sayde the moder of God : loo, doughter, thys woman gate mony-folde rewarde for hyr love, & so is euery day yeve rewarde to ychon after that god whyle he lyveth in this world.

[1] c iiij.   [2] MS. mankynge.

The Revelations of Saint Birgitta 41

How our lady & seynte Petre kept a woman fro fallyng to | synne, by whose [consell]¹ she changed hir lyf; & of special grace she fell in sekenes, & so was purgett and went to heuen. Cap. xv.

fol. 24 a
Revelations,
Book VI,
Chap. 93.

5 The spouse of Cryste seynte Birgitte see in sprite a woman sittyng in a rope, whos oo fote a fayr man bar upp, and a virgyn of mervelouse fayrenes bar vp the other fote.

Than our lady apperede and sayde : This lady that þu knoweste is wounde in mony bysenes of the flesh and the 10 worlde, and mervelously she hath be kepte that she fell nott. For she hath hadde often wyll to haue synned, bot neuer place nor tyme. And that made þe prayer of Petre the apostle² of my sonne, whom this woman loved. Some tyme she had tyme & space, bot thoo not wyll ; & þat made the lofe of me þat am 15 the moder of God. And þer-for now for hir tyme neghith nye, seynte Petre concellyth hir to take apon hir some sharpenes in clothinge and werynge, puttynge a-way softe clothing. For he was souerayne apostle ; and yette he suffered nakednes, prison, and hunger, all-though he war mighty in heuyn and erth. I also, 20 moder of God, þat passed neuer howr in erth with-owte tribulacion and dysese of herte, consell hir that she be nott ishamed to be meke and to obey the frendes of God.

After this anone saynte Peter the apostle appered and seyde to seynte Birgitte : Thu now, spowse of our lorde God, goo aske 25 of thys woman whom I haue loved and kepte, if she wyll all holy be my doughter.

When seynte Birgitte had asked, & she, consentynge, sayde, 'I wyll, with all myne herte,' seynte Petre aunswerede : I shall purvey for hyr as for my doughter Peronell, and take hir to 30 my kepyng.

Than anon as this lady herde thys, she changed hir lyf. And nott longe after, she fell seke that endured all the tyme of hir lyfe, tyll she was purged and wyth ryg[ht]³ grete deuocyon yaue vp the spritte. For when she come to the ende of hir 35 lyfe, she see seynte Peter arayde lyke a byshop, and seynte Petir þe martyr in habite of freer prechours, for he was of that ordre ;⁴ | whych both she loved enterly in hyr lyfe.

fol. 24 b

¹ Word omitted ; Latin quorum consilio.   ² Latin & Filii mei.
³ MS. rygth.   ⁴ c iij (foliation should be c v).

And than she sayde openly: what ar these [m]y¹ lordes?
When þe ladyes and wymmen that stode abowte hyr asked
her what she see, she aunswerede: I see, she seyth, mervelowse thinges. For I see my lordes Petre the apostle arayed
pontifically and Petre the martir in habyte of prechowres,
whom I haue euer loved and euer hoped in her helpe. And
anon, crying: blessed be God. Loo, I come, she paste to owr
lorde.

Revela-
tions,
Book I,
Chap. 3.

Owr lorde Ihesu Cryst steryth his spouse to love him, &
telleth hir how lyttell love mony hath to him, & how mych
to the werlde. Cap. xvi.

I am thy lorde God, whom þu wyrshyppest. I am he þat
by my power bere vp heuen and erth; and it is bor vpp with
non oþer arch nor pyllers. I am he þat ych day am offered on
the auter verray God and man. I am the same that hath
chose the. Worship my father. Love me. Obey to my sprite.
Do reuerence to my moder, as to thy lady. Wyrship all my
sayntes. Kepe the ryght feyth, which he shall tech the that
hath felde in himselfe þe stryfe of ij spirites of falsehod and
trewth; and be myn helpe he ouer-comyn.² Kepe thow verray
mekenes; that is, a man to shew him-selfe sych as he is, and
to yeve praysinge to God for hys yifte.

Bot now þer is mony that hateth me. My wordes and dedes
they holde bot sory and vanyte; and the auovterer, þe fende,
they halse and love. What-euer they do for me, it is with
gurching and bytterness. Ne they wold not knowleghe my
name, if thei shuld nott be confunded of me. The werlde they
love so clerly that they ar nott wery to labor ther-abowte nyght
and day; and alway they ar feruent in love þer-of, ther seruice
is so plesynge to me as yf a man yave his enmy mony to slee
hys own sonne. So doth they þat ȝeveth me a lytell almosse.
And they worship me with ther lippes to thentente þat thei
may encrese in wordely prosperyte, and abyde in wyrship and
fol. 25 a in synne; wher-for her good wyll | is slayne from profetyng in
God.

Bot if thu wyll love me with all thyne herte and desyre no

---

¹ MS. any.
² MS. ouer comercomyn; *Latin* deuicit.

thyng bot me, I shall draw the vn-to me by cherite, as the
adamaunte draweth to him irn. & I shall sett the in myne
arme, that is so stronge þat non may draw it owte, and so
myghty that when it is stretched owte, none may bowe it. It
is also so swete þat it passeth all swettenes ; and it haueth no
comparison with dilectaciones of the werlde.

How saynte Birgitte seē in gostely vision the dome of Revela-
a sowle whome the fende accused, and at the laste was Book IV.
holpe by our lady ; & how she see all hell and purgatorie Chap. 7.
& monye oþer mervelles ; & how nedefull it is to helpe hem
þat be in purgatorie. Cap. xvij.

It semed to a person wakynge in prayer and not slepynge, as
þough she had see in spirituell vision a palasse of vnspectable
gretenes, wher-in wer folke innowmerable, cladde in white and
shynyng clothes. And ech of hem semed to haue a propur sete
to him-self. In this palyse stode principally a seete of dome,
wher-in was as it had byn a sonne ; and the bryghtnes that wente
fro thet [1] sonne was mor þan may oþer be tolde or vnderstonde,
in lenght, depnes, and brede. Þer stode also a virgyn nygh þat
sete, hauyng a precyouse crown on hir hede. And all þat þer
wer seruede the sonne syttyng in þe seete, praysyng him with
ympnes and songes.

Then appered þer an Ethiope, ferefull in syght and beryng,
as þof he had byn full of envy and gretely anaungered. He
cried & sayd : O þu ryghtfull Iuge, deme to me this sowle, &
her his werkes ; for now hys lyf is nygh at the end. Suffer
me þer-fore to punysh the body with the sowle, till they be
departede in sunder.

When this was seyde, it semed to me that one stoode afor
þe sete as it had be a knyght armed clenly, and wyse in wordes,
& sobre in heryng, þat sayde : | Thu Iuge, loo, her ar his goode fol: 25 b
werkes that he hath do vn-to þis howr.

And anon ther was herde a voyce oute of the sonne syttynge
in the seete : her is vices, he sayth, moo then vertues. And it
is nott ryghtwosness þat vyce be Ioned to hym þat is souerayn
verteu.

[1] *Final t inserted above line.*

Then aunswerde the Ethiope: þer-for it is ryghtfull that þis sowle be Ioned to me; for if it haue any vyce in it, so in me is all wykkednes.

The knyght aunswerde: the mercy of God foloweth euery person vn-to[1] the laste poynte of hys lyffe, and then-after is the dome. And in this man that we speke of ar yett both sewle & body Ioned togeder, and dyscrecion abydeth in him.

The Ethiope aunswerde: the scriptur sayth, that may nott [li]e:[2] þu shalt love God above all thynges, and thy neghtbor as thy-self. See þu therfor, þat all the werkes of thys man be do of dred, and nott of love & cherite as they aught. And all the synnes þat he is shryve of, þu shalt fynde hem shrive with lytell contricion. And þer-for he hath deserued hell; for he hath forfett the kyngedome of heuyn. And þer-for hys synnes ar her open to-for the ryghtwosnes of God. For he gatt yett neuer contricion of goodely cherite for þe synnes that he hath doo.[3]

The knyght aunswerde; for-soth, he hoped and byleved to gete verray contricion to-fore his deth.

Thu, he sayde, hast gedered all the dedes þat euer he dyd well, and þu knowes all hys wordes and his thoughtes to the helth of his sowle. And all thes, what-euer þay be, may nott be lykened to þat grace had be contricion of the love of God with holy fayth and hope, and mych lasse they may nott do a-way all his synnes. For ryghtwyssnes is in God from with-owte begynnyng, that no synner shall enter heuyn þat | hath no per-fite contricion. And þer-for it is vnpossible þat God shuld deme ayanste þe disposicion ordened from with-oute begynnyng. Therfore the sowle is to be demed to hell & to be Ionede wyth me in euerlastyng payne.

When thes war sayde, the knyght helde his pees and aunswerde nott to his wordes. After thes appered fendes innowmerable, lyke vn-to sparkles rynnyng abowte oute of an hote fyr. And all they criede with one vyce sayinge to him þat satt in þe seete as a sonne: we, þay say, knowe that þu arte oo God in iij persones, with-oute begynnyng & ende, and ther is non oþer God but þu. Thu arte þat cherite to which is Ioned mercy and rightwysnes. Þu was in thy-selfe from with-oute

---

[1] MS. vn to & vn to.   [2] MS. be. See Notes.   [3] s cancelled.

The Revelations of Saint Birgitta

begynnynge, hauynge ryght nott lassede ne to lytell in the ne changeble, as it semyth God with-owte þe is right nott, and no thyng hath Ioy with-oute þe. Þer-for thy cherite made angelles of non oþer mater bot of the power of thy godhede. And þu
5 dedyste as mercy sterrede the. Bot after that we ware brente wyth-in with pryde, envye, and couetyse, thy cherite, louynge ryghtwosnes, keste vs oute of heuen with the fyr of our malyce in-to dyrke and vnspectable depnes that is now called hell. So dyde þi cherite, than, which shall nott yette be departed from
10 þe dome of thy rightwysnes, wheder it be after mercye or after equite. And yett we say mor, if that thinge that thu loveste to-fore all thinges, the virgyn þat bare the, þat neuer synned, hadde synned dedely & diede with-oute godly contricion, þu loveste so ryghtwysnes þat hir sowle shuld neuer haue gotte
15 heven, bot it shuld haue be with vs in hell. Ther-for, þu Jugge, why demeste þu nott this sowll to vs, that we may punysh it after his werkes?

After thes was herde as it had be þe sown of a trumpe, & | all fol. 26 b that herde it wer styll. And anon was herde a voyce seynge:
20 be styll and lysteneth ye, all angelles, sowles, and fendes, what the moder of God spekyth.

And than anon, the same virgyne apperinge to-fore the seete of dome and havynge vnder hyr mantell as it had be some grete pryve thinges, sayde: O O ye enmyse, ye pursue mercy
25 and wyth-owte cherite ye love ryghtwysnes, þof here apper defaute in goode werkes for which this sowle oweth not to gett hevyn, yett seeth what I haue vnder my mantell.

And when the virgyn hade opnede both the lappys of hyr mantell, vnder þe one appered one as it had be a lytell church,
30 wher-in semede to be some men of relygion; and vnder the oþer apperede women and men, frendes of god, religiose and other. And all thay cried with oo voyce saynge: haue mercy, mercyfull lorde.

Than after was kepte silence and the virgyne spake and
35 seyde: the scriptur seyth, he þat hath parfyte fayth may þer-by translate mountanes in the worlde. What than may and owe the voyces of thes do, that had fayth and also serued God wyth cherite? And what shall thoo frendes of God do, whom this man prayed to pray for him, that he myght be departede from

hell and gette heuen? And he sowght no noder rewarde for
his goode werkes bot heuynly thynges, wher all ther teres and
prayers may nott or be nott of power to take him and lyfte
him vpp so þat he gete godely contricion with cherite to-for his
deth, and forther-mor I shall adde to my prayers wyth þe 5
prayer of all sayntes that ar in heuyn, whom thys man specyally
wyrshipped. Yett than forþermor sayde the virgyn: o o ȝe
fendes, I commaunde yow by þe power of the Iuge to take kepe
to thes thynges that ye se now | in ryghtwysnes.

Then they all aunswerde as it had been with one mowth: we 10
see, thay seyde, that in the worlde a lytell water and a grete
ayer peese the ire of God. And so be thy prayer is God pesede
vn-to mercye wyth cherite.

After thys was herde a voyce from the sonne, saying: for the
prayers of my frendes shall now this man gete goodely contri- 15
cion to-fore his deth, in so mych þat he shall [not]¹ come ine
hell; bott he shall be purgett with him that sufferith moste
grevouse payn in purgatorie. And when the sowle is purgede,
he shall haue rewarde in heuen with hem þat had fayth & hope
in erth with ryght litell cheryte. 20

When thes was sayde, the fendes fledde her way. Then-
after, it semed vn-to the spowse as if þer had openede a ferefull
place and a dyrke wher-in appered a fornace all brennyng
with-in; and that fyr had not elles to brenne bot fendes and
quyke sowlys. And a-bove þat fornace aperede þat sowle whos 25
dome was ryght now to-fore. The feete of the sowle wer
festened to the fornace, and the sowle stode vp lyke a person.
It stode nott in the hyeste place nor in the loweste, bot as it
wer on the syde of the fornace. The shap of the sowle was
fereful and mervelowse. The fyre of the fornace semede to 30
come vp by-twyx the feete of the sowle, as when water ascendyth
vp be pypes. And that fyre ascended vp-on hys hede, and
vyolentely thryste him to-geder; so mych that the pores stode
as vaynes rennynge with brennyng fyr. Hys eres semede lyke
smythes belowes that mevede all his brayne with contynuall 35
blowyng. Hys eyn semede turnede vp so downe and sounke
ine as they had be festenede to the bake partye of the hede.
Hys | mowth was open and his tonge drawe owte by his noose

¹ Latin non.

The Revelations of Saint Birgitta 47

th[r]illes¹ and hynge doun to his lyppes. Hys teth wer as irn nayles fastenede be his palate. His armes wer so longe that they streched down to his feete. Both his hondes semede to haue & to presse to-geder a maner of 'fatnes with brennyng
5 pykke. The skynne þat semede apon the sowle semede lyke the skynne apon a body, and it was as a lynnen cloth al byshede wyth fylth; whych cloþe was so colde that yche on that see itt tremeld and shoke. And þer come þer-fro as whiter of a soor with corupte blode, and so wykked a stynk þat it myght nott be
10 lykenede to the werste stynke in the werlde. When his tribulacion was see, ther was herde a voyce of the sowle þat sayde v tymes, 'wo, wo, allas, allas,' cryinge with teres and all his mygthis.

Fyrst he sayde: alas and woo to me, þat I loved God so litell
15 for his ryght grete verteus and grace yove vn-to me. The secunde: allas and woo to me, þat I haue nott drede the ryghtwysnes of God as I aught. The thirde: allas and wo to me, þat I lovede the body and the luste of my synfull flesh. The ferte: allas and wo to me, for my wordely ryches & pride.
20 The vᵗᵉ: allas and woo to me, that euer I see yow, Ludowyke and Iohane.

Then sayde the angell to me: I wyll expowne to the this vysion. This paleys þat þu haste seen is the lykenes of heuen. The multitude of hem that þat wer in the seetes, cladde in white
25 and shynynge clothes, ar angles and sowles of seyntes. The sonne betokenes Criste in his godhede. The woman betokeneth the virgyn that bar God. The Ethiope betokeneth the fende that accuseth the sowle. The knyght betokenyth the angell that telleth the goode werkes of the sowle. The fornace be-
30 tokenyth hell, þat is so bren- | nyng with-ine, that yf all the fol. 28 a werld brynte with all thinges that be þer-in, it wer nott lyke the gretenes of that fornace. In this fornace a[r]² herde dyuerse voyces, all spekynge ayanste God, and all begynnyng her voyces with 'woo and allas', and endyng in lyke wyse. The
35 sowles appered as persones whos membres ar streched owte with-oute comforth and hath neuer reste. Know þu also þe fyre that semed to the in the fornesse brynnyth in euerlastynge derkenes, & the sowles that brynne þer-ine haue nott

¹ MS. thilles.   ² MS. as ; *Latin* audiuntur.

all one lyke payne. The derkenes that appered abowte the fornace ar called limbus, & it comyth of the derkenes that ar ine the fornes and yett they ar both one place and one hell. Who þat euer come ther shall neuer haue dwellyng with God. Above this derkenes is the gretteste payne of purgatorie that sowles may suffer. And by-yonde this place is a-noþer place wher is lesse peyne, that is none oþer bott lake of myghtes ine strenght, fayrnes, and such oder : as I telle the by a lykenes, as yf ther wer a seke man ; and when the sekenes and the payne wer sesede, he wer lefte so feble þat he had no strenghtes, tyll he recouerede by litell and litell. The thirde place is a-bove, wher is non oþer payne bot desyre of comyng to God. And that þu shuldeste the better vnderstonde in thy conscience, I telle the by a lykenes, as yf oþer metall wer medled with gold and brynte in moste hote fyr & shuld so longe be purgett, tyll the other metallys wer wasted away ; and the gold abode pur and clene the more that þe oþer metall were stronge and thikke, so mych it shuld nede the hottere fyr, tyll the golde wer as rennyng water, and all brynnyng. Then the master of the werke putteth þe golde in an oþer place, wher it shall take his trew forme and shappe ine syght and touchyng. And after that, he puttyth itt in-to the iij place, wher it is kepte tyll | it be presentede to the ower.

So it is gostely. In the fyrst place above the dyrkenes is the greteste payne of purgatorie, wher þu see þe sayde sowle be purged. Þer is towchyng of fendes. Ther is appere by lykenes venemouse wormes & lykenes of wode bestes. Þer is hete and cold. Þer is derkenes and confucion þat come of the payn þat is in hell. Þer have some sowles lasse payne & some mor, after that her synnes wer amended or noght, while tyme the sowle abode with the body. Then the mayster, that is, the ryght-wysnes of God, putteth the gold, that is, the sowles,[1] in oþer places, wher is not bot defaute of myghtes, ine whych sowles shall abyde tyll thay haue refreshing of her frendes or of con-tynuell suffrage of holy church. For a sowle, the more helpe it haue of fryndes, the rather shall it wax stronge & be de-lyuered from þat place. After thes, the sowle is bore to the iij place, wher is no payne bot desyre of comyng to the presence

[1] MS. þat is.

The Revelations of Saint Birgitta

of God & to his blessed syght. In this place abyde mony, and ouer-long, with-oute hem þat had perfyte desyr whyle they lyved in þe werld to come to þe presence and syght of God. Know þu also that mony dye in the worlde so ryghtfull and
5 innocentely, that anon they come to þe syg[ht][1] and presence of God. & some haue so amended her synnes with good werkes, þat her sowles shall fele no payn. Bot few þer be þat come nott in the place wher is desyr of comynge to Godde. Þer-for all sowles abydynge in thes iij places hath parte of the prayers
10 & goode werkes of holy church þat ar do in þe werlde : namle, of thoo þat thay dyd while thay lived, & of þoo that ar do of her frendes after her deth. Know þu also þat as synnes ar monye and dyuerse, so ar peynes mony and dyuerse. Þer-fore as the hungorie Ioyeth of mete when it comyth | to his mouth, fol. 29 a
15 and the thiristy of drynke, and as [2] he þat is hevy is glad of Ioy, and the nakede of clothinge, and the seke of commynge to his bedde, so sowles Ioy and be perteneres of the goode dedes at ar do for hem in the werlde.

Then sayde the angell forþermor : blessede be he þat in the
20 werld helpeth sowles with prayers, goode werkes, and labor of hys body. For the ryghtwosnes of God may nott lye þat sayth þat sowles oþer muste be purgede after her deth with peyne of purgatorie, or ells rather be lowsed be goode werkes of her frendes.

25 After thys was herde mony voyces oute of purgatorie, saynge : O lord Ihesu Cryste, ryghtfull Iugge, sende thy cherite to hem that gostely haue power in þe werlde ; for then shall we mowe haue more parte than we haue nowe, of her songe, redyng, and offrynge.

30 Above thys space fro when this crie was herde, semede as it had bene a howse in which wer herde mony voyces, sayng : rewarde be vn-to hem of God þat sende vs helpe in owre defautes.

In the same howse semede to go forth as it had bene þe
35 springe of a day, and vnder þat day springe apperede a clowde þat had ryght not of the lyght of the mornetyde. Oute of which come a grete voyce, saying : O lorde God, yife of thyne vnspekable power to ych of hem in þe world an hundreth fold

---

[1] MS. sygth.   [2] MS. as *inserted above line.*

rewarde, that with her good dedes lyfte vs vppe in-to the lyght of thy godhede, and in-to þe syght of thy face.

Revelations, Book IV, Chap. 8 and part of Chap. 9.
fol. 29 b

Then-after tellyth the angell the paynes of the sayde sowle, and seyth:

That sowle whos dispocion þu haste see, & herde his dome, is in the moste grevouse peynes of purgatorie. And that is þer-for, for it vnder-stondyth nott wheder it shall come to reste after purgacion, or ells be dampned; and this is the ryghtwysnes of God, for he had | conscience [1] and grete discrecion, which he vsede bodely to the worlde and not gostely to hys sowle. For he was to necligent and for-yette God to mych, as longe as he lyved. Þer-for his sowle suffreth now brennyng of fyre, and it tremeleth for cold. It is also blynde of darkenes and dredefull of the horrible syght of fendes. It is deffe of the fendes crie, hungrie & thiresty with-in-forth, and all wrapped in confusion with-owte-forth. Neuer-the-lasse, God 3affe it oo grace after deth; þat is, þat it shulde nott come to the touchinge of fendes. For he spared and for-3affe grevouse defautes to his cheffe enmyse, only for the wyrship of God; and he made frenship and a-corde with his cheffe enmye. Know þu also þat what euer he dyd of good and what euer he by-hyght & 3aff of well goten riches, & moste the prayers of the frendes of God, lassen and refreshen his payne, after it is determynede in the ryghtwysnes of God. Bott oþer goodes þat he yave, þat wer not well I-gotte, profyte þat to-for had hem ryght- fuly in possession gostely or bodely, if they be worthy after the dispocion of God.

After this þe angell calde, forþer-more, of the dome of the sayde sowle, & sayde: þu haste herde to-for that for þe prayers of the frendes of God, this man gatt goddely contricion of cherite for his synnes, a litle to-for hys deth; which contricion departed him fro hell. Þer-fore after his deth, the rightwysnes of Gode demede þat he shulde brenne in purgatorie be sexe ages þat he had, from that howr þat he dide fyrst wyttyngly dedely syn, vn-to the tyme þat he repentede fruytefully of godely cherite, bot he gatt helpe from Gode, of the world, or from þe frendes of God. The fyrst age was þat he loved nott God for

---

[1] MS. cons | conscience.

The Revelations of Saint Birgitta 51

the deth of his noble body, & for his monye folde tribulaciones, þat he sufferede for non oþer cause bot for the helth of sowles. The secunde age was þat he loved nott his own sowle as a cristen mann[1] | aught; nor he thonked not God for his baptem, for that he was neþer Iewe neþer hethenman. The iij age was þat he knew well tho thinges that God commaunded, and he had full litell wyll to fullfylle hem. The ferte age was þat he knew well tho thinges þat God for-bade hem þat wyll go to heuen; and bodely he dyde ayaynste hem, nott folowyng þe prikkynge of his concience, bot his own carnall affeccion. The fyfte age was þat he vsede nott grace and confession as longed to hym, while he had so longe tyme. The vi age was þat he rowght lytell of the bodye of Criste, nott wyllynge ofte receyve it, for he wold nott kepe him-selfe fro synne; neþer he had no cherite to receyve the body of Cryst tyll in the ende of hys lyfe.

After this appered one as it wer a man right sobre in syght, whos clothes wer white & shynyng as a prestes albe; he was gyrde with a lynnen gyrdele & a rede stole abowte his necke & vnder hys armes; & he began his wordes on this wyse:

Thu þat sees thes thinges, take kepe, merke, and commende to thi mynde tho thinges that þu seest and þat be sayde vn-to the. For ye þat be lyvyng in þe werld may not vnderstonde the power of God and the euerlastyng settyng þer-of, in the same wyse as we that ar wyth hym. For the thynges that ar anenste God do in a poynte of tyme, may not be vnderstonde ane[n]st[2] yow, bot with wordes and lykenes after the disposicion of the world. I am on of hem whom this man that is demede to purgatorie wyrshiped wyth his ʒiftes in hys lyfe. Þer-fore God hath granted me of hys grace þat yf ony man wolde do thes thynges þat I tell the, then his sowle myght be translate to an hier place, wher it shuld gett his trew | shappe, and fele non oþer payne bot as he shulde suffer that had a grete soore, and all the sorowes ware agoo, and he lay as a man with-oute strenght; and yett he shulde Ioye, for as mych as he shulde knowe certenly þat he shulde come to lyve.

fol. 30 a

Revelations,
Book IV,
Chap. 9
concluded.

fol. 30 b

---
[1] aught, catchword.   [2] MS. anest.

Þer-fore, as þu herde þe sowle of this man hath criede v
tymes woo and allas, so say I now to hym v thinges of comforth. The first wo was þat he loved God to lytell. Þer-fore,
þat he may be delyuered from this, be þer ȝeve for his sowle
xxx chalesse, wher-in the blode of God be offered, and God
him-selfe more wyrshipped. The secunde woo was þat he
drede nott God. Þer-for, for to do away this, be þer chose xxx
prestes þat after the dome of the man be deuote, & ych of
hem sey xxx masses, when they may: ix of marteres, ix of
confessors, ix of all sayntes, þe xxviij mass of angelles, þe xxix
of oure lady, and the xxx of the holy trinite. And all they
muste praye ententevously for his sowle, þat the ire of God be
swaged, and his ryghtwysnes bowed vn-to mercye. The thirde
wo was for his pride and couetyse. Þer-fore, to do away thys,
be þer receyved xxx poor men, whos feete be wesshede with
mekenes, and mete and drynke and mony & clothes be yeve
vn-to hem, wher-wyth they be comforted; and ych of hem,
both he þat wasshed, & thay þat ar wash, praye God mekely,
þat for his mekenes and bytter passion he foryeve this sowle þe
covetyse and pride þat he hath doo. The ferte woo, for the
lecherye of hys flesh. Þer-fore, who euer yife a mayden in-to
a monaster & a wydewe eke, & a mayde in-to trewe wedlok,
ȝevyng with hem so mych goode as they myght be sufficiently
founde in mete drynke & cloth; þane shuld God for-ȝeve the
synne of this sowle that he dyde in his flesh. For thes ar iij
lyves þat God | hath commaunded and chose to stonde in thys
world. The v woo was for he hath doo monye synnes in
tribulacion of many other. Þat is to say, for he did all hys
power þat tho tweyn named to-fore shuld come to-geder in
wedloke, which wer no less nye of kynne to-geder than yf they
hade be both of the nexte kynred; and this mariage he pro-
cured more for himself than for the realme, and with-owte
requeste of the pope, ayeynste þe prayseable [1] dispocion of holy
church. And for his dede, mony wer made martres, þat such
thinges shuld nott be suffered ayanste God and holy church
and cristen maners.

If any man þat wold do a-way þis synne went to þe pope,
and seyde: 'a certen man dyde sych a synne' (not expressyng

[1] MS. prayse able.

The Revelations of Saint Birgitta 53

the person), 'neuer-the-lasse in his ende he repented¹ & gatt absolucion, the synne nott amended. Puttyth to me þer-fore what pennance ȝe wyll, that I may ber; for I am redy to amende þat syn for him.' For-soth, if þer wer putt to him no
5 mor bot oo pater noster, it shulde be vayleable to þat sowle to the lessynge of his payn in purgatorie.

Wordes of praysyng bytwix our lady & hir son & what grace our lady getteth to hem that ar in purgatorie and in the werld. Cap. xviij.

Revelations, Book 1, Chap. 50.

10 Marie spak vn-to hir sonne and sayde: [blessede]² be thy name with-outen ende with thi godhed, which is with-oute begynnyng and with-owten ende. In thi godhed ar iij mervelowse thinges: þat is to say, power, wysdom, & vertue. Thy power is as fyre brynnyng moste hote, to-fore whos face all
15 that is seur and st[r]onge³ is as it were a drie strawe in the fyre. Thy wysdom is as it war the see that for gretenes may nott be drawe owte; which, when it encresyth and ouerflowyth, it hilleth⁴ | mountaynes and vales. So thy wysdom *fol. 31 b* may nott be comprehended ne full know. How wysely þu
20 haste made man and sett him above all thi creatures in erth! How wysely þu haste disposed birdes in þe ayr and bestes on the erth and fishes in the see, & to ych of hem þu haste ȝyve his tyme and ordre! How mervelously þu ȝeveste and takest away lyf to and fro all thinges! How wysely þu ȝeveste wys-
25 dom to the vnwyse and takeste it away from þe prowde! Thi vertue is grete as it wer þe lyght of the sonne þat shyneth in heuenes and fylleth all erth with hys light. So thy vertue fyllyth hie and low thynges, & all thynges. Þer-fore blessede be þu, my sonne, þat arte my God and lorde.
30 The sonne aunswerde: my moste der moder, thy wordes ar swete to me, for they come owte of thy sowle. Thu arte as the morentyde procedyng with clerenes. Þu haste yeve owte þi bemes above all heuenes, and thy lyght and clerenes passeth all angelles. Thu haste draw vn-to þe with thi clerenes þat
35 verray sonne þat is my godhed, so mych þat the sonne of my godhed, commyng in-to the, hath festened it-selfe in the. Of

---

¹ MS. repetented.   ² *Latin* Benedictum.
³ MS. stonge; *Latin* forte.   ⁴ d ij.

whose hete þu arte warmed with my cherite above all; of whos bryghtnes þu arte lyghtned above all oþer wyth my wysdom; and the derkenes of erth ar drive awaye, and all hevenes ar lyghtened be the. I sey in my trowth þat thi purenes, which plesed me above all angelles, drowgh my godhed in-to the, that thu shuldeste be enflamed with the hete of the holy goste, wherby þu closdeste in thy wombe verray god and man; wher throwe man is lyghtned, and angelles gladed. Þer-fore blessed be þu of thy blessed son. And þer shall no peticion be þat þu askes of me, bot þat it | shall be herde. And all that aske mercye with wyll to amende be the, they shall haue grace; for as hete procedyth fro the sonne, ryght so be the all mercye shall be yove. For þu arte as a well moste plenteous, oute of which mercy floweth vn-to wreches.

The moder aunswerde to her son: all verteu and glorie be to the, my sonne þat arte my God; & my mercye and all godenesse þat I haue is of the. Þu arte as a sede þat was nott sawe, and ȝit it ȝave of it-self a hondreth fold and a thousande fold fruite. For of the procedyth all mercye, which, for it is vnnowmerable and vnspekable, it may well be lykened in the noumbre of an hondreth, in whych is notted perfeccion; for of the is all p[er]feccion[1] and profett.

The sonne aunswerd to his moder: verely, moder, þu lykenest me well to a sede þat was nott sawe and yett it grewe, for I come in-to the wyth my godhed, and my manhode was nott sowe be eny medelyng of man. And ȝett it grew in the; wher-of mercye floweth vn-to all. Þer-fore þu saydeste well. And now, þer-for, for as mych as þu draweste mercye of me be the moste swete wordes of thy mowth, aske what þu wylte, and it shall be yove vn-to þe.

The moder aunswerd: my sonne, for I haue gote mercy of the, þer-for I aske mercye and helpe to wreches. For þer ar iiij places. Þe fyrst is hevyn, wher ar angelles and holy sowles; and they nede no thynge bot the, whom they hafe, and in the they have all goodenes. The secunde place is hell; and they þat dwell þer ar fyllede with malyce and excluded from all mercy; and þer-fore þer may be ryght nott of gode, noþer enter vn-to hem. The iij place is purgatorie; and they

---

[1] MS. profeccion.

The Revelations of Saint Birgitta

þat ar þer hath nede of iij folde mercye, fur they ar tormented in iij wyses. They ar trowbled in her heryng, for they here nott bot sorowes & paynes & [1] | wrechednes. Thei ar tormented in her syght, for they see ryg[ht] [2] noght bot her wrechednes. They ar tormented in her towchyng, [for they] [3] fele flaumes of fyre vnsuffereble and of grevouse payne. My lorde and my son, ȝeve hem thy mercye, for my prayers.

The sonne aunswerde : full gladely, moder, for þe I shall yeve hem iij folde mercy. First, her herynge shall be relesed ; her syght shall be esed ; and þe payne of felynge shal be more soft & esy ; and mor-ouer, from this tyme furth who euer be in þe gretteste payn of purgatorie shall come to the medell payn. And þay þat ar in þe medle payn shall come to the leste. And tho thatt ar in the leste payn shall passe in-to blysse.

The moder aunswerde : praysyng & worship be to the, my lorde. And then she sayde forþer: the ferte place is the world ; and the dwellers þer-in haue nede of iij thinges. Fyrst, contricion for her synnes ; secunde, satisfaccion ; thirde, strenght to do goode dedes.

The sonne aunswerde : who þat euer call apon thy name & hath hope in the, with purpose to amend that he hath do amysse, thes iij thinges shall be yove him & the kyngdom of heuyn þer-to. For þer is so mych swetenes to me in thy wordes þat I may not denye þat þu askes. For þu wyll no thing bot þat þat I wyll. For þu arte as a flawme bryght brynnyng, wherby candels quenched ar lyghtned. And þ[o] [4] þat ar not well brynnyng ar amended. Ryght so of þi charite, þat ascended in-to myn herte and drowgh me vn-to the, they þat ar dede in synne shall be arered to lyfe and tho þat ar leuke warme, as is blak smok, shall be made stronge in my cherite.

How our lorde lykneth our lady to a flour þat sprong in a vale and grew vppe above mountaynes. Cap. xix.

The moder of God spake vn-to hyr sonne : blessed | be thy name, my sonne Ihesu Criste. Wyrship be to thy manhode above all thynges made. Glorifie be to thi godhod a-bove all thinges, whych is with thy manhod oo God.

---

[1] d iij. [2] MS. rygth.
[3] Latin quia sentiunt. [4] MS. þu ; Latin & inaccensa conualescunt.

The sonne aunswerd: my moder, þu arte lyke to a flowr þat grew in a vale, a-bowte which vale wer v high mountaynes. And þat flour grew oute of iij rootes, with a ryght shafte þat had no knottes. This flowre had v leves full of all swettenes. And this vale grew vp with this flour above thes v moun- 5 tayns, and the leves of the flour sprede hem abrode above all the hyghnes of heuyn and above all the quores of angels. My loved moder, þu arte þat vale, for thy mekenes þe which þu haddeste a-fore all oþer. This vale passed v mountaynes. The fyrst mountayne was Moyses, that is called a mountayne for 10 power. For he hadde so grete power in the lawe apon peple, as if he had hade hem closed in his fyste. Bott thu closed in thy wombe the lorde of all lawes; þer-for þu arte hyer than that mountayne. The ij mountayne was Hely, which was so holy, þat wyth body and sowle he was take vp in-to an holy place. 15 Bot thu, my moste der moder, thy sowle was take vppe above all queres of angeles, vn-to the trone of God; and þer is thy moste clene bodye with thy sowle. Þer-fore þu art hier þan Hely. The iij mountayn was the high strength of Sampson, þat he had above all men. ȝett þe fende dyceyved him thro 20 his slyght. Bot þu ouer-come the fende with thy strenght; þer-fore þu arte stronger than Sampson. The iiij mountayn
fol. 33 b was Dauid, þat was a man after myn¹ | herte and wyll; and ȝett he fell in-to synne. Bot thu, my moder, foloweste all my wyll and synneste neuer. The v mountayn was Salamon, that 25 was full of wysdom; and ȝett he was fonned. Bot þu, my moder, was full of all wysdom and þu wer neuer no foole ne deceyved; þer-for þu art hier than Salamon. The flowr all-so spronge owte of iij rotes. For þu had iij thinges fro thy ȝonge age: that is, obedyence, cherite, and godely vnderstondyng. 30 Out of iij rotes grew a shafte moste ryght with-oute any knott: that is to say, thy wyll þat neuer was bowed bot after my wyll. This flour had also v leves that grew above all quers of angelles. For-soth, my moder, þu arte þe flour of these v leves. The fyrst leve is thin honeste, in so mych þat myn angelles þat ar 35 honeste to-for me, beholdyng thy honeste, see it be above hem and mor excellent than her honeste and holynes. Therfor þu arte hyer than angeles. The secunde lefe is thy mercye, þat

¹ d iiij.

The Revelations of Saint Birgitta 57

was so mych that when þu see þe wrechidnes of all sowles, thu
had compassion apon hem. In my deth þu sufferest most
payn. Angelles ar full of mercye, ȝett they suffre neuer sorow ;
bot þu, moste pitefull moder, had mercy on wreches when thu
5 felst all sorow of my deth. And for mercy þu woldest rather
suffer sorowe than be exempt þer-from. Þer-fore thi mercy
passeth the mercy of all angelles. The iij leve is thy myldenes.
Angelles ar myld and wyll gode to all. Bot þu, my moder
dere, to-fore thy deth had in thi body and sowle a wyll as a
10 angell, and dyd good vn-to all ; and yett þu denyeste non þat
askyth resonably to his profett. And þer-for thy myldenes is
more excellent than angelles. The iiij^{te} leve is thy fayrenes.
For angelles beholdes ych opers | fayrenes and they mervell þe fol. 34 a
fayrenes of sowles and bodies ; bot they see the fayrenes of thy
15 sowle above all thinges made, and the honeste of thy body passe
all men or wymmen þat euer wer. And so thy fayrenes passed
all angelles and all thinges made. The v leve was thy goodly
delectacion, be which no thinge delyted the bot God. Þer is no
thing þat delyteth angelles bot God, and ych on of hem feleth
20 his delyte in him-selfe. Bot when they see in the thy delyte
vn-to God, it semed to hem in her conscience þat her own
delyte brente in hem, as it had be a lyght in goddely cherite.
Bot thei see thi delyte in God, as it had bene a fyr most hot,
brynnyng with most fervente flaume, and so hie þat it neyght
25 vn-to my godhed. And ther-fore, moste swete moder, thy
goodely delectacion brynte hote above all queres of angelles.
This flour þat had thes v leves, þat is to sey, honeste,
mercye, myldenes, fayrenes, and souerayn delyte, was full of
all swettnes. For who þat wyll taste swettnes, he moste negh
30 vn-to swettnes & receyve it in-to him-selfe. And so did þu,
my good moder. For þu were so swete to my fader þat he
receyved þe all in-to his spirite, and thy swettnes plesed him
above all. A flowr also beryth a seede of he[t]e¹ and verteu
of the sonne, wher-of groweth fruyte. Bot blessede be þat
35 sonne þat is my godhed, that toke manhode of thy madynly
bowelles. For lik as sede, wher-euer it is sowe, bryngeth furth
sych flowres as the seede is, ryght so my membres wer lyk
vn-to thy membres in forme & in face. ȝett I was a man, & þu

¹ MS. hede ; *Latin* ex calore.

a virgyn woman. This vale was heved above all mountaynes with his flowr, when thi bodye was heved above all queres of angelles with thy [1] | moste holy sowle.

Our lady prayeth þat thes revelaciones mote be roten in mennys hertes and spred o-brode in the werld; and how our lorde prayseth owr lady and graunteth hir askyng, and byddyth þat thes be [2] bore to the pope & to oþer prelates. Cap. xx.

The blessed virgyn Marie spake vn-to hir sonne and seyde: blessed be þu, my sonne and my God, & lorde of angels and kynge of blys. I praye þe þat þe wordes þat þu hast spoke be roted in the hertes of thy frendis; and so sykyrly that they mote cleve in her myndes as the glewe whyt the which the shippe of Noe was glued, which neuer tempestes nor wyndes myght lowse a-sonder. Thy wordes mot also be spred in the world as branches and flowres moste swete, whos swete smell spredeth far o-brode. They mott also be fruytefull and swete as the date, whos swetenes delyteth mych mannes lyffe.

The sonne awnswerd: blessed be þu, my moste dere moder. Gabriell myn angell sayde vn-to the, 'Blessed be þu, Marie, to-fore all women,' and I bere the wyttnes þat thu art blessed and moste holy above all queres of angelles. Thu arte as a flowr in a garthen wher, þought mony swete flowres stonde abowte, ȝett it passyth all in swetenes, feyrenes, and verteu. Thes flowres are all þe chosen from Adam to the ende of the world, which wer planted in the garden of the werld and haue shyned and flowred with dyuerse verteus. Bot amongeste all þat euer war or shall be, þu wer moste excellente in swete smell of gode lyvynge and mekenes, and yn fayrenes of moste acceptable virgynyte, & in verteu | of abstynence. For I ber the wyttenes þat þu wer in my passyon more than martyr. In thyn abstynence þu arte more than any confessore. In mercye and goodenes þu arte more than a angell. Þer-fore, for the my wordes shal be roted as in moste stronge [glewe] [3] in the hertes of my frendes; they shall sprede o-brode as flowres smellyng most swete; and they shall sauor as a date alther swettyste.

Then sayde our lorde to his spouse, seynt Birgitt: sey to my

---

[1] d v.   [2] *Poorly written* bor *erased.*   [3] *Latin* bitumen fortissimum.

The Revelations of Saint Birgitta 59

frende, thy fader, hos herte is after myn herte, þat he expoune
dylygently thes wordes þat ar wryte ; and that he take hem to
the archebysshop and afterwarde to an oþer bysshoppe, and
when they ar wysely enformed, then þat he sende hem to the
⁵ thirde bysshoppe. Say also to him on my be-halffe : I am þi
maker and the raunsoner of sowles. I am he whom thu loveste
to-fore all oþer thinges. Be-hold and see þat the sowles which
I bowght with my blode ar as it wer þe sowles of hem þat
knew nott God. And they ar take prisoneres of the fende so
¹⁰ horribly þat he punyshet hem in all membres, as it were in a
streyte press. Þer-fore if my woundes sauour þe in thyn herte,
if þu sett ought be my scorgyng and by my sorowes, shew in
thyn werkes how mych þu loveste me ; and make my wordes
that I haue spoke with myn own movth to come in open, and
¹⁵ bere hem thy-self vn-to þe hede of the church. For I shall
ȝeve the my sprite þat wher-euer is eny debate by-twix tweyn,
thu shalt mow make hem acorded in my name by þe verteu
þat is ȝeve the, yf they ȝiffe fayth and credence to my wordes.
And for the more obydence of my wordes, þu shalt ber to the
²⁰ byshopes the wyttnes of hem | to whom my wordes sauour and fol. 35 b
delyte. For my wordes ar as it war fatt grece or talowe þat
melteth so mych þe sonner as a man hath with ine him more
kyndely hete ; for wher is no kyndely hete a man casteth oute
sych fattnes and receyveth it nott in-to his stomak. So ar my
²⁵ wordes. For þe mor feruent a man in his cherite that eteth
and choweth hem, þe more fatt he waxeth in swetenes of
heuenly Ioy and inwarde love, and the more he brennyth in
my love. Bot they to whom my wordes plese nott, haue as it
wer fattnes in her mouth which they taste, and anon they
³⁰ caste it owt & trede it vnder her fote. So my wordes are dispised of some, for the swettnes of spirituall thinges sauour hem
nott. The prince of the londe whom I haue chose in-to my
membre and made verely myn shall helpe the manfully ; and he
shall ȝeve the thin necessaries for the way of well gote goodes.

³⁵ **An angell tellyth seynt Birgitt a difference by-twyx þe** Revela-
good spirite and the evell ; and how a man shall do þat is Book I,
combered with þe evyll spirite. Ca. xxj. Chap. 54.

An angell spake vn-to the spouse of Cryst seynt Birgitt and

seyd : þer ar ij spirit*es*, on vnmade and a-noþer made.¹ The
spirite vnmade hath iij thing*es* : Fyrst, he is hote, secunde,
he is swete ; thirde, he is clene. He is hote, for he makyth
hoote not wi*th* eny thyng made, bot of him-self ; for he
is, wi*th* the fader and the sonne, maker of all thinges and 5
all myghty ; and than maketh he hoote when the sowll
brennyth all to the love of God. He is swete, when ryght
noght is swete ne plesyth þe sowle bott God allon and the
fol. 36 a mynde on hys werk*es*. He is clene, so þ*at* | [noo]² synne may
be founde in hym nor nothinge fowle, corrupt, nor changeable. 10
He makyth hoote, nott as mat*er*iall fyre, nore as the visible
sonne, þ*at* melteth thing*es* ; bot his hete is the inwarde born-
yng love of the sowle and a desyre fullfyllynge and swelowynge
the sowle in-to God. He is also swete to the sowle nott as
desiderable welth, luste, or any sych wordely thinge ; bot that 15
swettnes of the sprete is vnlykely to all temp*er*all swettnes and
the vnthinkable to all hem that neu*er* saue*r*ed it. Third, þ*at*
spirite is so clene as the bem*es* of the sonne, wher-in may be
founde no spott.

The secunde spirett, þ*at* is, a spirite made, hath also iij 20
thing*es* : for he is brennyng, he is bytt*er*, and he is vnclene.
Fyrst, he is brynnyng and wastyng as fyr. For þe sowle þ*at*
he hath in possessyon, he brennyth all wyth the fyre of lecherye
and of wyked desyr ; so that þe sowle may ryght noʒt think ne
desyr bot the fullfylly[ng]³ þ*er*-of ; so mych, þ*at* some tyme tem- 25
perall lyfe and all worshipp and comfort is loste þ*er*-by. Secund,
he is bitter as the gall ; for he enflaumeth the sowle wi*th* his
delectac*i*on, þ*at* þe Ioyes þ*at* ar to come seme to hem right
nought, and endeles good*es* seme to him folye ; and all thyng*es*
þ*at* ar of God and that he oweth to do to God ar bitt*er* to him and 30
abhorable, as if it wer a vomyte or gall. Thirde, he is vnclene ;
for he maketh the sowle so vile & redy to syn þ*at* he is ashamed
of no synne, ne he shulde leve noo synne, bot if he dred mor
shame of man then of God. And this spirite is brynnyng as
fyre ; for he is brynnyng in him-selfe vn-to wykednes & so 35
brynneth oþer wi*th* him. And he is bytter ; for all goode is
fol. 36 b bitter to him, and he makyth oþer bytt*er* wi*th* him. And he |

¹ MS. vn [made] *cancelled*.   ² *Latin* nullum.
³ MS. fully filly. *See Notes.*

The Revelations of Saint Birgitta

is unclene ; for he delyte[t]h [1] him in vnclenes, and he sekyth to haue oþer lyke to him.

Bot now þu myght aske & say to me : art nott þu a spirite made as he is ? Why arte þu þer-for [nott] [2] sych on as he is ?
5 I vnswer : for-soth, I am made of the same God þat he is ; for þer is bot on God, fader and sonne and holy goste, and they ar not iij Goddes bott on God. And we both wer well made and to a good ende, for God made neuer ryght noght bot goode. Bot I am as a sterr, for I stode in the goodenes and cherite of
10 God, where-in I was made ; and he is as a ded coole, for he wente from the cherite of God. Þer-fore as a sterr is not without outen bryghtnes and shynnyng, and a coole is nott with-oute blakenes ; so a good angell, þat is, a sterr, is neuer with-oute lyghtnes, þat is to say, the holy goste. For all þat he hath he
15 has of God, þat is, fader and sonne & holy goste, by hos love he is hote and by hos shynyng he is bryght. And to him he cleveth besyly and conformeth him to his wyll, and for he wyll neuer ony thinges bot as God wyll ; & þer-for he is hote and clene. Bot the devell is so fowle blak coole and mor fowll then
20 all creatures. For as [he] was mor fayr þan oþer, so muste he be fowler þen oþer ; for he was contrarie to his maker. And as the angell of God shyneth with-oute sesyng by the lyght of God & brynnyth in the lyght of his cherite, ryght so þe fend brynneth and is aungwesshed in hys malyce. & as his malice
25 may neuer be fylled, so þe goodenes of þe spirite of God and the grace of God ar vn-spekable ; for þer is non so rotted with the fende bott that the goode spirite some tyme vysetes and stirreth his | herte. So is þer also non so goode in erth bot þat fol. 37a þe fende is besy gladely to toch him with temptacion. For þer
30 ar mony good and ryghtfull þat ar tempted of the fende be þe suffrance of God. Bot þat is not for her harme, bot to þe more glorie. For þe sonne of Godd, þat is on in godhed with the fader and the holy goste, was tempted in his manhod. How mych rather his chosen muste be tempted to her more reward.
35 Þer ar also mony goode folke þat some tyme fall in-to synne ; and her conscience is derked be falsehed of the fende ; bot by verteu of the holy goste, they rise mor myghtly and stonde more strongely. Neuer-the-lesse, þer is non bott he vnder-

---

[1] MS. delyteh.   [2] *Latin* non.

stondeth in his conscience wheþer the suggestyon of the fende
leede to the fylth of synne or to goode, if he wyll besyly thinke
and examyn it. Þer-fore, þu spowse of my lorde, haste nott for
to dowte of the spirite of thy thoughtes, wheþer it be good or
evyll ; for thy conscience telleth the which thynges ar to be
lefte and which to be do. Bot what shall he do with whom the
fende is full ? For þe goode spirite may nott enter in him, for
he is full of the evyll spirite. iij thinges aweth he to do. Fyrst,
that he haue pure and hole confessyon of hys synnes which,
þof it may not be a-non in a contrite¹ herte for herdenes of
herte, ȝett for that confessyon þe fende yeveth stede to the
good spirite and a maner of sesyng and skyppyng away.
Secunde, he muste haue mekenes, þat he purpose to amende
the synnes which he hath don. Thrid, to thentent þat he gett
ayayn þe good | sprite, he oweth to praye God with meke prayer
and to be contrite for his synnes þat he hath do with verrey
cherite. For cherite to God fleeth the devell ; for he had leuer
die an hundreth tymes þan a man shuld yeve the leste goode of
cherite to his God, so envyous and malycyus he is.

After this spake þe blessed virgyn our lady to the spowse of
Cryste seynte Birgitt and seyd : thu new spowse of my sonne,
cloth þe in his clothes and sett thin owch on thy breste ; þat
is, þe passion of my sonne.

Seynt Birgitte aunswerd : my lady, sett thu þat owch on my
breste.

Our lady seyde : þat wyll I doo. For-soth, I wyll telle the
how my sonne was disposed and why he was so ferventely
desyred of holy faders. For he stode as a man be-twyx two
cytes ; þat is, heuen & hell. Oute of the fyrst cite cried a
woyse to him & sayde : ' Þu man þat stondeste in myde way
between the cites, þu art a wyse man and can be-war of perelles
þat fall. Þu arte stronge to suffer herde thinges þat þe betyde ;
and þu art myghty herted, for þu didest right noght.² We
haue desyred the and abydes the. Þer-fore open our ȝate, for
oure enmyse besege it þat it be nott opened.' Oute of the
secunde cite was herde a voyce, saying : ' Thu man moste man-
full and stronge, here our querell and weylyng. We sytt in

---

¹ MS. an vncontrite ; Latin contrito corde.
² Latin adds quia nihil times.

derkenes and we suffer hungur and thruste vnsufferable. þer-
fore be-hold our wrechednes and our wreched pouerte. For
we ar smyte as gresse þat is smyte with a syth; and we ar
dried from all goode, and all our strenght fayleth. Come to vs
5 and save vs; for the onely we haue abyde, and the we hope to
be our delyverer. Come and louse our pouerte and turne our
weyling in- | to Ioy. Be þu our helpe and our helth. O moste fol. 38 a
worthi and blessed body þat was bore of a pure virgyn, come.'
Those ij voyces herde my sonne oute of ij cites, heuen and hell;
10 and þer-fore he was moved with mercy; and by his moste
bitter passyon and ȝevyng oute of his blod, he opned the yate
of hell. Thes thinges, my dowghter, thinke þu; and haue hem
all way to-fore thyn eyn.

After owr lady hade sende mony reuelaciones to a kyng, Revela-
15 at laste she sente hym on and seyde þat it shuld be þe last tions, BookVIII,
letter that shuld be sente him. Bott in this reuelacion Chap. 48.
folowyng, our lady spekyth aȝayne to þe same kyng and
declareth her fyrst sayng, & enformeth seynt Birgitt why
þe wordes of God ar spok so derkely þat they may haue
20 dyuerse vnderstondynges. Here is also shewed þe blessed
trinite vnder lykenes of a pulpit; & of iij bemes of iij
dyuers colores; & of þe dome of iij kynges, of which on
was olyve, ane oþer was in hell, & þe thirde in purgatorie.
Cap. xxij.

25 The moder of God speketh to þe[1] spowse and seth: doughter, I told the to-for þat that shuld be my laste letter þat
shulde be sente to the kynge, my frend; that is to be vnderstonde of tho thinges that towches his syngler person and myn.
For if a man herde a profetable thinge song þat longed to his
30 frende, & he sat &[2] herde itt for to tell it to him, wheþer it
wer a songe of myrth or a letter of holsome blamyng, both he
þat endited it & he þat sounge it were worthy rewarde. Ryght
so þe ryghtwysnes of God, demyng in evennesse and Iustyfyyng
in mercye, wyll synge ryghtwysnes and mercy. And þer-fore
35 who euer wyll heer, heer he. For | it is no letter of blamyng, fol. 38 b
bot a song of ryghtwosnes & cherite. Some tyme when a letter
was sent one, it contened warnyng and blamyng; for it blamed

---

[1] MS. e *inserted above line.*   [2] MS. sat & *inserted above line.*

vnkyndenes of benefetez and warnde and stirred to conuersion
and amendynge of maneres. Bot now þe ryghtwysnes of God
syngeth a feyre songe, þat longeth vn-to all ho euer here it,
beleve it, & receyve it in werkyng, he shall fynde fruyte of
helth and fruyte of endeles lyffe.

Bot þu myght aske why þe wordes of God ar sayde so derkely
þat they may be dyuersely vnderstounde & some tyme thay ar
oþer-wyse vnderstounde of God and oþer while of men. I
aunswer : God is like to a man þat makyth brynnyng wyne.
For this man hath mony pypes, some goynge vpp and some
don, by which the wyne rynneth now vp & now down be
wyrkyng of the hete of the fyre tyll it be made perfyte. Ryght
so doth God in his wordes, for some tyme he goth vppe be
rightwysnes, and some tyme he comyth down be mercye ; as it
is shewed in kynge Ysache, to whom, I say, þe profett seyde of
ryghtwysnes þat he shuld dye, and yet afterwarde mercye
addyd to him mony ȝeres to lyve. Some tyme also God comyth
dovn be simple shewynge of wordes be bodely expressynge, bot
he goth vp ayayn be spirituall vnderstondyng ; as it was in
Dauid, to whom mony thynges wer seyde vnder the name of
Salamon which wer vnderstonde & fullfylled in þe sonne of
God. Some tyme also God spekes of thinges to come as it wer
of thinges paste, and towcheth both thinges presente and thinges
to com ; for all thynges, both present, paste, and to come, ar |
in God as oo poynt. And þu owe not to mervell þof God speke
in dyuerse wyse, for it is do for iiij causes. Fyrst, þat God
shuld shew his grete mercye, þat no man herynge þe rightwysnes of God shulde dispeyr of his mercye. For when a man
chongeth þe wyll of synne, þen Gode chaunges þe strettenes of
hys sentence. The secunde cause is þat they þat yeve fayth to
the ryghtwysnes and to the behestes of God shulde be crowned
& rewardede þe more largely for fayth and abydyng. The third
cause is for if the counsell of God wer know in certen tyme,
some shuld be gretely trobled be-fore, knowyng of contrarie
cases, and oþer for werynes shuld sesse of her feruour and
desyre. And þer-for when I write any wordes to ony, it is nott
expressed to the in þe conclusion wheþer tho wordes shall be
receyved & be beleved with effecte of him or noo. Ne it is
declared to the wheþer he shall beleve and fullfyl the wordes

The Revelations of Saint Birgitta 65

ine dede or no, for it is nott lefull to the to know it. The iij cause is þat non shulde presume bodely to discusse þe wordes of God, for he makyth him lowe þat is hyght, and of ane one he makyth a secunde. The fourte cause is þat he þat
5 sekyth occasion to departe from God may fynde itt, and thay that be fowle be mor fowle, and tho goode be made mor know.

After this, þe sonne of God spake to saynte Birgitt and seyde : yf a man spake be a pype þat hade iij howles, and seyde
10 to the herrer, þu shall neuer her my voyce be thys hole, he war not to blame þof he spake afterwarde be the ij other hooles. So it is now in our spech ; for þough the virgyn my moder sayde þat shuld be þe laste letter to be sent to þe kynge, þat is to be vnderstond | of his person. Bot now I God, þat am in the fol. 39 b
15 moder and moder in me, sende my messynger to the kynge, als well for hem þat ar now present olyve as for hem þat ar nott yett borne. For ryghtwysnes and mercye ar in God endelesse, for eternally this rightwysnes was in God, þat whill God was to-fore Lucyfer full of wysdom of gudenes and of power. He
20 wold þat mony shuld be pertyneres of his godenes. And þer-fore he made angelles ; of which some, beholdyng here feyrenes, desyred to be above God. & þer-for they fell and ar made vnder þe feete of God wykked fendes. And yett in hem God in a maner hath mercy ; for when the fende by the ryghtwysnes
25 and suffraunce of God fullfylleth the evell þat he desyrith, he is as it wer in a maner comforted of the prosperyte of his malice. Nott at the payne of the fende is lessned þer-bye ; bot as a seeke man that hath an enmye moste stronge is comforted be þe herynge of his deth, þof the peyne of his sekenes be nott
30 lessned be that heryng, ryght so the fende of Envye, wher-in he is hote brynnyng, Ioyeth and is glad when God doth ryghtwysnes ayenst men ; for the thruste of his malyce is in maner refresshed and esed. Bot after þe precypitacion of the fendes God, seyng lake ine his oost, made man, þat he shuld obey to
35 his preceptes and brynge forth fruyte, tyll as many men and women were ascended in-to heuen as angelles fell owte of heuen. Þer-for man was made perfyte ; which, when he had take þe comaundement of lyf, he toke no hede to Gode ne to his worship. Bot consentyng to the suggestyon of the fende, he

F

fol. 40 a trespased, sayng, 'Ete we of the tree of lyffe, and we shall[1] | know all thynges goode and evell'. Th[u]s[2] Adam and Eue wold nott herme to God, as the fende ; noþer they wold be above God, bot they wold be wyse as God. And the[y][3] fell, bot not as the fende; for the feende hadd envye to God, and hys wrechednes shall neuer have ende. Bot man wold oþer than God wolde he shuld wyll, and þer-fore he deserued and suffered rightwysnes with mercye. Than felt they ryghtwosnesse when[4] they had nakednes for clothyng of glorie and hunger for plente, styrryng of the flessh for virginite, drede for seekernesse, and labor for reste. Bot anon they gate mercye: þat is to say, clothynge aʒanste nakednes, mete ayanste hunger, sykernes of commyng to-geder for encresyng[5] of man-kynde. For-soth, Adam was of moste honeste lyffe, in that he had neuer wyf bot Eue, ne oþer woman bot hyr allon. Allso God hath shewed rightwysnes and mercy in bestes, for God hath made iij worthy thinges : fyrst, angelles þat hath sprete bot no bodye ; secunde, manne þat hath sowle and body ; thirde, bestes þat hath body bot noo sowles as man hath. Þer-fore angell, because he is a spirit, he cleveth contynualy to God and nedeth no mannes helpe. Bot man, for he is flesh, may not cleve contynually to God, tyll þe dedely bodye be departed from the sowle. And þer-for, þat man may lyfe, God hath made to his helpe vnresenable bestes to obeye and serue to his better. And in thes vnresenable bestes God hath grete mercye, for they haue no shame of her membres, nor sorow of deth tyll it come. And they ar content wyth simple lyvelod. Also after the flode of Noe was paste, God dyd ryghtwosnes with mercye. For God myght haue browght well ye peple of Israell in-to the lond of beheste in shorte
fol. 40 b tyme. Bot it | was ryght that the vesselles þat myght hold beste drynk shuld fyrst be preued and purged and after-ward halowed. To whom allso God dyd grete mercy, for by þe prayer of one manne, þat was Moyses, her synne was done away & þe grace of God ʒeff. On the same wyse, after myne Incarnacion, ryghtwysnes is neuer vsed with-owt mercy ne mercy with-oute ryghtwysnes.

[1] know all catchword.
[2] MS. thes ; Latin scilicet.
[3] MS. ther ; Latin ceciderunt.
[4] MS. when when.
[5] MS. encre syng.

The Revelations of Saint Birgitta

Then sewed þer a voyce on hie, sayng: O moder of mercy, moder of endeles kyng, purchase þu mercye; for to the ar comen thoo prayers and teres of thy seruant, the kynge. We know well þat right is þat his synnes be punyshed, bot gett þu
5 mercy þat he be conuerted & do pennaunce and wyrship to God. Then aunswerd oure lorde Ihesu Cryst and sayde: þer is iiij fold rightwysnes in God. The fyrst is þat he þat is made and is endelesse be worshiped above all thinges; for of him and in him ar all thinges lyve, and haue her beynge. The secunde
10 rightwysnes is þat to him þat euer was and is and was temperally bore, in tyme afore ordened, be do seruice of all; & for þat he be loved in all clannesse. The thirde rightwysnes is that he þat of himselfe may not suffer bot of hys manhode was made able to suffer; and in the dedelynesse þat he toke hath
15 deserued to man vndedlenesse, be desyred to man above all thinges þat may be desyred or ar to be desyred. The fourte rightwysnes is þat they þat ar vnstable do seeke verrey stablenes, and they thar in de[r]kenes[1] desir lyght, þat is, the holy goste, askyng his helpe with contricion and verrey mekenes.
20 Bot of this kyng, þe seruante of my moder, for whom mercye is now asked, rightwysnes seyth þat his tyme is nott | sufficiante fol. 41 a to purge worthely, as rightwysnes askyth, the synnes that he hath doo ayenste þe mercye of God, ne his body myght nott suffer the payn þat he hath deserued for his synnes.
25 Neuerthelesse þe mercye of the moder of God hath deserued and gatt mercye for the same, hir seruant, þat he shall her what he hath doo and how he may amende him, yf he wyll in happes be compuncte and conuerted.

Then anon, sayth seynte Birgitt, I see in heven a howse of
30 mervelouse fayrenes and grettenes. And in þat howse was a pulpite, and in the pulpite a booke. And I see ij stondynge to-for the pulpite; þat is to say, an angell and the feende.

Of which þe on, þat is, the feende, spake and seyde: my name, he sayth, is Waylleway.[2] For this angell & I folow oo
35 thing þat is desiderable to vs; for we see þe lorde moste myghty purposeth to byld a grete thing. And þer-for we labour; the angell to perfeccion of the thinge, and I to destruccion of þe same. But it happith þat when þat desiderable

---
[1] MS. dekenes; *Latin* tenebris.   [2] *Latin* heu.

thing comyth some tyme in-to my hondes, it is so fervent and
hote þat I may nott hold it; and when it comyth in-to þe
hondes of the angell, it is so cold and sliper þat anon it slydeth
oute of his hondes.

And when I, sayth seynt Birgitt, behelde besyly wyth all
consideracion of my mynd vn-to the same pulpite, myne vnderstondyng suffyced nott to conceyve it as it was, ne my sowle
myght nott comprehende þe fayrenes þer-of, ne my tonge
expresse itt. For the apering of the pulpite was as it had be
the sonnebeme, hauyng a red colour and a white colour and a
shynyng colour[1] | of gold. The golden colour was as the
bryght sonne. The white colour was as snow, most whyte.
And the rede colour was as a roose. And yche colowr was see
in oþer. For when I beheld the gold colowr, I see þer-wyth
the white and the redde colowr. And when I see the white
colowr, I see þer-in þe oþer two colowres. And when I byheld the rede colour, I see þer-in the white and the golden
colour. So that ych colour was see in oþer, and ȝett ych was
distincte from oþer and by it-self; and no colour was to-fore
oþer, ne after oþer, none lasse þan oþer, nor mor than oþer; bot
ouer all and in all thinges they semed even. And when I
loked vpwarde, I myght not comprehende þe lenghth and the
brede of the pulpyte; and lokyng downwarde, I myȝt nott see
ne comprehende þe grettenes ne þe depnes of it, for all was
incompre[hen]sible[2] to be consydered. After this I see a bok
in the same pulpite, shynyng as gold moste bryght, þat had
the shap of a boke. Which boke, and the scriptur þer-of, was
not write with ynke, bot ych worde in the boke was qwhik and
spak it-self, as yf a man shuld say, doo thys or that, and anone
it wer do with spekyng of the word. No man redde the scriptur
of that boke, bot what euer that scriptur contened, all was see
in the pulpyte and in the iij colours. To-fore þis pulpite I see
a kynge þat was o-lyve in the werld; and on the lyft syde of
the pulpite I se a noþer kyng þat was dede and in hell; and on
þe right syde of the pulpyte I se the iij kynge that was in
purgatorie. The sayde kynge þat was o-lyf satt crowned as it
had be in a vessell of | glasse close abowte. Above that glasse
hange an horrible swerde with iij egges, neyghyng contynually

[1] e ij.   [2] Latin incomprehensibilia.

The Revelations of Saint Birgitta

to þat glasse as a dyall in ane orelege neghith to his merke. On the ryght syde of the same kynge stode an angell that had a vessell of gold and his lapp open. And on his lefte syde stoode a fende þat had a peyr of tounges and an hommer. And
5 boþe þe angell and þe feend stroffe wheþer of her hondes shuld be mor ner the vessell of glasse when the iij egged swerde shuld touch it and breke it.

Than herde I an horrible voyce of the fende, saynge: how longe shall it be thus? For we both folow oo praye, and we
10 wot not who shall ouer-come.

Then anon þe ryghtwysnes of God spake to me and seyd: thes thinges þat ar shewed to the ar not bodely bot gostely. For neþer angell nor fende hath bodies; bot they ar shewed to the in sych wyse, for þu maiste not vnderstonde gostely thinges
15 bot by bodely lykenes. This lyving kynge aperyth to the as it wer a vessel of glasse, for his liff is bot as it wer frele glasse and sodenly to be ended, þe iij egged swerde is deth, for when it comyth it doth iij thinges. It febleth the body, it chongeth the conscience, & it fleeth all strengthes, departyng as a swerd
20 þe sowle from the body. That the angell and the fende seme to stryve abowte the glasse betokeneth þat eyther of hem desyrith to haue the kynges sowll, þat shall be demed to him to whos consell he is more obedyent. That the angell hath a vessell [1] | and a lapp betokeneth þat right as a child resteth fol. 42 b
25 in þe moder lappe, so laboreth þe angell þat the soule be presented to God as it wer in a vessell and reste in the lappe of endeles comforte. Þat the fende hath tonges and a hammer betokeneth that the fende draweth the sowle to him with the tonges of wykked delyte & brekyth it asonder with þe hammer;
30 þat is, with the consente and doyng of synne. That the vessell of glas is some tyme [2] ouer hote and some tyme ouer cold and slyper betokeneth þe inconstance and unstablenes of the kynge; for when he is in temptacion he thinkyth thus: þof I know well þat I offende God, if I fullfyll now þe conceyte of my
35 herte, ȝett a[t] [3] this tyme I shall fullfille my conceyte in dede. And so wyttyngly he synneth aȝanst his God, for he synneth so wyttyngly he cometh vn-to the hondes of the fende. After-

[1] e iij. [2] MS. is some tyme is some tyme.
[3] MS. as; Latin ista vici.

ward þe kynge takyth to him confession and contricion, & so
he ascapeth þe hondes of the fende and comyth in-to þe power
of the goode angell. And þer-for, bot if the kyng lefe his
inconstance, he stondeth full perlously, for he hath a feble
gronde. 5

After this I see on þe left syde of the pulpite þe dede kynge
þat was dampned in-to hell cledde in kyngely araye and
syttyng as it hadde be in a trone. Bot he was dede and pale
and ryght ferefull to loke on. To-fore his face was as it had
be a whele þat had iiij lynes in the ottmeste partye; and this 10
whele torned abowte att brethyng and blowyng of the kynge.
And ych of the iiij lynes ȝede vpwarde and donwarde as the
kynge wold, for þe mevyng of the whele was in the kynges |
power. The thre lynes wer wretyn bot in the fourte lyne was
writen right noght. On the right syde of this kynge I see an 15
angell as it had be a man most feyr, whos hondes wer voyde;
bot he serued to the pulpytt. On the lefte syde of the kynge
appered a fende whos hede was lyke to a dogg; his wombe
myght nott be fylled, his navyll was open and boyled out
venym, colowred with all maner of venemouse colours. And 20
in ych fote he hade iij clawes, grete, stronge, and sharpe.

Then was þer one þat shone mor bryght then the sonne,
that for bryghtnes was mervelouse to be-hold. And he seyde
vn-to me: This kynge whom þu seest is full of wrechednes,
whos conscience is now shewed to the as he was in his kyng- 25
dom, and whatt entent he was in when he dyed. Whatt hys
consciens was or he come to his kyngdome longeth nott to the
to know. Neuer-þe-lesse, know þu þat his sowle is nott to-for
thyne eyn, bot his conscience. And for the sowle & þe fende
ar nott bodely bot gostely, þer-fore þe fendes temptacions & 30
tormentes ar shewed to the [be]¹ bodely lykenes.

Tha[n]² onone þat dede kynge began to speke, not of his
mouth, bot as it had be of his brayne, and seyde thus: O ȝe my
conselleres, this is myn entent, that what euer is suggett to
the crown of my realme, I wyll hold it and kepe it. I wyll 35
also labor that the thinges þat I haue be encresed and nott
lessed. Bot in what wyse thoo thinges wer gote, þat I hold,

---

¹ Latin per similitudines corporales.
² MS. that; Latin et statim ille Rex.

what is it to me to aske? It is I-neught to me if I may
defende and encrese tho thinges þat I haue.
 Then cried the fende and seyde: lo, it is thorowght. What
shall my hoke do?
5 Ryghtwysnes aunswerde oute of the boke that was in the
pulpite, saynge to the fende;[1] | pott in thy hoke in the hoole fol. 43 b
& drawe to the.
 And a-non as the worde of ryghtwysnes was spoke, þe hoke
was putt ine. Bot þer-with in the same moment come to-for
10 the kynge an hammer of mercye with which the kyng myght
haue smyte away the hooke, if he wold have inquired the
trowght of all thinges and fruytefully haue chaunged his wyll.
 Then spak the same kynge ayane and seyde: O my conselleres and my men, ye haue me to be your lorde, & I haue take
15 yow to be my consellers. Þer-fore I tell yow þat þer is a man
in my realme þat is a treytour of my wyrship and of my lyf,
þat lyeth in wayte to hinder my realme and to distrowble peese
and the comyn peple of the realme. In this, seyth the kynge,
þer yave credence to me both lerned and lewed, both lordes
20 and comyn peple, belevyng the wordes þat I seyde to hem, in
so mych þat þat man þat I defamed of treson toke grete herme
and shame, and sentence of exile was yeve ayanste him.
Neuer-the-lesse, my conscyence wyste well what þe trowth was
in all this dede, and I wyst well þat I seyde mony thinges
25 ayanste þat man for ambicion of the kyngdom and for the
drede of lesyng þer-of, and that my wyrship shulde be spred
a-brode, & þat þe realme shuld cleve mor suerly to me and to
my successores. I thought also in myselfe þat þought I knew
þe trowth how this kyngdom is goten, and what wronge is don
30 vn-to him, yett if I receyve him aȝayn to my grace and | tell fol. 44 a
the trowth, then all þe repreve and herme shall fall apon my-
selfe. And þer-for I sett me seurly in myne herte þat I wold
rather die then tell the trowth or revoke myn vnryghtfull
wordes and dedes.
35 Then seyde the fende: O Juge, loo, how this kyng ȝeveth
me his tonge.
 The rightwysnes of God aunswered: put þer-on thy snare.
And when the fende had don so, anone þer hounge to-fore the

[1] e iiij.

kynges mouth an irne most sharpe, wher-with he myght if he had wolde haue kutt away the snare and all-to haue broke it.

Then spake þe same kynge and seyde: O my conselleres, I haue concelled with clerkes and lettred men of þe state of the realme, and they sey to me þat yf I shuld resigne the realme in-to oþer mennes hondes I shuld do herme to mony, and be a treytour of her lyves and godes and breker of the law of ryghtwysnes; and þer-for þat I myght kepe þe kyngdom & defende it from enmys, vs be-hoves to thinke and ymagyn some new thinges, for the old rentes of the escheker ar not suffyciaunte to gouernen and to defende þe realme. And thus I by-thought[1] me of new imposiciones of tributes and of gylefull exacciones to be putt in the realme, both to herme of hem dwellyng þer-in & of innocent peple þat went by the way and of marchauntes. And in thes Inuenciones I purposed to abyde to my deth, al-though my conscience told me þat they were ayanst God, ayanest all ryghtwysnes, and ayanst comyn honeste.

Then criede the fende and seyde: O Juge, loo, this kyng hath bowed both his hondes vn[der][2] my | vessell of water. What shall I do?

Ryghtwysnes aunswerd oute of the booke: putt thy venem þer-apon. And anon as the venem of the fende was putt apon his hondes, þer come to-fore þe kyng a wessell of oyntement wher-with the kynge myght well haue refreyned þat venym.

Then the fende cried owte strongely and seyde: loo, I see a mervelouse thinge þat passeth my wytt to vnderstonde. For my hoke is putt to the herte of the kynge, and anon þer is yeve him an hammer in his bosn. My snare is putt to his mowth, and þer is offred him an irne moste sharpe. My venym is powred apon his hondes, and þer is yeve him a vessell of oyntement.

Ryghtwysnes aunswerde oute of the boke of the pulpite and sayde: all thinges haue tyme; and mercye and ryghtwysnes shall mete to-geder.

After this the moder of God spake to me and seyde: come, doughter, and heer & see what the good sprete styrreth to, and whatt the evell; for euery man hath infuciones and visitaciones,

---

[1] MS. by thought. [2] MS. vn; Latin sub.

The Revelations of Saint Birgitta

some tyme of the good spirite and some tyme of the evell. For þer is not bot þat he is visitted of [God][1] longe as he leveth.

And anon þer appered ayane þe same dede kynge, whos sowle þe holy goste enspired while he lyved in this wyse: O frende, þu owest to serue God with all thy strenghthes, for he [y]aue[2] lyff, conscience and vnderstondyng, helth and wyrship; and yett he suffreth the in thy synnes.

The kynges conscience aunswerd, spekynge by a lykenes: it is trew, he sayth, þat I am hold to serue God, be hos power I am made and bowght, and hos mercy I lyfe and haue my beyng.

Bot her ayaynste the wyked sprete styrred the kyng and sayd: Broþer, I ȝeve þe good consell. Doth as he doth þat paryth ane apple | for þe parynges, and the coor he casteth away, & þe pyght and the beste he kepeth to him-selfe. So do þu. God is meke and mercyfull and pacyente and nedeth nothing. Þer-fore yeve him of thy goodes such as þu maste esely forber, and oþer goodes þat ar mor profitable and desiderable kepe to thy-self. Do also what þe lyste after thy flesh, for it may lyghtly be amendett. And þat þat þe lyste nott to do, þough þu be bounde to do it, lefe it; and in-stede þer-of yeve almes. For þer-by may mony be comforted.

The kynges conscience aunswerd: this, he sayth, is a profetable consell. For I may yeve some thinges þat I haue withoute any grete harme to me, and yett God settyth right mych þer-by. And oþer thinges I shall kepe to myn own vse & for to gete me þer-wyth frenshipe of mony oþer.

After this þat good angell þat was yeve to kepe the kynge spake vn-to him by inspiraciones, sayng: O þu frende, thinke þat þu, dedely, shall dye. Thinke also that this lyff is shorte and God is a ryghtfull and pacyent Juge þat examineth all thy thoughtes, wordes, and dedes from the begynnyng of thyn vnderstondyng age un-to the ende, which also demeth all thy wylles & ententes and leveth right noght vndyscussed. Þerfor vse thy tyme and thy strenghthes resonably and gouerne thy membres to the profett of thy sowle. Lyve sobrely, not

fol. 45 a

---

[1] *Latin* a Deo.   [2] MS. haue; *Latin* dedit tibi.

fullfyllynge the luste of thy flesh in desyres, for they þat lyven after the flesh and after her own wyll shall not come to the kyngdom of God.

 Bot her ayayne anon þe fende wyth his suggestyones stired
fol. 45 b þe kynge and sayde: O þu broþer, | yf þu shalt yeve a reken- 5
ynge to God of all thy tymes and momentes, whan shalt þu than Ioy? Bot here my consell. God is mercyfull and may esely be plesed, for he had nott bowght the if he wold haue lost the. Ther-for the scriptur of God sayth þat all synnes ar foryeve be contricion. Do þu þer-for as dyd he þat aught an- 10
oþer xx pounde of gold. And when he had nott wher-of to pay, he come to his frende and asked him consell. And he conseled him to take xx pound of copur and gilt hit with oo pound of gold, and with þat gilte mony pay his creditour. & he dide after þe consell I-yeve him & payde his creditour xx pounde 15
of coper ouer gylte; & xix pounds of pure gold he kepte to him-self. So do þu. Spende xix howres to thy delyte, luste, and Ioy; and on howr is suffyciante for the to be sory and compuncte for thy synnes. Þer-fore do þat delyteth the both a-fore [& after] [1] confession; for as coper þat is gylt semeth 20
gold, so þe werkes of synne þat ar betokened in coper, when they ar ouer gylte with contricion, shall be do away, and all thi werkes shall shyne as golde.

 Then aunswerd þe kynges conscyence: this consell semeth to me delectable and resonable. For if I do thus I shall mowe 25
dispose all my tymes to myne own Ioy.

 The good angell spake ayayn to the kyng be his enspiraciones, saynge: O frende, thinke fyrst with what mastre God browght the oute of the streyte wombe of thy moder. Secunde, thenke with how grete pacyence God suffreth the to lyfe. 30
Thirde, thinke with how grete bytternes God hath bowght the from endeles deth.

fol. 46 a Bot ayane-ward | the fende styrrede the kynge, sayng: O brother, if God haue browght the oute of the streyte wombe of thy moder in-to the brede of the world, thenke also þat he shall 35
lede þe ayayn oute of the world be herde deth. And yf God suffer the to lyff longe, thinke also þat þu hast in thy lyff

[1] *Latin* audacter ergo ante, & post confessionem. *Note that* audacter *is omitted in translation also.*

mony dyseses and tribulaciones ayanste thy wyll. Yf God
haue bought the with his herde deth, hoo compelled him?
Praydeste þu him? Than the kynge aunswerd as it had be by spekyg with-in in
his conscyence: it is trew, he sayth, þat þu sayste. For I
sorowe more þat I shall die þan þat I was bore of my moderys
wombe. It is also more grevouse to me to bere the aduersites
of the world and tho thinges þat ar contrarie to my wyll þan
any oþer thing. For I wold, and I myght chese, rather to lyve
in the world with-oute tribulacion and to abyde in comforte
þer-of, than to be departed from the werld. And rather I wold
desyre to haue endelesse lyff in the werld with wordely felycite
þan þat Cryst had bowght me with hys blode. And I rowght
nott [þ]of[1] I come neuer in heuen, if I myght haue the werld
at my wyll in erth.

Then herde I a word oute of the pulpyte, sayng thus: take
now away from þe kynge þe vesell of oyntement. For he hath
synned in God the fader. For God the fader þat is endeles in
the sonne and in the holy goste ȝaffe a trew and a ryght law be
Moyses. Bot this kyng hath made an evell and a contrarie
lawe. Neuer-the-lesse, for this kyng hath done some goode [2]
dedes, all though he dyd hem nott with good entent, þer-fore he
shall be suffered to haue possession of the kyngdom whill he
lyveth, and so be rewarded in the world. Secunde tyme the
worde spake oute of the pulpite and sayde thus: bere a-way
the most sharpe Irne from this kynges eyn. For he hath
synned ayanste þe sonne. For he sayde[3] in his new lawe that
doome shall be do wyth-oute mercy to him þat doth no mercye.
Bot this kynge wold not do mercy to him þat was vnryght-
wysly vexed ne amende his errour ne chaunge his evyll wyll.
Neuer-the-lesse, for some good dedes þat he hath doo, be it
yeve to him for reward þat he haue wordes of wysdom in his
mowth and þat he be hold wyse of mych peple. The thirde
tyme the worde of ryghtwysnes spake owte of the pulpite and
sayde: the hammer be take awey from the kynge, for he hath
synned in the holy goste. For the holy goste foryeveth synnes
to all repentaunte, bot this kynge purposeth to persuer in his

[1] MS. of.   [2] MS. some good | some good.
[3] MS. for he sayde for he sayde.

synne vn-to the ende. Neuer-þe-lesse, for he hath do some
goode dedes, þer-for þat thing be yeve to him þat he desyreth
moste to the delyte of his body, þat is, þat woman which he
desyrith to be his wyfe, þe delyte of his eyn, and þat he haue
a fayr and desyderable ende after þat werld. 5

After this,[1] when þe ende of his lyff neghed, the fende cryed
and sayde: loo, the vessell of oyntment is bore a-way. þer-
for shall I now make his hondes hevy, þat he shall do no fruyte-
full goodes. And anon as the worde of the fende | was seyde,
þe kynge was prived of his strenghth & heleth. And then anon 10
the fende cryed and sayde: loo, the sharpe Irne is take away;
þer-for I shall aggrege my snare apon him.

And anon the kynge was prived of hys spech. And in þe
poynte of hys priuacion, ryghtwysnes spake to the good angell
that was yove to the kyng to be his keper, and seyde: seeke in 15
the whele and see what lyne þer-of goth vpwarde, and rede the
scriptur þer-of.

The angell loked and the fowrte lyne yode vpwarde, wher-in
was ryght not wryte, bott all it had be rased. Then seyde
ryghtwysnes: for this sowle hath l[o]ved[2] þat is voyde, þer- 20
fore go he now to the delyte of his rewarde. And anon the
sowle of the kynge was departed from the bodye.

And anon as the sowle was gon owte, the fende cried and
sayde: now shall I brek and all-to rente þe herte of this kyng,
for I haue his sowle in possession. 25

And then I see how the kynge was all chaunged fro the
toppe of the hede vn-to the sowle of the foote, and he semed
horrible as a beste all flayn. His eyn wer oute and his flesh
all clobbed to-geder. Then his voyce was herde, saynge: wo
vn-to me, for I am made blynde as a whelpe þat is bor blynde, 30
sekynge the hynder partyes of the moder. For be myn vnkyndenes I se nott the moderes tetis. Woo vn-to me, for I see
in my blyndenes þat I shall neuer see God, for my con-|scyence
vnderstondeth now fro whens I am fall, and what I awght to
haue do and dyd nott. Wo vn-to me, for by the providence of 35
God I was bore in-to the werld and bore ayane be baptem. And
yett I was neclygent and foryett God. And for I wold not
drynke of the mylke of the swettenes of God, þer-for I am now

[1] MS. neghe *cancelled*.   [2] MS. leved. *See Notes*.

The Revelations of Saint Birgitta 77

mor lyke to a blynde dogge þan to a whyke and a seyng chyld. Bot now ayanest my wyll, þowgh I wer a kynge, I am compelled to sey trowth. For I was bound as it had be with thre ropes for to serue God : þat is to say, for baptem, for wedloke,
5 and for the crown of kyngdom. Bot the fyrst I dispised when I turned myn affeccion and wyll to the vanyte of the world. To the secunde I toke non hede when I desyrede a-noþer mannes wyff. The thrid I dispised when I was prowde of erthely power and thought not of the power of heuen. Þer-
10 fore, þough I be now blynde, I se in my conscience þat for the contempte of my baptem I owe to be bounde to the hatefullnes of the fende. And for the inordinate sturryng of the flesh I owe to suffer þe fendes luste. And for my pride I owe to be bounde to the fendes feet.
15 Then aunswerde the fende : O brother, now it is tyme þat I speke and with my spekyng I shall wyrke. Therfore come vn-to me, nott with cherite bot with hate ; for I was fayrest of angelles, and þu wer a dedely man. & God most myghty[1] | fol. 48a yave me fre chose my wyll. Bot for I meved it vnordynately
20 and wold rather hate God and passe him in wyrship than love him, þer-fore I fell as he þat hath his hed downward and his feet vpwerd. Bot þu, as ych oþer man, wer made after my fall and gatteste a specyall preuelege above me, in as mych as þu wer bowght with the blode of the sonne of God. Þer-fore, for
25 þu haste despised the cherite of God, turne thine hede to my feete and I shall take thine feet in-to my mowth ; and so be we Ionede to-geder as they ar wher the one hath a swerde in the oþers herte, and the other hath a knyffe in his maly[t]e.[2] And for I had an hedde, þat is to sey, vnderstondyng, to wyrship
30 God if I had wold, and þu haddeste feete, that is to sey, strenghth to goo to God and wold nott, þer-fore my fyerye hede shall waste thy cold feete, and þu shall be deuored wyth-oute cesynge, bot not consumed, for þu shalt be reveved ayane to the same. Ioyne we vs also to-geder wyth iij ropis, of which
35 the fyrst shall be in the myddes, with which þi navell aud myn shall be bounde to-geder : so þat when I breth, þu draw my venym in-to the, and when þu bretheste, I shall drawe thyne

---
[1] ʒaffe me, catchacord.
[2] MS. malyce ; Latin cultrum in visceribus alterius. See Glossary.

entrelles in-to me. And worthily, for þu loveste more thy-selfe than thine ayane-byar, as I loved more my-selfe than my maker. Thy hede shal be bounde to my feete with the secund rope, and wyth the thrid rope my hede shall be bounde to thy feete.

After this, I see the same fende hauyng iij sharpe clawes in ych fote, saynge to the kyng:[1] | for þu, brother, hadeste eyn to see the way of lyf and conscience to discerne be-twyx good and evell, þer-fore my two clawes shall enter and thirlle thyn eyn; and þe thrid clawe shall enter thy brayne, with which þu shalt be so strangled þat þu shall be all vnder my feete. For þu wer made to haue be my lord, and I the stole of thy fote. Thu haddest also þoo erres to here the way of lyf, and a mowth to speke þe profett[2] of thy sowle. Bot for þu hast dispised to here and speke the helth of thi [sowle],[3] ther-fore ij clawes of myn oþer foote shall enter in-to thyn eres, and the thrid in-to thy mowth, wher-in þu shalt be so tormented þat all thinges shall be to the moste bitter þat semede to the before moste swete, when þu offendeste God.

When thes thinges wer sayde, anon the hedde and the feete and the navell of the kynge wer Ioyned in maner for-sayde with þe heed & feete and navell of the fende, and so both bounde to-geder fell dovn in-to hell.

And then herde I a voyce, saynge: O, O, what hath the kynge now of all his riches? Certenly no thinge bot herme. And what has he now of all hys wyrshipp? Certes, nott bot shame. And what hath he now of his couetyse, by which he desyred so mych þe kyngdom? For-soth, right not bot payn. For he was anounted with holy oyle and sacrede with holy wordes and crowned with kynges crowne, þat he shuld worship þe wordes and dedes of God, and defende and gouerne the peple of God, know him-selfe vnder þe feete of God, and God his rewarder. Bot he despised to be vnder þe feete of God ; þer-fore he is now vnder þe feet | of the fende. And for he wold not bye ayane his tyme with fruytefull werkes while he myght, þer-fore from hens-forth he shall haue no fruyte-full tyme.

After this spake ryghtwysnes oute of the boke þat was in the pulpite, saynge to me: all thes thinges þat ar thus seriosly

[1] f j.   [2] MS. propfett.   [3] *Latin* animae.

shewed ar do anenste God in a poynte. Bot for þu arte bodely, þer-fore it is nedefull þat sp[irit]uell[1] thinges be shewed vn-to the [throwgh][2] bodely lykenes. For þat þe kyng and þe angell and the fende semede to speke to-geder is no thinge elles but
5 inspiraciones of the good & evell sprite made be hem to the sowle of the kyng, or by hys concellores or frendes. That the fende cried and sayde, 'It is trowth,' it is to mene þat when the kynge seyde þat he wold hold and kepe all that longeth to the crowne, how euer it wer I-gott, and nott to reke of ryght-
10 wysnes, then the kynges conscience was thrilled throwgh with the irne of the fende, þat is to say, with the hardnes of synne, when he wold nott speke and dyscusse which wer tho thinges þat longed rightfully to þe realme, and which nott, and when he rought nott to examyn what ryght he hadde to the crown.
15 And then was the hoke pot to þe kynges sowle, when the fendes temptacion prevaled so mych in his sowle þat he wold abyde in his vnryghtwysnes vn-to þe deth. Bot þat þer come an hammer to the kynges bosn after the hoke, betokeneth tyme of contricion yeve to the kynge ; for if the kynge hade had
20 sych a thought, saynge : 'I haue synned ; I wyll no lenger wittyngly hold evell goten goodes, bot I wyll amend | me from fol. 49 b hens-furth,' anon the hoke of ryghtwysnes had be broke with the hammer of contricion, and the kynge had comen to good lyf and good way. That the fende cryed, 'loo, the kyng ȝeveth
25 me his tonge,' and anon the snar was putt þer-apon, was when the kynge wold not do grace to the man þat he had defrauded. Þat is thus to vnderstonde, þat who euer wyttyngly[3] blameth and deffameth his neghtbor for to encrese his own fame, he is governed with the sprete of the fende, and to be
30 snared with a snare of a thefe.

Bot that þer come a sharpe irn to-fore the kyng after the snar betokeneth the tyme of chongyng & of correccion of his wyll and werke. For when a man corre[c]teth[4] his trespase with amendement and with good wyll, sych wyll is an irne
35 moste sharp, wher-with the snare of the fende is kytt I-sonder and remyssyon of synne is gotte. Ther-for if this kynge had

---

[1] MS. spuell ; abbreviation mark omitted.
[2] Latin tibi per corporales similitudines.
[3] MS. witttyngly.   [4] MS. corretteth.

chonged hys wyll and done grace to the man þat hadde wronge
and was sclandered, anon þe snare of the fende hadde be kytt
away. Bot for he formed his wyll in evell purpose, þer-fore the
rightwysnes of God was þat he shuld be mor harder in synne.
And þat when the kynge thought to pott newe exacciones of
tributes in his realme, þu see venym powred apon his hondes,
betokeneth þat his werkes wer gouerned by the sprite of the
fende and by evell sugesstiones. For as venym makyth cold
& sekenes in þe body, so was the kynge labored & vnrested
with wykett suggestiones & thoughtes, sekynge menes how he
myght gette goodes and possessions of oþer men and gold of
hem þat wente by the way. For when wayferynge men slepte
and trowed þat her gold had be in her purse, when they awoke,
they founde þat it was in þe kynges power.

Bot that the vessell of oyntement come after þe venym betokeneth the blode of Ihesu Cryste, by which seke sowle is
quykened. For if the kynge had weyte his werkes in consideracion of the blode [1] of Cryst, and prayed God to be his helpe,
and sayde: 'O lorde God, þat haste made me and bowght; I
know þat by thy suffraunce I am comen to þe kyngdom and
crown, þer-fore werre þu þe enmyse þat warr ayanste me, and
pay thu my dettes; for the goodes of the realme ar nott suffi-
ciaunte,' I sothely shuld haue made his werkes and his birthen
more esely to ber. Bot for he desyred oþer menes goodes and
wold be see ryghtfull wher he wyst well þat he was vnrightful,
þer-fore the fende gouerned his herte & stirred him to do ayanste
þe ordinaunce of the church, & to meve werr & defraude Innocentes, till ryghtwysnes oute of the pulpite of Goddes mageste
cried dome and equite.

The whele þat was meved at the [2] kynges brething betokeneth his conscience, which was stirred in maner of a whele, now
to myrth and now to hevenes. The iiij lynes þat war in the
whele betokeneth the fourefold wyll þat ych man oweth to
haue: þat is to say, a perfyte wyll, a stronge wyll, a right wyll,
& a resonable wyll. The perfyte wyll is to love God & have
him above all thinges; and this wyll oweth to be in þe fyrst
line above. The secunde lyne is to desyr & to [do] [3] gode to

---

[1] MS. of the blode of the blode.   [2] MS. at þe at the.
[3] Latin facere.

The Revelations of Saint Birgitta 81

his neghtbour & to him-self for God. This wyll muste be so stronge þat it be noþer broke with hate or with covetyse. The thrid wyll is to a[b]stene[1] fro fleshly desyris and to desyre endeles thinges. And this will muste be right þat it be not
5 doo to þe plesaunce of man, bot of God. The fourte will is nott to wyll haue þe werld, bot resonably and only to þe nede.

Þer-fore when the whele was turned, þer appered in the laste lyne goynge vpwarde þat the kynge loved the delytes of the world, & sett nott by the love of God. In þe secunde lyne was
10 write that he loved þe men of the world. In the thrid lyne was write þe love þat he had vnordinately to wordely rechesse & possessiones. In the iiij lyne was write right nott, bott all was voyde wher-in aught to haue be write the love of God. Abofe all thinges, therfor, þe voydenes of the iiij lyne betokenes
15 ye defaute of love and drede of God ; for by drede God is draw in-to the sowle, and by love God is festened in a good sowle. For yf a man had neuer loved God in all hys lyf tyme, and in his laste ende myght say or thinke in his herte, ' O god, me forthinketh with all myn herte þat I haue synned ayanste þe ;
20 yeve me thy love & I shall amende me fro hens-forth ', a man of sych love may nor shall not goo to hell. Bot for the kynge loved him nott whom he aught to haue loved, þer-for he hath now | þe rewarde of his love.   fol. 51 a

After this, I see toþer kyng on the ryght syde of rightwysnes,
25 þat was in purgatorie, þat was lyke to a chyld new bore þat myȝt nott styrr him-selfe, bot onely lyft vp his eyn. & I see that the fende stode on the kynges leeft syde, whos hede was lyke to a payr of belowes with a longe pype, his armys wer as ij serpentes, and his knees lyke a presse, and his feete lyke
30 a longe hoke. On the right syde of the kynge stode an angell moste fayr, redy to help him.

And then I herde a voyce sayng : this kynge apperith now sych as his sowle was disposed when it departed from the bodye.

35 And a-non the fende cried to the boke in the pulpite, saynge : here is see a mervelose thinge. This angell and I haue abyden the byrth of this chyld, he with his clennes, and I with my fylth. Bot now the child is bore, nott in bodye, bot from the

[1] MS. astene.

G

bodye, vnclennes in him appereth which þe angell, lothinge, myght not towch the chyld. Bot I toch him, for he is fall into myn hondes. Bot I wote nott wheder to lede him; for my derke eyn see him nott, for the lyȝt of a clerenes þat cometh owte of his breste. The angell seeth him and wote wheder to leede him, bot he may nott towch him. Þer-fore þu, þat art rightful Iuge, departe our stryfe.

The worde aunswerde oute of the boke þat was in the pulpite, & seyde: tell, þu þat spekys, for what cause this sowle of this kyng come to thine hondes.

The fend aunswerd: þu arte rightwysnes, & þu saydest þat non shuld enter heuen that makyth not fyrst restitucion of thinges vnryghtfully gote. Bot this sowle is all defowled[1] | of wronge gotten godes. Secunde, þu saydeste þat þoo tresours shuld not be gedered þat rusteth and maughtes destrie, bot thoo þat lesteth with-outen ende. Bot in this sowle þat place was voyde wher heuenly tresour shuld haue byn gedered & þat place was full wher wormes and [f]rosses[2] wer noryshed. Thride, þu saydest þat a manes neghtbor shuld be loved for God. Bot this sowle loved his body mor then God, & of the love of his neghtbour he rowght right not; for he, abydyng in body, was gladd of the takyng away of hys neghtborr goodes. He wonded the hertes of hys sugettes, nott takyng hede to the harmes of oþer, so he him-selfe had plente, & he dide what euer him lyste, & comaunded what he wold, and toke litell hede of equite. Thes ar the principall causes, after which folow oþer innowmmerable.

Then aunswerde the worde oute of the boke of ryghtwysnes, saynge to the angell: O þu angell, keper of the sowle, þat arte in lyght and seeste [light],[3] what right or power haste þu to helpe thys sowle?

The angell aunswerde: this sowle, he sayth, had holy fayth, & byleved and hoped þat all þat he had synned shuld be do away by contricion & confession. And he drede the, his God, þof it wer lasse þan he owght.

Then spake ryghtwysnes ayayne and sayde: O þu, myn angell, now it is graunted the to toch the sowle & to þe, þu

---

[1] f iiij. [2] MS. throsses; *Latin* ranae. *See Glossary.*
[3] MS. high; *Latin* lucem.

The Revelations of Saint Birgitta

fende, to see the light of the sowle. Enquyreth þer-fore both what this sowle loved when it lyved in body & had all his membres hole. The angell and the fend aunswerde both: he loved men & riches.

5   Then seyde rightwysnes ayane out of þe boke: what loved he when he was aungwyssed with þe payne of deth? |

Then aunswerde both: he loved him-selfe, for he was mor fol. 52 a aungwyssed of the sekenes of his body and of tribulacion of his herte, than he was of þe passyon of his ayayne-byer.

10   Than spake ryghtwysnes ayane and seyde: yett sekyth and lokyth what he loved and thought in the laste poynte of hys lyffe, while he had hole conscience and vnderstondyng.

Onely the goode angell aunswerd: the sowle thought thus. 'Woo', he sayde, 'vn-to me, for I haue be ouer-bold ayanste 15 my ayane-byer. Wold God I had now tyme in which I myght thonke God for his benefettes. For it greveth me more that I haue synned ayanste God then the payn of my body; and þof I shulde neuer haue heuen, ʒett wold I serve my God.'

Ryghtwysnes aunswerde oute of the boke: for as mych as 20 þu, fende, mayst nott see the sowle for bryghtnes of his lyght, and þu, my aungell, may nott towch the sowle for his vn-clennes, þer-fore this is the dome: þat þu, fende, purge it; and þu, aungell, comforte it tyll it be brought in-to bryghtnes of blysse. And to the, þu sowle, it is graunted to loke to the 25 good angell & to haue comforte of him; and þu shalte be per-tener of the blode of Cryste & of the prayers of his moder and of the church.[1]

Then sayde the fende to the sowle: for þu art comen to myn hondes full of metes and evell gote gudes, þer-for I shall now 30 avoyde þe wyth my presse.

And then the fende putt the brayns of the kyng by-twyx his kneys, lyke a presse, and streyned it strongly in length and brede, tyll all the merowth was as thyne as the lefe of a tre.

Secunde, þe fende sayde to the | sowle: for the place is fol. 52 b 35 voyde wher verteus shuld be, þer-for I shall fyll it.

And then he putt the pype of his belowes in the kynges mouth, and blew strongely, and fylled him myghty full of

---

[1] MS. church of; *but Latin sentence ends with* Ecclesiae.

horrible wynde; so mych þat all the kynges beyng and synewes wer wrechedly broken and breste o-sonder.

Thrid tyme, the fende sayde ayane to the kynges sowle: for þu wer cruell and with-oute mercy apon thi sugettes, which owght to haue be to the as thy sonnes, þer-fore myne armes 5 shall bytyngly grype the to-geder; þat lyke as þu grevest thy suggestes, so shall myn armes, lyke [1] to serpentes, all-to rende the with moste grevouse horror and sorow.

After thes iij paynes, þat is to say, of the presse, of the belowes, and of the serpentes, when the fende wold haue 10 aggreged the same paynes ayane, begynnyng at the fyrst, then I see the angell [of] [2] God putt owte his hondes apon the fendes hondes, that he shuld nott make the peynes so grevouse as they wer at the fyrste tyme. And so att ych tyme, the angell of God esed þe paynes; und after ych payne, the sowle lyft vp his eyn 15 to the angell, no thing sayng, bot shewyng in his beryng þat he was comforted be him; and þat he shuld hastely be saved.

Then sayde the worde oute of the pulpyte vn-to me: all thes thinges that thus seriosly ar shewed vn-to the ar do anenste God in a poynte; bot for þu arte bodely, they ar shewed to the 20 be bodely lykenes. Bot this kynge, þof he wer couetouse to haue þe wyrshipes of the world and for to gete godes þat wer nott his, ʒett, for he dredde God and lefte for that drede some thinges þat wer lusty to him, þer-fore þat drede drough him to fol. 53 a the love and cherite | of God. For know þu well that mony 25 þat ar entriked with mony grete synnes gete right grete contricion afore her deth, whos contricion may be so perfyte þat not only her synne is foryeve hem, bot also the payn of purgatorie, if they die in the same contricion. Bot the kyng gatt nott cherite till in the laste poynte of his lyf; for then his 30 strengthes and his conscience fayling, ʒett he gatt of my grace goddely inspiracion, by whych he sorowed mor of the vnwyrshipyng of God þan of his own sorow and herme. And this sorow betokeneth that lyght be which the fende was blynded & wyst nott wheder to lede the sowle. ʒett he sayde nott þat he 35 was so blynded for lake of gostely vnderstondyng, bot for he merveled how þat in þat sowle shulde be so grete clerenes of lyght and so mych vnclennes. The angell wyst well I-nogh

[1] MS. the *cancelled*.   [2] *Latin* Angelum Dei.

The Revelations of Saint Birgitta

wheder to lede the sowle, bot he ne my3t towch it till it wer purged. As it is write, 'No man shall see þe face of God bot he be fyrst made clene'.

Then the worde oute of the pulpite spake ayane to me and sayde: that þu see þe angell putt out his hondes apon the sowle &[1] of þe fende that he shuld nott aggrege þe peynes betokeneth the power of the angell above the power of the fende be which he refreyneth þe fendys malyce. For the fende shuld haue no mesur nor ordor in ponyshyng bot if he wer refreyned by þe vertue of God. And þer-for God doth mercy in hell; for þough þer be no redempcion, remission, nor comforte to hem þat ar dampned, 3ett in als mych as they ar not punyshed bot after her desertes and after | rightwysnes, þer-for in that is shewed grete mercy of God. Els þe fende shuld haue no temperaunce ne mesur in his malyce. That the kyng was see as a child þan bor be-tokeneth þat who wyll be bor out of the vanite of the world vn-to the lyf of heven, he muste be innocent, & by þe grace of God grow in verteus to perfeccion. That the kyng lyft vp his eyn to the angell betokeneth þat by the angell, his keper, he had his comforth; and of hope he had Ioy, in as mych as he hoped to come to endeles lyf. And thes ar spirituall thinges vnderstonde be bodely lykenes; for fendes nor angelles haue non such memberres ne noo such spekyng to-geder, for thay ar spirites. Bot by sy[ch]e[2] lykenes her goodenes or wykednes ar shewed to bodely eyn.

Also the worde spake out of the pulpyte, sayng to me: the pulpyte þat þu seeste betokeneth þe self god-hed: þat is to say, fader and sonne and holy goste. That[3] þu myght nott comprehende the lenghth, brede, depnes, and hyghnes of the pulpite betokeneth þat in God is nott to fynde begynnyng nor ende. For God is and was wyth-outen begynnyng, and shall be with-outen ende. And þat ych colour of the iij colours seyde was see in oþer and yett ych colour was dyscerned from other, betokeneth that God the fader is endelesse in the sonne and in the holy goste, and þe sonne in þe fader and in the holy goste, and the holy gost in hem both, which ar verely one in natur and distincte in propurte of persones.

---

[1] *Latin* Angelus extendere manus suas super manus Diaboli.
[2] MS. syde; *Latin* per tales similitudines.   [3] MS. that þt.

That on of the colours semede to be sanguyn and redde be-
tokeneth þe sonne, þat with-oute hurte of his godhed | toke
mannes natur in-to his person. The white colour betokeneth
the holy goste, be whom is wesshing away of synnes. The
golden colour betokeneth the fader, þat is the begynnyng and [1]
þe perfeccion of all thinges. Not that ony perfeccion is mor in
the fadre þan in the sonne, ne þat the fadre is to-fore þe sonne ;
bot þat þu vnderstonde þat þe fader is nott the same in person,
þat is þe son. For other is the fader in person, & oþer is the
sonne in person, and oþer is the holy goste in person ; bot on in
natur. Ther-fore iij colours ar shewed vn-to þe boþe departed
and Ionede togeder ; departed for distinccion of persones, and
oned to-geder for oned of natur.

And as in ych colour þu see þe oþer colours, and þu myghtes
nott see one with-oute an-oþer, and þer was nothinge in þe
colours to-fore nor after, more or lasse, ryght so in the trinite
is nothing to-for mor or lasse departed or medeled ; bot one
wyll, one endeles, on power, & on glorie. And þof the sonne
be of the fadre, and the holy goste of both, ȝett þe fader was
neuer with-oute þe sonne and the holy goste, ne the sone and
the holy goste with-oute the fader.

Also þe worde spake vn-to me & seyde : þe boke þat þu seest
in þe pulpite betokeneth þat in þe goodhed is endeles rightwysnes and wysdom, wher-to no thinge may be added or lassed.
And this is þe boke of lyffe, þat is nott write as the scriptur.
Þat is & was nott ; bot þe scripture of this boke is alway. For
in þe godhed is endeles beyng and vnderstondyng of all thinges
present, passte, and to come, with-outen any variance or
chaungyng. & no thing is inuysibile þer-to, for it seeth all
thinges. That the word | spake it-self betokeneth þat God is þe
endeles word, of whom ar all wordes, and in whom thinges
haue lyf and beynge. And this same worde spake þan visibly
when the worde was made man and was conuersaunte amongest
men. Loo, this goodely vision hath the moder of God gote to
be shewed vn-to þe ; and this is the mercy behight to the kyngdom of Sweth, þat men dwellyng þer-in shuld her the wordes
þat procede oute of the mouth of God. Bot þat few receyve
and beleve thes heuenly wordes I-ȝeve þe from God, þat is nott

[1] MS. and to ; *Latin* qui est principium, & perfectio omnium.

Goddes defaute, bot mennes. For they wyll nott leve þe cold
of her aune sowles. Neuer-the-lesse, the wordes of the gospell
wer nott fullfilled with the fyrst kynges of þat tyme; bot the
tymes shall ȝett come when þai shall be fullfylled.

5 **How þe fader of hevyn shewed to seynt Birgitt an herde
dome apon a kynge þat was vnkynde & vnobedient to þe
conselles of God. And how they þat ar in heuen, in erth,
in purgatorie, & in hell ask wreth apon kynges & princes;
& how our lady prayeth for hem. Cap. xxiij.** Revelations, Book VIII, Chap. 58.

10 God the fader spake to the spouse seynt Birgitt and seyde:
here þu þoo thinges þat I speke, & speke þo thinges þat I byd
the; not for thy wyrship, ne for thy repreve. Bot onely and
even hold þu in thine herte þe prayser & þe reprever, so þat
neþer þu be meved to ire for reprefe, ne hyued to pride for
15 praysyng. For he is worthi wyrship þat is & was endelessely
in himselfe, which hath made angelles and men only to that
ende, þat | mony shuld be perteneres of his glorie. I am now fol. 55 a
he, & þe same in power and in wyll þat I was than when the
sonne.¹ toke mankynde; in which sone I am and was, & he in
20 me, and the holy goste in both. And þof it wer preuey to the
world þat he was þe sonne of God, yett it was know to some,
þof it wer fewe. And know þu þat þe ryghtwysnes of God,
þat had neuer begynnyng nor ende, no more than God him-
selfe, was fyrst shewed to angelles as lyght or þei see God; for
25 they fell nott for ignouraunce of the law of the rightwysnes of
God, bot for they wold nott hold it & kepe itt. For they
vnderstounde þat all þat love God shuld see him and abyde
with him for euer, and they þat hated God shuld be punyshed
endelesly and neuer see him in his glorie. & yitt her ambicion
30 and desyre of wyrship ches rather to hate God & to haue þe
place wher they shall be punyshed, þen to love him þat they
myght Ioy endelesly. And lyke rightwysnes is of a man as of
angelles. For man oweth fyrst to love God and afterwarde see
him,² þat he shuld mowe be see in manhode; for he myght
35 nott be see in his godhed. And free ches is yove also to man

¹ MS. some; Latin Filius meus.
² Latin clause omitted; propterea Filius meus ex charitate nasci voluit post legem iustitiae.

as to angell, þat they shuld desir heuenly thinges & despyce erthely. Þer-for I, God, visett mony in mony maneres, all þough my godhed be nott see. And in mony parties of the world I haue shewed to mony persones how the synne of ych londe myght haue be amended, and how mercy myght haue be 5 gotte, or euer I dyde dome & my rightwysnes in t[h]oo[1] places. Bot men take non hede to thes thinges, ne sett not þer-by. Þis ryghtwisnes is also in God, þat all þat ar apon erth first hope seurly tho thinges þat they see nott, & þat they beleue to the church of God and to the holy gospell. And forþer-|mor that 10 they love God above all thinges, that hath yove hem all thinges; and himselfe he hath yove for hem to deth, þat all shulde endelessly Ioy with him. Ther-for I myselfe, God, speke to such as me luste, þat it be know how synne owe to be amended, and how payne may be lessed and blys encresed. 15

After this I see, sayth seynte Birgitt, as yf all heuenes had ben on howse, wher-in saate a Iuge in a trone. & the howse was full of seruantes and prayseres of the Iuge, ych of hem in hys voyce. And vnder this heuen was see a kyngdom. And anon þer was herde a voyce þat all myght her it, þat sayde: 20 come ye, both angell and fende, to the dome; þat is to say, þu angell þat arte keper of the kynge, and þu fende þat arte gouernor of the kyng.

& anon as the worde was spoke, an angell and an fende stood to-fore þe Iuge. Þe angell semed as a man trowbled, 25 and þe fende as a man Ioyng. Þen seyd þe Iuge: O þu angell, I putt the to be keper of the kyng, when he made couenaunde of pees with me and made confession of all his synnes þat he had do from his younge age, þat þu shuldeste be mor ner to him þan the fende. How is he now þer-for so fer from the? 30

The angell aunswerd: O Iuge, I am brennyng in the fyr of thi cherite, with which þe kynge was warmed for a tyme. Bot when the kynge lothed & dispised tho thinges þat thi frendes sayde to[2] him, & it was tediouse to him to do tho thinges þat þu concelst him, þan went þe kyng as his own lyst[3] | drowhe 35 him, afer from me, and neghed ych hour vn-to þe enmye.

The fende aunswerde: I am the selfe cold, & þu art the selfe

---

[1] MS. too; Latin eisdem.
[2] MS. to to.
[3] drowght him catchword.

The Revelations of Saint Birgitta 89

hete and godly fyre. Þer-fore lyke as ych þat neghis to the is mor feruent to gode werkes, so þe kyng, neghyng to me, is made mor cold vn-to thy cherite & more hote to my werkes. Then aunswerd the Iuge: the kynge was stirred to love God
5 above all thinges, and his neghtbor as him-self. Why þer-for haste þu take from [me][1] the man þat I bought with myn own blode, and makys him to nye his neghtbour, not only to his temperall godes bot eke to his lyf? The fende aunswerde: O Iuge, now longeth it to me to speke,
10 & þe angell to kepe silence. For when the kynge went fro the & fro thi consells & come to me, þan I conceyled him to love himselfe mor than his neyhtbour; & that he shuld nott rech of the helth of sowles, if he hadde the wyrship of the world; and that he shuld nott take hede ho wer nedy or defrauded, if
15 his frendis had plente. Then sayde þe Iuge to the fende: ho so wyll go fro the, they may; for þu mayst hold non with vyolens. Þer-for I shall yett sende some of my fryndes to the kynge, þat shall warne him of his perell.
20 The fende aunswerde: ryghtwysnes is þat ho euer wyll obey to me, he oweth to be gouerned by me; & þer-fore I shall sende my concelleres also to the kyng, & it shal be see to hos conceyles he shall rather gyf stede. Then sayde þe Juge: goo, for my ryghtwysnes is to deme to
25 þe tormentour þat is his, as well as to him þat hath accion of þat þat is dew to him in his cause. After this, sayth seynt | Birgett, when certen ȝeres wer fol. 56 b paste, I see ayayn þe same Iuge with his heuenly hoste, more moved than he was wonte to be, & as he had be wroth. & then
30 he seyde to þe aungell & to the fende: telleth, he seyth, wheder of yow hath ouercomen. The angell aunswerd: when I come to the kynge with goddely Inspiracion, & thi frendes with sprituell wordes, anon þe messyngeres of the fende rowned in his eres, and seyde:
35 'Wyll þu spar temperall goodes or thi wyrship or sowles or bodyes, þat thi frendes whom þu loveste more than thi-self may haue wyrshipe and prosperyte?' To this sterryng þe kynge assented, and to the styrrynges of the freendes

[1] *Latin* a me.

he, saynge, aunswerd:[1] 'I am suffyciaunte I-nogh and wyse I-nowgh of consell with-owte ȝow. Go ȝour wayes fro me with shame.' And so þe kyng torned his bake to the, & his face to the enmye, & putte from him frendes with dishonest repreve and scorne of the frendes of the world.

Then cried the fende and sayde: O Juge, loo, now longeth it to me to gouerne the kynge & to yeve him consell by my fryndes.

The Juge aunswerd: go; and as mych as þu art suffered, punyshe the kynge. For he hath provoked me to indignacion ayaynst him.

Too ȝer after this, the Iuge appered ayane, & the angell & the fende to-for him. Then sayde the fende: O Juge, deme þu now I shall pronownce rightwysnes. Þu art verely the self cherite, & þer-for it longeth not to the to dwell in that herte wher-in Envye and wroth is roted. Thu art also | verry wysdom, & þer-for þu owest nott to be in the herte of him þat desyrith to nye the lyf of his neghtbores, her goodes, and her wyrship. Thu art also verry trouþe, & þer-for it semeth the nott to dwell with þat man þat hath bounde him with oth to do treson & deceytes. Þer-for for this kynge hath spitte þe oute from him as þat thing is spitte owte þat is abhomynable, þer-for suffer me to stirr him and oppresse him, þat he be all oute of his wytt & deede. For my conselles he holdeth wysdom, and thy counsell he takyth for scorne. & with sych mede I desyre to reward him, for he hath do my wyll. Neuer-the-les I may nott do to him with-oute thi suffrance.

And when this was herde, þe Juge semed to haue a mervelouse chongyng; for then he appered bright as the sone, & in that sone wer see three wordes: þat is, vertue, trowth, & rightwysnes. Vertue spake & sayde: I haue made all thinges with-oute merettes goyng to-for. & þer-fore I am worthy to be worshiped of my creatur & not to be dispised. I am also worthi praysing of my fryndes for my cherite. I owe also to be wyrshiped and dred of myn enmyes, for I supporte hem pacyentely with-outen her merettes, wher they haue worthely deserued dampnacion. And þer-for, þu fend, it longeth to me to deme all after my rightwysnes and not after thy malyce.

[1] MS. aunswerd aunswerd.

The Revelations of Saint Birgitta 91

Then anon spake trowth eke and seyde: I in my godhed toke manhod of a virgyn, in which manhod I spake & [prech]ed[1] to peple. I sent also þe holy gost to þe apostoles, & I spake by her tonges. As I speke ych day by spirituell infusion to such
5 as me list, þer-fore my frendes mote know þat I my-selfe that am trowth hath sende my wordes to a kynge, which he hath dispiced. Þer-for, þu fende, her now; for I wyll speke þat it be know wheder the kyng hath obeyde to my concell or to my stirrynges. For I wyll tell all the concell I 3ove to the kynge,
10 rehersyng now in few wordes þat I expressed to-for mor largely. For the kynge was sterred & concelled to be-war of all synnes forbode of holy church, & to haue moderate fastynges, so þat he myght her and aunswer his sugettes compleyntes, & be redy to do right to rich and poor þat aske it; so þat for mych
15 abstinence þe goode of þe comynte of the peple of the realme and þe gouernance of the comyn profett be nott lassed, ne þat he shuld nott be þe mor sleuth for ouer-mych excesse to yeve audience to all. Also the kynge was conceyled & stirred how he shuld serue God & pray, and which dayes and tymes he
20 shuld lefe oþer occupaciones & entente to the comyn profett of his realme. Also þe kynge was concelled which days he shuld ber þe kyngely crown to the wyrship of God; & þat he shuld treete all his conceylles with men þat loveth trowþe & with the frendes of God; and þat he shuld neuer wyttyngly passe trouth
25 ne law; & þat he shuld nott putt non vn-wounte greuaunce to þe comyn peple of his realme bot for defence of the same, & for werr ayaynest the paynemes. Also the kynge was conceyled to haue an nowmbre of seruauntes in howsehold, acordyng to þe faculte of lyfelod and rentes of the cheker of his realme.
30 & all þat left over, he shuld departe with his knyghtes and frendes. Also the kyng was conceyled wysely to monysh hem þat wer insolente & lewde with cheritable wordes, and manfully to correkke hem; & þat he love in goodely cherite hem þat wer prudente and sadde; & that he shuld defende þe peple
35 dwellyng in his realme and yiff his yiftes with discrecion; & all tho thinges þat longe to the crown he shuld nott lessen nor alyene; that he shuld deme rightfully both men of the lond and strangeres; þat he shuld love the clergye, & cheritably

[1] *Latin* praedicabam; MS. purchesed.

gadre to him his chyualrye, and norish in peece þe comen peple of his realme.

When thes thinges wer herde, The fende aunswerde to the Iuge & sayde: and I conceyled the kynge to do some synnes priualy which he durst nott do in open. I conceyled him also to say longe & mony prayers and psalmes with-oute attendaunce and deuocion of herte, þat so[1] he shuld prolonge & occupie þe tyme in vayne, & nott her anye þat wold compleyn, ne do any ryght to such as suffered wronge. Also I styrred þe kynge to leve & despice oþer goodemen of the realme; & to lyft vpp and preferr oo man above all oþer; & to love him with all his herte, mor than him-self; and to hate his one sonne; & to greve the comyn peple of the realme in his exacciones; & to slee men & spoyle churches. I stirred the kynge also to dissimile rightwysnes; and to suffer ych man to nye oþer, þat he shuld aliene & yeve londes longynge to his crown to a grete prince of a noþer realme, my swor brother; and this I conceyled to þat ende þat treson and werr shuld be arered; þat goodemen & rightfull shuld be caste done; wyked peple shuld be drowned þe depper in hell; & thay that shall be purged in purgatorie shuld be the | more grevously tormented; women shuld be defowled; shippes in the see shuld be robbed; sacramentes of the church shuld be dispiced; lecherouse lyf shuld þe mor boldely be contynued; and all my wyll mor. frely fulfilled. And thus, þu Juge, be thes synnes, & mony oþer now I-do & fulfilled be the kynge, it may be preved & know wheder the kyng hath obeyde to thi concele or myne.

After this spake rightwysnes, aunsweryng, & seyde: for the kynge hath hated verteu & dispised trowth, þer-for it longeth now to þe to encrese some of thyne conceyles ȝove to the kyng. & I owe after rightwysnes to lassen & with-draw from him some of my graces I ȝove to him.

The fende aunswerd: O Iuge, I shall multiplie & mor my ȝiftes to the kynge. & first, I shall sende him necligence, þat he take non hede of the werkes of God in his herte, & þat he thenke nott on the werkes & exsamples of thy frendes.

Ryghtwysnes aunswerd: & I shall lasse vn-to him þe Infu-

---

[1] MS. longe cancelled.

The Revelations of Saint Birgitta 93

ciones of the holy gost, & I shall wit*h*draw from him the goode
thoughts & comfortes þat he had to-for.

Þan seyde þe fende: I shall sende him boldenes to thinke &
to do dedely synnes & venyall wit*h*-out bashment or shame.
5 Ryghtwysnes aunswerd: I shall lessen his reson & discre-
c*i*on þat he discerne nott ne discusse þe rewardes and domes
of dedely synnes & venyall.

The fende sayde: I shall yeve him drede þat he dar nott
speke ne do right ayanste þe enmyse of God.
10 Ryghtwisnes aunswerde: I shall lessen his prudence &
knowynge*s* of thing*es* to be do so lewdly, þat he shall seme
mor like a foole & a Iape*r* in wordes & dedes than a wyse man.

Then seyde the fende: I shall putt to him angwysse and
tribulac*i*ones of herte, be-cause he hath not p*r*osp*e*ryte | after fol. 59 a
15 his wyll.

Ryghtwysnes aunswerde: I shall lesse to him gostely comfortes, which he had some tyme in p*r*ayeres & in his dedes.

Þe fende sayde: I shall put to him fellnes to thinke sotell
invenc*i*ones, by which he may begyle and disceyve hem whom
20 he desyrith to destrie.

Ryghtnes aunswerd: I shall lesse his vnderstondynge so
mych þat he shall take non hede of his own wyrship ne of his
own p*r*ofyte.

The feende sayde: I shall putt to him such Ioy of herte þat
25 he shall nott reke of his own shame, ne of the herme and
pe*r*ell of his sowle, while he may haue tempe*r*all p*r*ospe*r*ite
afte*r* his wyll.

Ryghtwysnes aunswerde: I shall lessen his thinking to-for
& þat consyderac*i*on that wysemen have in her word*es* & dedes.
30 Then seyde the fende: I shall yeve him a womannes boldenes, & an vnsemely drede, and sych beryng þat he shall seeme
mor lyke a ribold or an harlott than a crowned kynge.

Ryghtwysnes aunswerd: sych dome is he worthy, þat
depa*r*teth him frome God. For he oweth to be despised of
35 his frendes, & to be hated of the comentye of his peple, & to
be caste down of Godd*es* enmys; for he hath myssevsed þe
ȝeft*es* of Godd*es* cherite, both gostely and bodely.

Than spake verteu [1] ayane and seyde: thes thinges þat ar

[1] *Latin* veritas.

shewed to the ar nott for the merettes of the kynge, hos sowle is nott ȝett demede ; bot it shall be demed in the laste poynte of his lyfe.

After thes thinges wer sayde, I see þat tho iij, þat is to say, verteu, trowth, & rightwysnes, wer lyke to the Iuge þat spake to-for.

& then I herde the voyce, as it had be of a bedell saying : O ye, all heuenes with all planettes, yeveth silence ; & all ye fendes þat | ar in derknes, listeneth ; and all ye other þat ar in derkenes, hereth ; for the souerayne emperour proposeth to here domes apon the princes of erth.

And anon the kynges that I see wer nott bodely bot spirituell. & my gostely eres and eyne war opned to her and see. And than I see Abraham come with all sayntes þat war bor of his generacion. Than come all patriarkes and profettes. & afterwarde I see the iiij euangelistes, hos shapp was lyke to iiij bestes, as they ar paynted apon wallys in the world, save they appered quyk and nott dede. After this, I see twelfe seetes, & in hem the xij appostoles, abydyng þe comyng of the power. Then come Adam and Eve with martires & confessores and all oþer sayntes þat come of hem. Bot the manhod of Criste was nott yett see, ne the body of his blessed moder ; bot all abode her comyng. The erth and the water s[e]med [1] to be lyft vp to heven, & all thinges þat wer in hem meked hem, & with reuerence bowed hem to the power.

Then, after this, I see an awter þat was in the seete of the maieste, & a chalesse with wyne and water and brede in lykenes of a hoste offered apon þe auter ; and then I see how in a church of the world a preeste be-gan masse, arayd in a prestes araye. & when he had do all þat longed to the masse, & come to the wordes with which he shuld blesse the hoste, I see as if the sone and the moone & þe sterres with all oþer planettes, & all heuenes with her courses and mevynge, sownede with swetteste noote and with sondery voyces. And all the songe [2] and melodye was herde, and semed as it had be vnnowmmerable maners of musyk, whos most swete sowne was impossible to be comprehended of mannes wytt | or to be spoke. They þat wer in lyght be-held the preste & enclyned hem to the

[1] MS. somed. [2] MS. and all the songe and all the songe.

power with reuerence and wyrship, and they þat wer in derkenes horred and dredde. Bot when the wordes of God wer sayde of the prest apon the hoste, it semed to me that the same sacred hoste was in the seete of the maieste in iij fygures, abydynge neuer-the-lesse in the honde of the preste. And the same holy hoste was made a quyke lombe, and in the lomb appered a face of a man. And a brynnyng flawme was see with-in & with-owte the lombe and the face. And when I festened my syght besyly in by-holdynge the face, I se the lombe in the face. And when I behold the lombe, I see the same face in the lombe. & the virgyn sate crowned by the lombe, and all angelles serued hem, which wer of so grete multitude as þe motes in the sonne. And a mervelouse shynyng proceded fro the lombe. Ther was also so grete multitude of holy sowles, that my sight myght nott behold hem in length, brede, heght, and depnes. I see also some places voyde, þat ar ȝyt to be fulfilled to the wyrship of God.

Then herde I a voyce oute of the erth, of vnnowme[ra]ble[1] thousaundes, crying & seying : O lorde God, rightful Iuge, ȝeve dome apon our kynges and princes, and take hede to the shedyng of our blode, and be-hold the sorowes and wepynges of our wyfes and children. Be-hold our hungre & shame, our woundes & our prisonmentes, brynnyng[2] of our howses, & the vyolacion of the chaste maydens[3] & women. Be-hold the wronge doo to churches and to all the clergye. & se þe false byhestes and deceytes of kynges & of princes, & the pillage þat they wrayste to hem with vyolence & Ire. For they reke nott how mony thousaundes die, so they may spred o-brode her pride.

Þan cried ther oute of hell as it had be vnnowmerable thou- | sandes, saynge : O Iuge, we know þat þu art maker of all fol. 60 b thinges. ȝeve dome þer-for apon the lordes whom we serued in erth. For they haue drowned vs in hell depper than we shuld haue be, and þowghe we wyll the harme, ȝett ryghtwysnes compelleth vs to compleyn & say trouth. For our erthely lordes loved vs with-oute cherite ; for they roght no more of

---

[1] MS. vnnowmeble.
[2] MS. brymñyng (*five strokes*).
[3] MS. n *above line*.

our sowles than of doggis. & it was allon to hem wheder we
loved þe, our maker, or noo, desyringe euer to be beloved &
served of vs. Þer-for thay ar vnworthi heuen; for they reke
nott of the. & they ar worthy hell, bot thy grace helpe hem.
For they haue deceyved vs; & þer-for we wold suffer mor 5
grevous paynes þan we suffer, that her payn shuld neuer haue
ende.

Afterward, they that wer in purgatorie, spekynge be lykenes,
cryed & sayde: O Juge, we ar demed to purgatorie for contricion & gode wyll þat we had in þe end of our lyf. And þer- 10
for we compleyn apon the lordes þat ȝyt lyff in erth. For they
aught to haue gouerned vs, & to haue warned vs with wordes
& blamynges, & to haue taught vs with holsom conseyles &
exsamples. Bot they comforted vs rather, & prouoked vs
rather to evell dedes and synnes. And þer-for our payn is now 15
the mor grevouse for hem; & the tyme of payne is þe larger;
& our shame & tribulacion is the mor.

Then spake Abraham with all þe patriarches, and seyde: O
lorde, amongest all thinges desiderable, we desyre that thy [1]
sone shuld be bor of our lynage, þat is now despised of þe 20
princes of erth. Þer-for we aske dome apon hem, for they take
no hede to thy mercye, ne they dred nott thy dome.

Then spake the profettes and seyde: we profecyed of the
comyng of the sonne of God; and we seyde þat for the delyuer-
aunce of þe peple was nedefull that he shuld be bor of a virgyn 25
& suffer tre-|son and be take and be scorged & be crowned
with thornes & att laste dye on the crosse, that heven shuld be
opened & synne do away. Wher-for thoo thinges ar now fulfilled þat we seyde; þer-fore we aske dome apon the princes of
the erth þat despyce thy sonne þat of thy cherite dyed for hem. 30

The[n] [2] spake the euangelystes & sayde: we ar wyttnes þat
thi sone hath fullfylled in him-selfe all thinges þat wer for-
sayde of him.

Also the appostoles spake and seyde: we ar Iuges, þer-for it
longeth to vs to deme after trowth. Wher-for he that despices 35
the bodye of God & his preceptes, we deme to perdicion.

After all this, þe virgyn that saatt by the lombe sayde: O
moste swete lorde, haue mercy apon hem.

[1] MS. they; *Latin* Filius tuus.   [2] MS. the; *Latin* tunc.

The Revelations of Saint Birgitta

To hir the Iuge aunswerd: it is nott right, he seyth, to denye the eny thing. Ther-for they that sesen from synne and do worthy pennaunce shall fynde mercy; and dome shall be torned away from hem.

5 After this I see that the face þat was see in the lambe spake to the kyng and seyde: I haue do grace with the, for I haue shewed the my wyll: how þu shuldest ber and demene the in thy gouernaunce, & how þu shuldest gouerne thi-self honestely and worthely. I cheresed the also with swete wordes of cherite 10 as a moder, & I fered the with warninges as a pitevos fader. Bot thu, obeyng to the fende, hast cast me from the, as a moder casteth away a dedebor chyld whom she deyneth noþer to touch ne putt her tetes to his mouth. & þer-for all þe goode þat is byhyght þe shall be take from the & yove to one þat 15 shall come after the.

After this, the virgyne þat saate with the lambe spake to me and sayde: I wyll tell the how vnderstondynges of spirituell visiones is yeve vn-to þe; for the | sayntes of God receyve the holy goste dyuersely. For some of hem knowe to-fore the 20 tyme when tho thinges shuld fall þat wer shewed to hem, as holy profettes. Other knew to-fore what ende any batell shuld haue, or euer they that shuld fyght entered bateyle. Oþer knew in spirett what they shuld aunswer to persones that comen to hem when any thinge was asked of hem. Oþer 25 knew wheþer they wer dede or quyke þat wer fer frome hem. Bot it is not lefull to the to know other thinges, bott to her and see gostely thinges, & to write þe thinges þa þu seeste, & to tell & say hem to such persones as þu [art]¹ bode. And it is nott lefull to the to wete wheþer they be olyve or dede, to whom þu 30 art bode write; or wheþer they shall obey or nott to the conceyles of thy wrytyng I-yeve to the from God in spirituell vision for hem. Bot þough this kyng haue dispiced my wordes, 3yt þer shall [come]² anoþer þat shall receyve hem with reuerence and wyrship and vse hem to his helth. Amen.

35 **Our lorde Ihesu Cryst blameth & treteth herde sentence apon all maner of peple, of what state or degre euer they be, for her synnes & vnkyndenes, be-hotyng mercy if they wyll** Revelations, Book VII, Chap. 80.

---

¹ *Latin* quibus tibi praecipitur; *and cf. below.*   ² *Latin* veniet.

amende hem. & this revelac*i*on o*ur* lord bad seynt Birgitt
write laste of her revelac*i*ones, affirmyng þat his dome
shall be fullfylled apon all peple þat torne not to him wit*h*
wery mekenes, like as it is shewed in this same revelac*i*on. Cap. xxiiij.

I see a grete pales like to a bryght heuen, wher-in was an
hoste of heuenly chevallrye, vnnowme*r*able as motes of the s*u*ר*n*ə,
shynnyng bright as the sonne bem*es*. Ine this paleys þer satt
fol. 62 a in a marvelouse trone, as it wer | a pe*r*son of a man of incom-
pr*e*hensible feyrenes, & as lord of grete power, whos clothes
were mervelouse and of vnspekeable clerenes. And a virgyn
stode to-fore him þat sate in the trone þat was brighter than
the sonne, who*m* all they that wer ther of heuenly chevalrye
wyrshoped reue*r*ently as the quene of heyvenes.

Then he þat sate in the trowne opned his mowth and sayde:
her ye, all my enmyes lyvyng in the world ; for I speke not
now to my frendes þat foloweth my wyll. Her ȝee, all clerk*es*,
archbysshopp*es*, bishopp*es*, and all þat ar of lowr degre of the
church. Here ȝe eke, all religiose peple of what-eu*er* order ye
be. Hereth eke, ȝe kyng*es*, princes, and Iuges of the erth, and
all soue*r*aynes and s*er*uantes. Hereth eke, ȝe women, pr*in*-
cesses, ladies, wyves, maydenes, and all peple of what eu*er*
condic*i*on or degre þat ȝe be, grete or smale, þat dwell in the
world. Here thes wordes which I my-selfe þat made yow
speke now vn-to yow. I compleyne, for ȝe ar go a way fro
me, & ye haue yeve fayth to the fende, myn enmye. ȝe haue for-
sake myn comaundementes, & ȝe follow¹ the wyll of the fende
and of his sugestyones. ȝe take non hede þat I, vnchaunge-
able & endeles God, yo*ur* maker, come downe from heven vn-to
a virgyn, takyng of hir a body, and was conue*r*saunte wit*h* yow.
& I be my-selfe opned yow þe way & shewed yow concelles be
which ȝe shuld go vn-to heuen. I was naked, scourged, and
fol. 62 b crowned wit*h* thornes, & so strongly | streched o-brode and
lengtht on the crosse þat all ȝe synow*es* & Ioyntes of my
body wer as they had bene lewsed in sounder. I herde all
repr*e*ves and suffered moste despisable deth & bytt*er* sorow of
herte for yo*ur* helth. O ȝe myne enmyes, of all thes thing*es*
take ȝe no hede, for ye ar deceyved. & þ*er*-for ye ber the yoke

¹ MS. fololow.

and the byrden of the fende with disseyveable swettenes, & ȝe
knowe nott nor fele not thoo thinges, tyll endeles sorow neghe
apon yow; & ȝytt þese thinges suffice nott to yow. Bot þer-to
your pride is so mych þat yf ȝe myȝt ascende above me, ȝe wold
5 gladely do it; and the luste of your flesh is so mych þat ye
wold rather be with-owte me þan ȝe wold leve your inordinate
delyte. And also your couetyse may nott be fylled, as a sakke
þat is open att both endes; for þer is nothing þat may fyll
your couetyse. Þer-fore I swer in my godhed þat if ye dye in the
10 state þat ȝe ar ine now, ȝe shall neuer se my face, bot for your
pride ye shall be drowned so depe in hell þat all fendes shall
be above yow & torment yow with-outen comforth. For your
lecherye ȝe shall be fylled with horrible venym of the fende,
and for your couetyse ȝe shall be fylled with sorow and
15 angwysse and be parteners of all evells þat is in hell. O ye
myne Enmyes, abhomynable, vncurteys, and vnkynde, I seme
to yow as a worme dede ine wynter; and þer-for ye do what
ye wyll, and haue prosperyte. Bot I shall aryse in Soumer,
and then ȝe shall be stylle; and ye shall nott flee myn
20 honde. Nethlesse, O ȝe Enmyes, for I haue bowght yow with
my blode, and I seke right noght bot your sowles, þer-for
torneth yett aȝayne to me with mekenes, & I | shall receyve fol. 63 a
yowe gladely, as my children. Shakyth from yow the grevouse
yokke of the fende and hath mynde on my cherite; and ȝe
25 shall see in yowr conscyence that I am esy and myld. Amen.

Assint laudes deo.

[The rest of fol. 63 a and fol. 63 b blank; another hand com-
mences at the top of fol. 64 a.]

How oure blissid lady is redy to helpe alle, bothe fol. 64 a
30 **wyues, widowes, and maydens.** Revela-
tions,
Here thou,[1] saith the modre of God to seint Birgitte, that Book IV,
prayest God with all thyne herte that thi children may please Chap. 53.
God. Truely, suche prayer is plesyng to God. For there is
no modre that loueth my son aboue all thynges and askith the
35 same to hir children, but þat I am anone redy to helpe hir to

---

[1] MS. what *incorrectly inserted above line between* thou saith; *Latin* audi tu
(inquit) mater Dei, quae toto corde rogas Deum.

þe effect of hir askyng. There is also no widowe þat stably prayeth aftir the helpe of God to stonde in widowhod to þe worship of God vn-to hir deth, but that anone I am redy to fulfille hir wille with hir. For I was as a widowe, in þat I hadde a sone in erthe that had no bodily fadre. There is also no virgyn that desireth to kepe hir maydenhode to God vn-to hir deth, but þat I am redy to defende hir and to comforte hir. For I myself am verrayly a virgyn. Nor thou owest not to meruaile whi I say these thinges. It is write that Dauid desyred kyng Saules doughter, whan sche was mayde. He resceyued hir also, whan sche was widowe. He had also the wyf of Vrye, while hir husbonde lyued. Neuirtheles, the desyre and lust of Dauid was not with-oute synne. But that gostly dilectacion of my sone, which is lorde of Dauid, is withoute all synne. Therefor, as these thre lyves, that is, maydenhod, widowhod, and wedlok, plesed Dauid bodily, so plese it my sone to haue hem in his moost chast delyt gostly. Therefor no meruail though I helpe hem and drawe her gostly delyte in-to the delyt of my sone, for his delyt is vn-to hem.

The mantelle of mekenes.

Revelations, Book II, Chap. 23.

Oure lady seint Mary spekith vn-to the spouse of Crist, seint Birgitte, and saith : many meruaillen why I speke to þe. Certayne therefore it is that my meknesse be schewed, for as þe hert ioyeth not of a membre of the body þat is seeke to-fore it resceyue helthe ayene, and whan it is hole, the herte is more glad ; so I, synne a man neuer so moche, yf he turne ayene to me with[1] alle his herte and with veray amendement anoon, I am redy to resceyue hym. And I take noo kepe how moche he hath synned, but with what entent and wille he turneth ayene. I am cleped of alle modir of mercy. Forsothe, doughtre, the mercy of my sone made me m[e]rcifull,[2] and þe disese of hym made me to haue compassion. And therefor schall he be wreched þat cometh not to mercy while he may. Therefor, thou my doughter, come and hide the vndir my mantell, whiche is dispisable outward, but ynward it is profitable for thre thinges. First, it schadowith from tempest of wyndes. Seconde, it kepith from bytyng colde. Thridde, it

fol. 64 b

[1] MS. of cancelled, and with inserted above line.   [2] MS. mrcifull.

The Revelations of Saint Birgitta

defendith fro reyne. This mantel is my mekeneɔ. This semeþ to þe louers of the worlde full despisable and veyn to folue. What is more despisable þanne to be cleped a foole, and not be wroth nor speke ayene? What is more despisable þanne to
5 leue and forsake alle thinges, and to be nedy in all thinges? What is more sorowful amonge wordly peple than a man to suffre and dissimile wronge doon vn-to hym, and to bileue and holde hym-selfe lower and more vnworthy þan alle othir? Suche, doughtre, was my mekenes. This was my ioye, this
10 was all my wille, that [I][1] wolde plese noone but my sone.

And this, my mekenes, is vaylable vn-to thre thinges. First,[2] for tempest of wynde and wedir; þat is, for þe repreef and despyt of men, for as wynde and wedir that is full of tempest and stronge greueth a man on eche syde and makith hym colde, so
15 repreues beren donne lightly a man that is vnpacient, and thenkith not on þe tyme and thinges þat arne to come and maken his herte colde from charitee. But who euer take kepe besily to my mekenes, he most thenke what I, lady of alle, herde, and seche my praysing and not his, and considre þat
20 wordis arne but wynde; and anoone he schall haue refresshyng and fynde eese. For why are wordly peple so vnpacient to suffre wordes and reproves, but for þey seche more their owne | praysing than the praysing of God? And there is no mekenes in hem, for they haue their eyen sperde from biholding of hir
25 synnes. Ther-for, though the rightwysnes that is write say that a man is not bound to suffre or to here repreuable wordes withoute cause, it is vertue and worthy reward to here and to suffre paciently contrarious thynges seyde or doo vn-to hym.

Seconde,[3] my mekenes defendith from bytyng colde, þat is
30 to say, from carnal frenschip and fleschly loue. There is a manere of frenschip and loue by which a man is loued oonly for these thinges that arne present, as þei that seyen thus: ' Fede thou me, and I schall fede the in this lyf. For I recke not who fede the aftir thi deth. Worship þou me & I schall
35 worship the, for I charge litil what worship folue here aftir.' This frenschip is colde and with-oute hete of þe loue of God. And it is as snowe frore in the loue and compassion of his

[1] *Latin* cogitabam.   [2] MS. j *in margin.*
[3] MS. ij *in margin.*

neighburgh that hath nede. And vnfruytfull to rewarde, for whan hir felaschip is departid and þe table layde doune, anoone all the profyt of hir frenschip and loue is dissolued and þe fruyte there-of agoo. But who euere folue my mekenes, he doth wele to alle for God, bothe to enmyes and to frendes. [To frendes],[1] for they abyde stablely in the worship of God ; and to enemyes, for they arne the creatures of God, and in happes they schullen be-come goode.

Thridde[2] is the beholdyng of my mekenes defendith from reyne and from vnclennesse of water that cometh of cloudes. Whereof cometh cloudes or skyes, but of humours and moisture goyng oute of the erthe, and arne lifte up in-to þe firmament, and there waxe thicke? And so comen thre thinges of hem: rayne, hayle, and snowe. This cloude betokeneth mannes body, þat cometh of vnclennesse. This body hath thre thinges with it, as hath the cloude: for the body hath heryng, seyng, and felyng. In that þat the body hath sight, it desyreth tho thinges þat it seeth ; it desyreth goode thinges and fayre faces, and it desyreth large possessiouns. And what arne alle thise thinges but as reyne comynge of cloudes, defoulyng the herte in desyre and loue to gadre goodes to-gedre, vnrestyng the herte by many besynesses, disperplying the herte by many and vnprofitable thoughtes, and troublyng it in leuyng of tho thinges þat it hath gadrid to-gidre. In þat that the body hath heryng, it herith gladly the owne worschip and loue and frenschip of the worlde. It herith also all þat is delitable to þe body and noyous to þe soule. And what arne all thise thinges, but as snowe þat sone is dissolued and makith þe soule colde to God and harde to mekenes ? In that that the body hath felyng, it felith gladly þe owne lust and eese of þe flessh. And what is this but hayle frore to-gidre of waters of vnclennesse, makyng þe soule vnfruytfull to gostly þinges, stronge to wordly thinges, and softe to þe desyre of þe body? Therefor who euer desyre to be defendid from this cloude, fle he to my mekenesse and folue it ; for by þat he schall be defended from couetise of sight, that he desyre not vnleful

---

[1] *Latin* amicis. Amicis. *The* MS. *has omitted the second* Amicis, *which is necessary for the sense.*

[2] MS. iij *in margin.*

thinges; and from delyt of hering, that he here not ayenst
trouthe; and fro lust of the flessh, that he be not ouercome in
vnlefull steringes.

Forsoth, I say to þe that the beholdyng of my mekenes is as
5 a good mantell, makyng hote hem þat bere it. That is to say,
not hem that bere it only in thought, but also in dede; for a
bodely mantell makith not a body hote bot if it be bore, nor
my mekenes profiteth not hem to thenke it, but yf eche of hem
studie to folue it in dede to her power. There-for, my dough-
10 ter, doo vp-on the this mekenes to þy power; for wymmen of
þe worlde bere mantels that haue moch pryde outward and
with-in, but litil profyt. Suche clothinge fle þou in all wyse;
for but yf þe luf of the worlde be first foule[1] | and lothsom vn- fol. 66 a
to þe; and but yf þou thinke continuelly the mercy of oure
15 lorde God schewed vn-to þe, and thyne vnkyndnesse ayen to
hym; and but yf thou thinke alwey tho thinges þat þou hast
doo and þat þou doest, and what sentence of dome þou deseruest
ther-fore, thou maist not gete the mantel of my mekenes. For
where-to meked I me so moche, of where-of deserued I so
20 moche grace, but for I thought and knewe wele þat I was right
nought nor had right nought of my-self? There-for I wolde not
myn oune preysyng, but þe praysyng and worschip of hym
only that was yeuer and maker of all. Therefor, doughter,
flee þou to þe mantel of my mekenesse, and thenke and hólde
25 thy-self a synner aboue all othir. For þough thou see ony
wykked, thou wost not what schall come vn-to hem to-morowe.
Also þou wost not with what entent nor with what knowyng
thei do it, wheþer it is of freelte or of purpos. Therfore preferre thi-self to-fore none; and thou owist to deme none in
30 thyn herte.

Oure lorde Ihesu Cryst techith vs to meke vs in foure *Revela-*
maners. *tions,*
Book IV,
The sone of God spekith vn-to seint Birgitte and saith : *Chap. 91.*
Thou owest to meke the in foure manere wyse. First,[2]
35 anempst hem that haue power by estat or by office in þe

---

[1] *Marg. gloss*: A schort lesson : | how þou schalt arraie the in þe mantel of mek[e]nesse.
[2] MS. j *in margin.*

worlde. For sithe man despisid and lefte to obeye God, it is
worthie þat he obbeye to man. And for folke mowe not be
with-oute gouernours, therefor reuerence and worschip most be
youe to þe power. Seconde,[1] þou most meke the anempst hem
that bene poure gostly, that is to seye, anempst synners,
prayeng for hem and thonkyng God for in happes thou art not
ne hast be noon suche. Thridde,[2] anempst hem that bene riche
gostly, that is to say, anempst þe frendes of God, thenkyng
thy-self vnworthy to serue hem or to be conuersaunt amongst
hem. Fourthe,[3] anempst þe pore of þe worlde, helping hem
and clothing hem and wasching her feet. |

fol. 66 b
Revelations,
Book VI,
Chap. 52.

This is a reuelacion sende to the holy spouse of Crist,
saint Birgitte, in whiche oure lady saint Marye repreueth
the pryde of wymmen in her porte, beryng, speche, array,
and oþere gouernaunce, by example of thre wrecched
wymmen; of whiche one was in helle, anothir in pur-
gatorye, and the thridde alyue.

The[4] holy spouse of Crist, saint Birgitte, spekith vn-to oure
lorde Ihesu Crist wordes of louyng and praysyng for the grete
grace þat he wrought with hir, and saith: praysing be vn-to þe,
almyghty God, for all thinges þat bene made, and worschip for
alle thi vertues. Seruice be youe vn-to þe of all creatures for
thi grete loue and charitee. I, ther-fore, vnworthy and sinfull
euer fro my youthe, thonke þe, my God, that thou denyest
grace to no synners that asken hit; but thou sparist and hast
mercy on alle. O my suettest God, it is full merueillous that
thou workist with me; for whan it plesith the, thou bringist
my body in a spiritual slepe, and than þou excitest and rerist
vp my soule to see and here and fele gostly thinges. O my
God mooste swete, how suete bene thy wordis to my soule,
which sualwith hem as mete althir suettist. And thei entren
with ioye in-to myn herte, for whan I here thy wordes, I am
bothe full and hungry; fulle, for me delitith no thinge but thi
wordes; hungry, for the more I here hem the more feruently
I desyre hem. Ther-for, blesful God, yeue me helpe euere to
do thy wille.

[1] MS. ij in margin.   [2] MS. iij in margin.   [3] MS. iiij in margin.
[4] Marg. gloss: Oure lorde appering vn-to saint Birgitte.

[First]

and lothsom vn to þe and but yf þou thinke contynuelly þe mercy   holy þou schalt
of oure lorde god enclosed yn to þe and thyne vnkyndnesse ayen   arise þe m pa
to hym and but yf þou thinke alwey thys thyng os yf þou hast   mantel of mek
doo and þat þou doest and what sentence of some þou deser   nesse
uest therfore thou mayst not gete the mantel of my mekenes
for where to meked y me so moche or where of despised y
so moche grace but for y thought and knewe wele yf y
was right nought nor had right nought of my self · therfor
for y wolde not myn owne preysing but þe preysing and
worschip of hym only that was power and maker of all
therfor doughter flee þou to þe mantel of my mekenesse
and thenke and holde thy self a synner aboue all other
for þough þou see ony wykked · then wost not what
schall come on to hem to morowe Also þou wost not yit
what entent nor with what knowyng þei do it whether
it is of feeble or of purpos · therfore preyse thi self to
fore none and thou offist to deme none in thyn herte

Oure lorde Ihū gyft techith vs to meke vs in fowre maners
The sone of god spekith on to seint Augustine and saith
yf þou desire to meke the m fowre man wyse first
anemptz hem that haue power by estat or by office m þe
worlde for aþe man despisid and lefe to obeye god · it
is worthie þat he obeye to man · And for folke molde not
be with oute gouūours · therefor yeuence and worschip·
must be yone to þe power · Seconde þou most meke the
anemptz hem that bene pouere goostly that is to seye · anemptz
synneres prayeng for hem and thankyng god for m happes
thou art not · me hast be noon suche · Thirde anemptz hem
that bene riche goostly that is to sey · anemptz þe frendes of god
thankyng thy self onwerthy to seyne hem or to be conuersant
amongst hem fowrthe anemptz þe pore of þe worlde helpyng
hem and clothyng hem and wasshyng her feet ·

Oure lorde Ihesu Crist ansuerith and seith: I am with-outen begynneng and withouten ende. And alle thinges that are arne made by my power; all thinges arne disposed by my wisdom and all thinges arne gouerned be my doome and wille; and alle my workes arne ordeyned by charitee. Ther-fore to me is right nought impossible. But that herte is ouer-harde that nothir loueth me ne dredith me, sith I am gouernoure of all þinges, | and Iuge. And ȝit man fulfilleth rathir the wille of þe deuell, whiche is my turmentour and a deceyuour, whiche yeueth oute venym largely by the worlde, for which soules mowen not lyue, but thay arne drouned doune in-to the deth of helle. This venomos synne, which, though it be bitter vn-to þe soule, ȝit to many it sauoreth swetly, and eche day it is drowe oute of þe deuels honde vpon moche people. But whoo herde euere ony[1] suche thingis, that lyf is offred vn-to alle, and thai chesen rathir deth þan lyf. Neuertheles I, God of alle, am pacient and haue compassion of her wrecchidnesse. For I doo as a kyng þat sendith wyne vn-to his seruantis and saith: 'Brille it forth to many, for it is holsom. It yeueth helthe vn-to þe syke, myrthe vn-to hem þat bene heuy, and a manful hert to them þat bene hoole.' Bot ȝit þe wyne is not sente but by an able vessell. So I haue sent my wordes, whiche arne likned to wyne, vn-to my seruauntes by the, that art my vessell, whiche I wille fille and drawe oute aftir myn owne wille. Myne holy spirit shall teche the wheder thou schalt goo and what þou schalt saye. Ther-fore speke thou ioyfully and with-oute fere tho thinges that I bidde the; for there is none that schall preuayle ayenst me.

Thanne ansuerde the spouse, seint Birgitte: O king of all glorie and blisse, yeuer of all wisdom and graunter of all vertues, why takist thou me to suche a werk, that haue wasted my body in synnes? I am as an asse, lewde and vnwyse and defectif in vertues; and I haue trespassid in alle thinges and no thyng amendid.

Oure lorde Ihesu Cryst answerde: if money or othir metall be presented vn-to a lorde, who schulde meruaille, though he | made hym there-of crounes or ringes or peces to his owne profite? So is it not to meruaille though I resceyue þe hertis

---

[1] MS. ony *inserted above line.*

of my frendes presented vn-to me, and doo my wille in thaym.
And for as moche as one hath lesse vndirstonding and anothir
more, there-for I vse the conscience of eche as is expedient to
my worschip. For the herte of a rightfull man is my money;
therfor be thou stable and redi vn-to my wille. 5
Than[1] spak the modir of God to seint Birgitte, sayeng:
What sayen þe proude wommen in thy kyngdome?
Saynt Birgitte ansuerd: O lady, I am one of thaim, and
ther-fore I am aschamed to speke in thy presence.
Than sayde the modir of god: though I knowe it better þan 10
thou, ȝet I wole here it of the.
Saynt Birgitte ansuerde: whanne, sche saith, verray mekenesse was prechid to vs, we seide that oure progenitours
enherite vs, and yaue vs in heritage large possessions and fayre
nortur of maneres and condicions. Why ther-fore schulde I not 15
folue them? My modir saat with the first and the highest and
was clad and arrayed noblely, hauyng right many seruauntes
and norsshyng thaim with worschip. Why schulde I not also
enherite suche thinges to my doughter, whiche hath lerned to
bere hir noblely and to lyve with bodily ioye and to die with 20
grete worschip of the worlde?
The modre of God ansuerd: iche womman that hath thise
wordis and sueth hem in dede gooth by the verry way vn-to
helle. And ther-for suche ansuere is full harde. What profiteth to haue suche wordis, whan the maker of all thinges 25
suffred his body to abyde and duelle in erthe with all mekenesse fro the tyme of his birthe vn-to his deth, and there come
neuere cloth of pride vpon hym. For-sothe, suche wommen
considren not his face, how he stoode lyvyng and dede vpon | the
crosse, blody and pale for paynes; nor that rekken not of his 30
repreues whiche he herde, nor of his despisable deth whiche he
chees; nor thei haue not in mynde the place where he ȝaaf vp
the spiryt, for where theues and robbers had resceyued many
woundes, there was my sone wounded. And I, that to-fore all
creatures am moost dere vn-to hym, and in me is all mekeness, 35
was there present. And there-fore thay that done such proude
and pompous thinges, and yeuen othir occasion to folue thaim,
bene liche vn-to a sprenkle; whiche, whanne it is put to

[1] *Marg. gloss*: Oure lady and saint Birgitta.

a brennyng licour, it brenneth & defouleth alle theim that it
sprenklith. Right so the proude ʒeueth ensample of pryde,
and full greuously they brenne soules by euel exsamples.
And ther-fore I wil now doo as a good modre whiche, fering
5 hir children, makith hem to see þe rodde, whiche the seruauntes
seeth also. But the children, seyng the rodde, dreden to offende
hir modre, thonkyng hir that sche wolde threten hem and not
bete thaim. The seruauntes dreden to be beten yf thay tres-
passe. And so of þat drede of the modre the children doon
10 moo good dedes than they dedyn to-fore, and the seruauntes
doon lasse euell. So sothly, for I am modre of mercy, ther-for
I wole schewe to the the rewarde of synne, that the frendis of
God may be more feruent in the charitee of God. And synners,
knowyng thaire perell, flee synne, atte leest, for drede. And
15 on this manere wyse I haue mercy bothe of good and euel; of
the good peple, that thay obtene and gete more croune and
reward in heuen; of the wicked, that thay suffre lasse payne.
And there is none so moche a synner, but þat I am redy to
helpe hym; and my sone to yeue hym grace, yf he aske mercy
20 with charite.

Aftir this, there appered three wymmen:[1] that is to sey,
the modre, and the doughter, and the nyfte, that is, the
doughteris doughter. But the modre and the nyfte appered
dede, and the doughtir aperid o-lyve. The saide deed modre
25 se-|med to comme crepyng oute of a foule and derke clay diche; fol. 68 b
whos herte was drawe oute of hir body, hir lippes kut of, and
hir chyn tremeled; hir teth, schynyng, white, and longe,
grinted and chatred to-gidres; hir nose thrilles weren all-to
gnawe; hir eyghen put oute, hangyng doune on hir chekes
30 betwene senowes; hir forhed was holowe; and instede of hir
forhed was there a grete and derke depnesse. In hir hede the
hede panne fayled and was away, and the brayne boyled vp as
it had be leed, and flowed oute as blak picche. Hir nek turned
a-boute as a tree that is turned in the instrument of a turnour,
35 ayenst whiche was sette an Irne alther sharpest, kittyng and
shaving away with-outen ony comfort. Hir breste was open
and full of wormes longe and smale; and eche of thaim
walowed hider and thider vp-on othir. Hir armes were liche

[1] *Marg. gloss*: the apperin[g] of thre wym[men].

vn-to the haftes or handlis of a grynding stone. Hir hondes weren as keyes full of knottes and longe. The chynes of hir bak weren alle dissolued, eche from othir; and one goyng vp, anothir goyng doune, they cessed neuere of mevyng. A long and a grete serpent come forthe by the nethir partie of hir stomak vn-to þe ouerparties; and ioyneng the heed and taylle to-gidre as a rounde bowe, wente rounde aboute hir bowels continuelly, as a wheel. Hire hippes and hir legges semed as two roughe staues of thorne full of prickes moost sharpe. Hir feet weren as it hadde bene toodes.

Thanne[1] this dede modre spak vn-to hir doughter þat was o-lyve, sayeng: here thou, alto torne and my venomos doughtre. Woo to me that euere I was thy moder. I am sche that sette the in þe nest of pryde, in whiche thow, maad hoo[t],[2] waxist til thou come to age. And þan it was plesyng to the that thou haddist spent thyne age in that nest. Therefor I say to the that as often as thou turnest thyn eyhen with lokyng, or sight of pryde whiche I taught the, so ofte castist thou boyling venom in myn | eyghen with vnsuffrable brennyng hete. As often as thou spekest wordes of pride whiche thou lerndest of me, so often swalowe I moost bitter drinke. As often as thyne eren arne fillid with wynde of pryde whiche the wawes of arrogance and pryde exciten and stiren vp in the, that is to say, to here praysinges of thyn owne body and to desyre worschippes of the worlde, whiche thou lernedest of me; so often cometh to myn eres a feerful and dredfull soune, with wynde blowyng and brennyng. Woo there-fore to me, poure and wrecched: ther-fore poore, for I haue nor fele right nought of good, and ther-for wrecched, for I haue habundaunce and plentee of all euell. But thou, doughtir, art liche vn-to the taille of a cowe whiche, goyng in foule claye, as often as sche moeueth hir taille, so often sche defouleth and bys[p]renglith[3] thaim that been nye aboute hir. So thou, doughtre, art lyke vn-to a cowe; for thou hast not no goodly wisdom, and thou

---

[1] *Marg. gloss*: the dede modre and the doughter o-lyve.

[2] MS. maad hood; *Latin* in quo calefacta crescebas, donec ad aetatem pervenisti.

[3] MS. bystrenglith; *Latin* aspergit. *Cf. N.E.D.* bespringild (c. 1440); *the* g *is influenced by M.E.* besprenge[n], *to besprinkle.*

The Revelations of Saint Birgitta 109

goest aftir the werkes and sterin*ges* of thy body. Ther-for as
often as thou foluest the werkes of my custome, that is to say,
tho synnes which I taught the, so often is my payne renewed,
and the more greuously it brenneth vp-on me. Ther-fore, o þu
5 my doughtre, why art thou proude of thy generacion and
ky*n*ne? For it be honour and worschip vn-to the that the
vnclennesse of my bowelles was thyne pilowe, my schamefull
membre was thyne oute goyng, and the vnclennesse of my
bloode was thy clothinge whan thou were bore? Ther-for now
10 my wombe, in which thou lay, is alto eten with wormes. But
why, doughtir, playne I vp-on the, whych I aught more to
playne vpon myself? For thre thynges ther arne that turmenten
me moost greuously in myne herte. The first is that I, maad
of God to heuenly ioye, mysvsid my conscience and haue dis-
15 posed me vn-to the sorowes of helle. The seconde is that God
made me fayre as an aungell, but I deformed and haue forschape
my-self so that I am more | liche vn-to the deuel than to an   fol. 69 b
aungel of God. The thridde is þat in the tyme youen to me,
I made a full euel chaunge. For I resceyued a litil thing
20 schort and transitorie, that is to say delectacion of synne, for
whiche I fele now endles euel, that is, þe payne of helle.

Thanne[1] saide this deed modre vn-to the spouse of Cryst,
saint Birgitte: thou, sche saith, that seest me, seest me not
but by bodily liknesse. For yf thou schuldest se me in that
25 fou*r*me in whiche I am, thou schuldest dye for drede; for alle
my membres arne deuels. And there-for the scripture is trewe
that saith that as rightfull men arne membres of God, so
synners arne membres of the deuel. Right so haue I now in
exp*e*rience that deuels arne fastned vn-to my soule; for þe
30 wille of my herte hath disposed me vn-to so moche filthe,
deformyte, and myschap. But here now furthermore. It
semeth to the that my fete arne as toodes. That is for I stode
stablely in synne; there-for now fendes stonden stablely in
me. And alwey bytyng and gnawyng me, thai arne neue*r*e
35 full. My legges and my thyes arne as staues fulle of prickyng
thornes, for I hadde a wille aftir flesshly delectacion and myn
own lust. That iche chyne of my bak is loose, and eche of
hem moued ayenst othir; that is therfor for the ioye of myn

[1] *Marg. gloss*: [t]he dampned [m]oder spekith to [S]aint Birgitte.

herte sometyme went vpward ouermoche for wordly solace and
comfort, and somtyme ouermoche dounward by to moche
heuynesse, grucchyng, and wratthe for aduersitee and disease
of the worlde. And therefor as the bak is moued and sturid
after þe moeuyng of þe hede, so aught I to haue be stable 5
and moeuable aftir þe wille of God, which is heed of all good.
But for I did not soo, there-for I suffre rightfully these paynes
that þou seest. That a serpent crepeth forthe by the lower
fol. 70 a parties of my | stomak vn-to the hier parties, and standyng as
a bowe turneth aboute as a whele, thore-for it is for my lust 10
and delyte was inordinat; and my wille wolde haue had alle
worldes goodes in possession, and in many wyse to haue spent
hem, and vndiscretly. Ther-for now the serpent serchith
aboute myn entreils withoute comfort, grawyng and byting
with-outen mercy. That my brest is open and alle-to gnawe 15
with wormes, that schewith the verray rightwisnesse of God;
for I loued foule and roten thinges more þan God; and þe loue
of myn herte was all youen to transitori and passing thinges
of the flesshe and the worlde. And there-for as of smale
wormes arne brought forthe lenger wormes, right soo my 20
soule; for the foule stinking thinges that I loued is fulfilled
with deuels. Myn armes semen as they were haftes; that is
for I hadde my desyre as two armes; þat is to say, for I desyred
long lyf, that I myght haue lyued longe in synne. I wolde
also and desyred that the dome of God had be more esy than 25
the scripture saith. Neuertheles, my conscience tolde me wele
that my tyme was schorte and þe doome of God vnsuffrable.
But ayenward my desyre and delyt that I had to synne stired
me to thenke that my lyf schulde be longe and the doome of
God suffrable. And of suche suggestions my consciens was 30
subuerted and turned vp so doune, and my wille and reson
folued lust and delectacion. And ther-for now the deuell is
moeued in my soule ayenst my wille, and my conscience
vndirstondith and feleth þat the dome of God is rightfull. My
hondes arne as longe keyes. And þat is for the preceptes and 35
comaundementes werne not delitable to me; and therfor myn
handis arne to me now grete birden, and to noon othir vse.
fol. 70 b My necke is turned aboute as a tree | that is turned ayenst
a scharpe yren; that is for the wordes of God weren not swete

The Revelations of Saint Birgitta

vn-to me to swalue and taste thaym in the charitee and loue of myn herte; but thay weren ovir bitter, for thai argued and repreued the delectacion and wille of myn herte; and therfore now a scharpe Iren stondith ayenst my throte. My lippes arne cutte of, for they werne redy to wordes of pride, vayne, gameful, and vnhonest; but naughtfull they weren and full irkesom to speke the wordes of God. My chynne apperith tremelyng, and my teeth grintith and betith to-gidre; that is for I was of full wille to yeue mete vn-to my body, þat I myght seme faire and desirable, hoole and stronge to alle the delites and plesaunce of the body. And there-for now my chynne tremlith and quaketh with-oute comforte, and my teth beten to-gidre; for all þat thay wasted was but an vnprofitable labour as to þe fruyt of the soule. My nose is cutte of; for as amongest you it is wonte to be do vn-to thaym that trespassen in suche a caas to thaire more schame, right so is the mark of my shame sette vpon me endelesly. That myn eyghen hange doune bytwene senowes vp-on my chekes, it is rightfull that right as the eyghen ioyed of the fairnesse of my chekes for ostentacioun and schewyng of pryde, so now of moche wepyng thay arne putte oute and hange doune to my chekis with schame and confusion. And right wisly is my forhed holowe, and in-stede of it there arne grete derknesse. For aboute my forhed was sette the veyle and the arraye of pryde; and I wolde appere gloriouse, and be seen of fairnesse, and seme fayre. And ther-for my forhed is now derke and foule, deformed and misseshape. That my brayne boyleth vp and flowith oute as leede and picke, it is wel worthy. For as lede is softe and may be bowed aftir the wille of hym that vsith it, right so my conscience, whiche lay in my brayne, was bowed to þe wille of myn herte, although I vnderstode wele tho thinges þat |[1] I fol. 71 a schulde haue doo. And the passion also of the sone of God was no thinge fastned in myn herte, but it flowed owte as a thynge that I knewe wele and toke none hede of. And furthermore, of þat holy blood that flowed oute of the membres of þe sone of God, I toke no more kepe than of picke, and fledde as picke þe wordes of charitee and of the loue of God, lest they schulde turne me or trouble me from the delites of

[1] I schulde haue *catchword*.

the body. Neuertheles, oþere while I herde the wordes of God for schame of man; but as lightly as thay entrid, so lightly thay went oute of myn hert ayene. And therfor now my brayne flowith oute as brennyng picke, with moost hoot boylyng. My eres arne stopped with harde stones, for woordes of pride entrid in thaim ioyfully, and softly and suetly they wenten doune in-to the herte, for the charitee of God was sperd oute of my herte. And for þat I did all that I myght for pryde and for the worlde, ther-for now ioyfull woordes bene sperd oute from myn eeres.

But thou may aske yf I did ony meritorie or goode dedes. And I aunswere the I did as doth a chaunger of money, which clippeth or kitteth the moneye; and sith resigneth or taketh it ayen to the lorde þat oweth it. So I fasted and did almes and suche othir goode werkes; but I did hem for drede of helle, and for to escape thaduersitees and disease of the body. But for the charite and the loue of God was kutte of from my workes, therfore such workes werne not vaillable to me for to geten heuen, although thay ware not with-outen reward. Thou myghtest also aske hou I am with-inforthe in my wille, whan so moche foulnesse and mysshappe is with-outeforthe. I answer: my wille is as the wille of a mansleer or of hym that wolde gladly slee his owne modre. So I coueyte and desyre the worst euel vn-to God, my maker, which hath be to me best and moost swete.

fol. 71 b Thanne the dede | nyfte,[1] þat is, the doughtres doughter of the same deed Beldame, spak vn-to hir owne modre that was ʒit than o-lyve, sayeng: here, thou scorpion my mooder, woo to me, for thou haste euel deceyued me. For thou scheudest me thy mery face, but thou prickedest me ful greuously in myn herte. Thre counsails thou yaf me of thy mouthe, thre thinges I lerned of thy workes. And thre wayes thou scheudest me in thy processe and forth goyng. The first counseill was to loue flesshly for to gete carnall loue and flesshly frenschip. The second was to spende temporall goodes ouere largely for worschip of the worlde. The thridde was to haue reste for delectation and delyte of the body.

These counsailles weren to me ful noyous and grete hind-

[1] Marg. gloss: [s]pekith vn-to hir modre.

ringe. For I loued carnally, ther-fore haue I now shame and spirituel enuye. And for I spent wastfully temporell goodes, therfor was I pryued of grace and the yeftis of God in my lyf, and aftir my deeth I haue goten me grete confusion and shame.
5 For I delited in the quyet and rest of the flesshe in my lyf, therfore in the houre of my dethe began vnrest of my soule with-outen comfort.

Thre thinges also I lerned of thy workes. The first was to doo somme goode dedes, and neuertheles vse forthe and not to
10 leue þat synne that delyted me: as a man shold doo that delid hony with venym, and offerd it vn-to a Iuge; and he, therby moeued to wratthe, shedde it vp-on hym that offerid it. So am I now experte in many-folde anguysshe and tribulacion.

The seconde is þat I lerned of the a merueillous manere of
15 clothinge me; that was to hille myn eyghen with a kerchif, to haue sandales on my | feet, gloues on my hondes, and the necke all nakid with-out-forthe. This kerchif hilling myn eyghen betokeneth fairnesse of my body, which so beschadowed my gostly eyghen that I toke none hede nor see not the fairnesse
20 of my soule. The sandals whiche kepen the fete vndirnethe and not aboue betoken the holy faith of the chirche, whiche I helde faithfully, but there folued it no fruytfull workes. For as sandals furtherne my fete, right so my consciens, stondyng in faith, promoted my soule. But for good workes folued not,
25 therefor my soule was as naked. The gloues on the hondes bitoken a veyne hoope that I hadde; for I extendid my workes, whiche arne tokened in the handes, in-to a so greet and large mercy of God, which is noted in the gloues, that,[1] whanne I groped the rightwisnesse of God, I felte it not nor toke none
30 hede there-of. There-fore I was ouer bolde to synne. But whan deth cam, than fille doune the kerchef from myn eyghen vp-on the erthe, that is to say, vp-on my body. And thanne the soule see and knewe it-self that it was naked, for fewe of my dedes weren goode, and my synnes weren many. And for
35 schame I myght not stonde in the paleys of the endles kyng of blisse, for I was schamefully clothed. But þanne deuels drowe me in-to harde payne, where I was scorned with schame and confusion.

[1] *Latin* quia.

The thridde thinge, modre, that I lerned of the was to clothe the seruaunt in the lordes clothes, and to sette hym in the lordis seete, and to worschip hym as a lorde, and to ministre vn-to þe lorde the releefs of the seruaunt and alle thinges that weren despisable. This lorde is charitee and the loue of God. The seruaunt is a wille to synne. Sothly in my herte, where owed to haue regned godly charitee was sette þe |seruaunt, that is, dilectacion and lust of synne, whomme I clothid thanne whan I turned vn-to my wille all temporall thing that is maad. And the releefs and the parynges and moost abiect thinges I yaue vn-to God, not of charitee, but of drede. So ther-for was myn hert glad of fulfilling and dilectacion of mine own wille, for the charite and the loue of God was excluded frome me, and the goode lorde spered oute and the euel seruaunt closid with-inne. Loo, modor, þise thre thinges lerned I of thy workes.

Thre wayes thou scheudest me also in thy forthegoyng. The first was bright. But whan I entred in it, I was blendid of þe brightnesse there-of. The seconde was compendiouse and sleper as Ise, in whiche, whan I wente oo stappe forward, I sloode ayene bakward an hool paas. The thride way was ouer longe, in whiche, whan I wente forthe, ther come aftir me a scharpe rennyng floode and baar me ouer vnder an hille in-to a depe diche.

In the first way is noted the forth-goyng of my pryde, which was ouere bright; for the ostentacion and schewyng which proceded of my pride shined so moche in myn eyen that I thought not the ende of it, and ther-for I was blynde.

In the seconde way is noted inobedience[1] in this lyf is not longe; for aftir deth a man is compellid to obbeye. Neuertheles, to me it was longe, for whan I went oo stappe forward in mekenesse of confession, I slood bakward a paas. For I wolde þat the synne confessid schulde haue be foryoue, but aftir confession maade, I wolde not flee þe synne. And therefor I stode not stably in the steppe of obedience, but I slode ayene in-to synne, as he þat slideth vpon yse; for my wille was coolde and wolde not aryse and flee froo tho thinges þat delited me. So therfor whan I went | a steppe forward shryuyng of

---

[1] MS. in obedience.

The Revelations of Saint Birgitta 115

my synnes, I slood a paas bakward; for I wolde falle ayene to thoo synnes and dilectacions that delited me, of whiche I was confessid.

The thridde way was that [I][1] hooped a thinge which was 5 impossible; that is, to mow do synne and not to haue longe payn; to mowe also lyue longe, and the hour of deth not to nyghe. And whan I went forthe by this way, þere cam after me an hasty rennyng floode; that is to say, deth, whiche froom oo yere to anothir caught me and turned my feete vp so doune 10 with payne of syknesse. What were these feete, but, whan syknesse come vp-on, I myght litill take hede to the profyt of the body and lasse to the helthe of the soule? Ther-for I fille in-to a deepe diche, whan my herte that was high in pride and harde in synne braste, and the soule fille doune lowe in-to the 15 diche of peyne for synne. And therfor this way was longe; for aftir þe lyf of the body was ended, anoon ther began a longe peyne. Woo, therfor to me, my modre; for alle thoo thinges that I lerned of the with Ioye, nowe I wayle hem with wepyng and sorowe.

20 Thanne spak this same deed doughter[2] vn-to the spouse of Cryst, saint Birgitte, whiche sigh all þise thinges, sayenge: here thou that seest me. To the it semyth that myn hede and my face is as it were thondre, thondri*n*g and leuennyng with-inne and with-oute; and my necke and my breste as it were putte 25 in an harde presse, with longe sharpe prickes; myn armes and my feete arne as it were longe serpentes; and my wombe is smyte*n* with harde hamers; my thyes and my legges arne as it were flowing water oute of the goters of a roof; and my fete allto frore to-gidre. But ȝet ther is oo payne with-inneforthe | 30 that is bitter[3] to me than alle thise. Right as yf ther were ony fol. 73 b persone of whom alle the brethes of his leving spiritis weren stopped and alle the veynes, fulfilled with wynde, arted hem vn-to the herte, whiche for violence and strengþe of thoo wyndes schulde begynne to breste; so am I disposed with-35 inneforth ful wrecchidlye for the wynde of my pryde, whiche was to me full dere beloued. Neuertheles, ȝit I[4] am in the waye

[1] *Latin* sperabam.
[2] *Marg. gloss*: The deed nyfte spekith to saynt Birgitte.
[3] *Latin* amarior.   [4] MS. I I.

of mercy, for in my moost greuous syknesse I was shryve in
the best wyse I coude, for drede of peyne. But whan deeth
came neer, than com to my mynde the consideracion and
beholding of the passion of my God, hou that was moche more
greuous and more bitter than all that I was worthy to suffre
for my synnes and demerites. And with suche consideracion,
I gate teeres and wepte waylled that the charite and the loue
of God was so moche to me and myn so litil to hym. Than I
behelde hym with the eyghen of my conscience and saide: 'O
lorde, I beleue the, my God. O thou sone of the virgine, haue
mercy vp-on me for thy bitter passion ; for now from hens-
forward wolde I amend my lyfe, yf I hadde tyme, full fayne.'
And in that poynte of tyme was ther accendid and kyndelid in
myn herte a sparcle of charitee, by whiche the passion of Cryst
semed more bitter to me þan myn owne deth. And so than
brast my herte, and my soule come in-to the hondes and power
of deuels to be presented in the doom of God. Therfor it come
in-to þe hondes of deuels, for it was not worthy that the
aungels of fairnesse schulde come nere the soule of so moche
foulenes. But in the doome of God, whan the deuels cryed
and asked that my soule schulde be dempte and | dampned
vn-to helle, the Iuge ansuerde : 'I see, he saith, a sparcle of
charite in the herte whiche owith not to be quenched, but it
most bee in my sight. Therfore I deme the soule vn-to purgacion, vn-to þe tyme that it be so worthely purged and made
clene that it deserue and haue foryefnesse.'

But now myght thou aske yf I schall haue parte of all the
goodes and goode deedes that be done for me. I aunswere the
by a lyknesse. Right as yf þu see two balaunces hange, and
in that one were naturelly bering dounward and in the tothir
were some light þing goyng vpward, the gretter thinges and
fayre that were put in the voyde balaunce, so moche the rathir
scholde þai lifte vp the tothir balaunce þat is hevy and of grete
weight. Right so is it with me ; for the depper that I was in
synne, the more greuously am I goo doun into payne. And
therfor what euere be doo to the worschip of God for me, it
liftith me vp from peyne ; and specially that prayer and good
that is doone be rightfull men and the frendes of God, and
benefetes þat be doon of wele goten goodes and dedes of

charitee. Such thinges, sothly, thay bene that maken me eche daye to nygh more nerre to God.

Aftir this spak the holy modre[1] of God vn-to the spouse of Cryst, saint Birgitte, and saide: Thou meruaillest how I that am Quene of heuen and thou that lyuest in the worlde and that soule that is in purgatorye and that othir that is in helle speken to-gidre. This schall I wele tellen the. I, sothly, goo neuere from heuen, for I schall neuere be departid from the sight of God. Nor that soule þat is in helle schall not be departed from payne. Nor that soule that is in purgatorie, nothir, til it be clene purged. Nor thou schalt not come to vs to-fore the departyng of thy bodily lyfe. But thy soule with thyn vndirstonding, by vertue of the spirit of God, is lyfte vp to here the wordes of God in heuen; and thou arte suffred to knowe som paynes in helle and in purgatorie, for warnes | and fol. 74 b amendement of euel lyuers and to the comforte and profyte of thaim that bene good. Natheles, knawe thou that thy body and thy soule arne Ioyned to-gidre in erthe, but the holy gooste that is in heuen yeueth the vndirstonding to vndirstonde his wille.

Aftir this, this thridde womman that was o-lyve lefte all the worlde and entred in-to Religion, and lyved all hir lyf aftir in grete perfeccion and holynesse.

How our lady tellith saint Birgitte of the doome of Sir Charles hir sone; and what allegeaunce oure lady and his good aungel made to-fore Cryste for his soule; and what the feende allegged ayenst the soule; and of the sentence that Cryst yaf for deliueraunce of the soule. Revelations, Book VII, Chap. 13.

Owre lady saint Marye speketh vn-to saint Birgitte and saith: I wole tell the hou I did to the soule of Charles thi sone. When it was departid from his body, I did as a womman that standith by another womman whan sche childeth, to help the chylde that it dye not of flowyng of bloode ne be not slayne in that streight place were it cometh oute; being also ware that the childes enemyes that bene in the hous slee it not. On the same wyse did I; for I stode nygh the saide sone a litel to-fore he yaf vp the spirit, that he schulde not haue no flesshly

---

[1] *Marg. gloss*: Oure lady a[pperith] ayene vn-to s[aint] Birgitte.

loue so in mynde that it schulde cause hym to thenke or say onythinge ayenst God ; nor that he schulde wille leeue¹ ony thinges that weren plesing to God ; nor wille to do tho þinges that myght in ony wyse be contrarie to the wille of God and hindring to his soule. I halpe hym also in that straite place 5 þat is in the goyng oute of the soule from the body ; so that he schulde not suffre so harde payne in deeth that schulde cause hym to be vnstable or to dispeire in ony wyse, ne þat he schulde not foryeten God in his dyeng. I kepte also his soule in suche wyse from his dedly enmyes, that is to say, from 10 fendes, that none of hem myght touche it. But anoone as it was goo oute from the body, I toke it in-to my keping and |
fol. 75 a defence. And than alle the company of feendes hastely fledde and wente awaye, which of thaire malice desireden to haue worwed the soule and euerlastyngly to haue putte it in tor- 15 ment. But how the doome was of the soule of the same Charles after his deeth, it schall be schewed the plainly whan it pleseth me.

Thanne, aftir a fewe dayes, oure lady saint Marie appered vn-to saint Birgitte wakyng in prayer, and sayde : now it is 20 leeful vn-to the, by the goodnesse of God, to see and to here how the doome was doo vp-on the saide soule whan it was departid from the body, and that that was done thanne in a momente of tyme, that is, in a right schort whyle, to-fore the vnspecable magestee of God schall be schewed vn-to the by 25 order and by layser, by bodily liknesse, so that thyne vndirstonding may conceyue it.

Thanne anoone saint Birgitte was rauysshed into a grete and fayre paleys, where sche sigh oure lorde Ihesu Crist sitting to deme as a crouned Emperour, with vnnumerable company of 30 aungels and sayntes seruyng hym. And by hym sche sigh standing his moost worthy moder, listnyng vn-to the doome. It semed also that a soule stoode a-fore that Iuge in grete feere and dreede, and naked as a childe than bore, and as it had be blynde in all wyse, so þat it sigh nothing in conscience. But 35 ȝit it vndirstode what was saide and done in the paleys. There stode also an aungel on the right syde of the Iuge by the soule,

¹ *Latin* vellet omittere.

The Revelations of Saint Birgitta 119

and a feende on the lefte syde. But neither of hem touchid the
soule nor come nye it.

Aftir this the feende cried and saide: here tho, almyghty
Iuge. I playne to-fore the that a womman, which is bothe my
5 lady and thy moder, whom thou louest so moche that thou
haste made hir myghty a-boue heuen and erthe and a-boue vs
alle feendes of helle; for sche hath do me wronge and vnright
of this soule that stondeth now here. For I aught of right to
haue take this soule to me anoone aftir it was | goo from the fol. 75 b
10 body, and with my felaschip to haue presented it vn-to thy
doome. And loo, thou rightfull Juge, that womman, thy
modre, toke this soule in-to hir stronge keping or it was fully
oute of his mouthe, and hath brought it vn-to thi doome.

Thanne the holy virgine, oure lady saint Mary, modir of
15 God, aunsuerd thus: here myne ansuere, thou deuel. Whan
thou were maade, thou vndirstode that rightwisnesse þat was
in God euerelastingly with-outen begynnyng. Thou haddist
also free choys to do what the list beste. And though thou
chees rathir to hate God than to loue him, yet thou vnder-
20 stondist welle alwaye what owith to be doo aftir rightwisnesse.
Therefor I say to the that it longed more to me than to the to
presente this soule to-fore God, verray Iuge. For while this
soule was in the body, it hadde grete charitee and loue vn-to
me, thenkyng ofte in his herte that God vouched sauf to make
25 me his modre, and þat he wolde enhaunce me hye a-boue alle
thinges that he made. And for this cause he began to loue
God with so moche charitee that he said thus in his herte: 'I [1]
ioye so moche that God loueth the virgen Marie his modre
a-boue alle thinges that there is no creature nor bodily delite
30 in this worlde that I wolde chaunge for that ioye; but I schuld
preferre that ioye to-fore alle erthely delytes. And yf it were
possible that sche myght be hindrid in the leest poynte from
that worthynesse that sche is inne anempst God, I schulde rathir
chese to me in letting there-of to be tormentid euerelastingly in
35 the depnesse of helle. And therefore endles thonkyng and
euirlasting blisse be vn-to almyghty God for þat blissid grace
and grete glorie that he hath youe vn-to his moost worthy

[1] *Marg. gloss*: (*in different hand*); [marke] how thu shall [loue o]wre
lady.

modre.' Ther-for, thou deuel, see now with what wille this knight dyed. And what semeth the; whethir was it more right that his soule scholde come in-to my | defense to-fore the doome of God, or to thyne hondes, wikkedly to be tormentid? The feende aunsuerde: it is not my right that that soule that loueth the more than it-selfe schulde come to myn hondes or than the doome be youe. But though thou haue oo right to doo this grace with hym to-fore the doome, yet aftir the doom be youe, his werkes schulle deme hym to myne hondis to be punisshed. Now, thou Queen,[1] I aske of the why thou drofe so alle vs fendes from the presence of his body in the passing of the soule that none of vs myght make there ony horrour, ner bringe hym in no feer ne drede. The virgin Mary aunsuerde: that did I for that brennyng charite and loue that he hadde vn-to my body and for the ioye that he hadde that I was the moder of God. Therfor I gat hym that grace of my sone that none euel spirit schulde come nerre hym where euere he were, nor ȝit where he is now.

Aftir this, the feend spake vn-to the Iuge and saide : I know wele that thou arte rightwisnesse and power. Thou demest nomore vnright to the deuell than to an aungel. Deme þou ther-fore and dampne this soule to me. In that wisdome þat I hadde whan þou madist me, I haue write alle his synnes. I haue also kepte alle his synnes in that malice þat I hadde whanne I felle from heuen. For whan this soule come first to suche age of discrecion that it vndirstode wele that it was synne that it dide, than his owne wille drow hym more to lyve in wordly pryde and flesshly delite than to withstonde suche thinges.

The aungell aunsuerde:[2] whanne his modre vndirstode firste that his wille was flexible and redy to bowe to synne, anoone she socoured hym with workes of mercy and longe prayers that God scholde vouche sauf to haue mercy vp-on hym, that he fille not ferre from God. And by[3] thise[4] workes of his moder

---

[1] *Marg. gloss in different hand*; marke this qu[estion] of þe feende [and owre] ladysse aw[nswere] þer to.

[2] *Marg. gloss in later hand*; Marke how þe [modres] prayers purchesyth /disposicion to [contri]cion of hyr [sone].

[3] for *cancelled, and* by *written above by hand that made marginal glosses.*

[4] i *changed to* o *by same hand that made marginal glosses.*

he gat the drede of God, so that as often as he felle in-to synne,
anone he hastid | hym to schryve hym therof.
The feende ansuerde: me behoueth to telle his synnes. And
anone as he wolde haue be-gonne to telle, he began to crie and
5 waille and to seke besyly in hym-selfe, bothe in his heede and
in alle the membres that hym semed to haue. And it semed
that he alle-to trembled and schoke, and of grete trouble he
cryed: allas and woo vn-to me, wrecche. How haue I loste
my long labour? For not onely I haue loste the texte, but
10 also all the matere is brente where-inne alle thing*es* werne
writen. The matere betokneth the tymes in which he synned,
where of I haue nomore mynde than of the synnes þat weren
writen there-inne.

The aungell aunsuerde: this haue wepi*n*ges and longe labour
15 of his modre and many p*r*ayers doo; so that God, hauyng compassion of hir wailinges, yaue hir sone suche grace that for eche
synne that he did, he gat contricion and made meke confession
of godly charitee. And ther-for tho synnes arne foryete and
putte oute of thy mynde.

20 The deuel aunsuerde, affermyng that he hadde yet a sak full
of writing*es* of suche sy*n*nes as the knyght hadde purposid to
haue mendid, but aft*er* he tooke no kepe thereof. And ther-
fore he most be tormentid til he haue I-done satisfaccion by
payne for suche synnes as he amendid not in his lyfe.

25 The angell ansuerd: open thy sak and aske me dome of tho
synnes for whiche thou moste chastice hym.

Thanne the feende cryed as he hadde be woode, and saide: I
am spoiled in my power; for not only my sak is taken a-weye
from me, but also the synnes that weren ther-inne. This sak
30 was slouþe, where-inne I putte alle his synnes that I most haue
punished hym fore. For for slouthe he lefte many goode dedes
vndone.

The aungell aunsuerd: The teres of his modre haue spoiled
the and broken thy sak and distroied thy wryting, so moche
35 hir teeres plesed God.

The fende ansuerde: yet haue I here some thinges to say
ayenst hym; that is to say, his venyal synnes.

The aungel ansuerde: he gate a wille to goo on | Pilgrimage
oute of his contree, leuyng his goodes and his frendes, visiting

holy places with many labours. And thise he fulfilled in dede. He arraied him also in suche wyse that he was worthy to resceyue indulgence and pardon of holy chirche. And he desired to plese God, his maker, by the amendement of his synnes. Wherefor alle thoo causes that thou saist that thou haste write arne foryoue.

The feende ansuerde: yet, at the leest, I moste punische hym for suche venial synnes that he did, for thay arne not alle done away by indulgences; for they arne thousand thousandes whiche arne writen in my tonge.

The aungel aunsuerde: putte oute thi tunge and schewe thy wryting.

The feende ansuerde with grete yellyng, wailyng, and cryeng, and saide: allas and woo vn-to mee, for I haue not oo worde to speke; for my tunge is cutte a-way by the rootes with all his strengthes.

The aungel aunsuerd: that hath his modir do with hir besy prayers and labour. For sche loued his soule with alle hir herte. And ther-for, for hir charitee, it hath plesed God to foryeue alle his veniall synnes that he did from his childehode vn-to his dethe. And therefore thy tonge is withouten strengthe.

The fende aunsuerd: yet haue I oo thinge bisely kepte in my herte that may not be done a-way. And that is that he gate thinges vnrightfully, not takyng hede to restore thaim.

The aungel aunsuerde: his modir dide satisfaccion for suche thinges with almes and prayeris and dedes of mercy, so that the rigour of rightwisnesse bowed it vn-to the softnesse of mercye. For God yaue him a parfyte wille, with-oute sparing of alle his goodes, to doo full satisfaccion aftir his power to thaim fro whom he had take ony thinge vnrightfully. And this wille God acceptith for theffecte of dede, for he myght lyue no lenger. And there-fore his heires most do satisfaccion for suche thinges to thair power.

The feende aunsuerd: than, yf I may not punysshe hym for his synnes, yet | me behoueth to chastice hym; for he did not goode workes and vertuos aftir his power, whan he hadde full witte and hoole bodye. For vertues and good workes arne that tresour that he schulde bere with hym to suche a king-

The Revelations of Saint Birgitta 123

dome; that is, the gloriouse kingdome of God. Suffre me therfore to fulfille with payne that that faileth hym in vertuose workes.

The aungele ansuerde: it is I-write that to the asker it schall
5 be youe and to the knocker with perseueraunce it schall be opened. Here, therfore, thou fende. His modir knocked for him at the yate of mercy perseuerantly with prayers of charitee and dedes of pitee more than thritty yere, weping many thousand teres that God scholde vouche sauf to yeue the holy goost
10 in-to his herte, so that he schulde with glad wille yeue his goodes, his body, and his soule to the seruyce of God. And so God did. For this knyght was made so feruent in charitee that it pleasid him to lyve for none othir thinge but for to folue and to doo the wille of God. For God was prayed so longe
15 that he yaue his blessid spirit in-to his herte. Also the virgyn Mary, modir of God, yaue him of hir vertue alle that failed hym in goostly armure and clothing þat longen vn-to kynghtes whiche schullen entre in-to þe kyngdome of heuen vn-to þe hye and soueraigne Emperour. Saintes also þat bene in þe kyng-
20 dome of heuen, whiche this Knyght loued leuyng in the worlde, haue youen hym comforte of thair merites. For he gadred tresour as thoo pilgrymes that chaungen euery day temporal goodes into euerelasting richesses. And for he did soo, therfor he schall haue ioye and worschip euerelasting;
25 and specially for that feruent desyre þat he had to goo on pilgrimage to the holy citee of Jherusalem; and for he desired feruently to haue yofe his lyf in bataile that the holy lande myght be reduced vn-to þe lordeschip of cristen men, so þat the glorious sepulcre of God myght be had in due reuerence, End of
30 yf he had be sufficient to haue brought it aboute. And | fol. 77 b

British Museum MS.
Julius F. II, f. 238 b, 1. 14 ff.

[And] þerfore, þou deule, þu has none right to fulfelle tho thinges þe whech personally he did nat. Than þe deul hering
35 þat cried impaciently and rorid: wo to me! for all myn memory is ablat fro me. For I have for-getyn his name.

The aungel ansuerd: his name is callid in heuen 'the son of teeres'.

The deul cried and seide: O cursid be þat modir of him þat had so gret a wombe þat so meche water was in. And cursid be she of me and all myn felaschep.

The aungil ansued: Thin curs is the Honour of God and blissing of all his frendis. 5

Than Crist the iuge spac thus, seinge: Thou deule, go thin way. Furdermore he seide to þe knight: Come, myn wel belouyd.

And so a-noon the deule fled.

Than the spowse seeing[1] these thinges, she seyd: O ever- 10 lasting vertu and in-comprehensibil, þu myn lord Ihesu Crist, thou yetes all good thoughtes to hertis with preyours and teeris. Therefore honour and grace be to þe of all thinges þat thou has creat. O þu myn suete God, þu art most deere to me and truely derer to me þan myn body or myn soule. 15

And þan the angel seid to þe spowse: thou owis to knowe þat this vision is nat only shewid of God to þe for thin comfort, but also þat þe frendis of God may vndirstonde what he wil doo for the prayours, wepinges, and laboures of his frendis, fol.239a þe whech prayours cheritefully for | odir men and laboris with 20 perseuerans and good wil. Thou may knowe þat þis knight thin sone shuld[2] not have had soche grace but that he had wil fro his youþe to love God and his frendis and to eschewe gladly fall of synne.

[1] MS. seinges.   [2] MS. sh shuld.

NOTES

1/1. The chapter headings in the Garrett MS. usually differ from the Latin text; these differences are not usually mentioned in the notes, as the headings do not form an integral part of the revelations. References to the Latin text are always to the 1628 edition of the Durantus (see Table of Abbreviations).

The literary independence and originality of Birgitta, mentioned in the Introduction, pp. xxvii–xxviii, is more fully discussed in a letter written by Knutt B. Westman to Bishop Wordsworth, and printed by him (John Wordsworth, *The National Church of Sweden*, A. R. Mowbray & Co., 1911):

'Unfortunately the notices in this regard [about the books Birgitta studied or owned] are very few and not very significant. She has surely known the following books: The Bible; Historiae Scholasticae (which I suppose to be the Historia Scholastica by Petrus Comestor); Diologus Gregorii; Vitae patrum; Pseudo-Bernhard, Liber de modo bene vivendi, and Speculum Virginum (an ascetic book, later on translated into Swedish, now edited by Geete, Stockholm, 1897-8).

'There is scarcely anything more to mention, if not some Italian heretical and apocalyptic books—no doubt emanating from the Fratelli—which she disapproves (Bk. III, ch. 33; Bk. VI, ch. 67, ch. 68).

'So there is no explicit trace of any literary influence from any of the earlier female mystics. To the question whether any such influence on the text of the revelations—for instance, from Gertrude, or either of the two Mechthild's—is, on inner reasons, to be supposed, I would personally answer in the negative. At least, no such influence is needed to explain those rather unliterary writings of Birgitta. If there can be found any detail, a thought or parable or something like that, that could be best explained by supposing such an influence (a possibility which I do nôt deny, though I have not found any), it must always be remembered that Birgitta and the above-named mystics are religious types of a very different kind. They are ecstatic, with their visions centred around a bridal mysticism on the lines of Bernhard's Sermones in Canticum, partly (Mechthild of Magdeburg) also devoted to the metaphysical trend of Dionysius Areopagita and the Victorines. She, even in her visions, is prophetical and practical, intent on finding and interpreting the intensely active and world-reforming will of God. To this type belongs, for instance, Savanarola, and, in some degree also, Hildegard of Bingen.'

6/10. **enmy**: Latin, immitior, more harsh. Immitior was mistaken for inimicior by a Latin transcriber or by the translator.

8/29. **accipiunt**: Latin, recipiunt.

11/32. **and while he that**: Latin, qui. The translation is awkward, since this clause and the preceding one are correlative.

14/3. **enim** is not in the Latin text.

14/17. **fowle**: Latin adds 'ei', which clarifies the sense.

27/2. **profetying**: Latin, perfectio erit.

27/34. **seke**: Latin adds, id est verba consolatoria cum charitate Dei.

31/5. **goyng abowte seketh**: Latin, circumiens monticulos inquirit.

34/23. **apostata**: Latin, apostata. The form in the MS. is probably due to the Latin.

35/4. **for he yafe Ioyfully himself**: Latin, Nam ipsa gaudenter dedit seipsam mihi. Marie and Martha are feminine throughout in the Latin; but the translator evidently felt that as long as the two were considered abstractly, as typifying the contemplative life and the active life, they should have the masculine gender. But in the following passage (35/5-24), where the Bible story is retold and the two sisters are individualized, the translator uses *she* and *hyr*. The symbolization of the lives of Mary and Martha (vita contemplativa et vita activa) began very early in Biblical exegesis. Augustine (ser. civ. 4, Migne, *Patrologia Latina* xxxviii, col. 617) writes: Duae vitae in Martha et Maria figuratae... quae ambae fuerant Domino gratae... duas vitas esse figuratas, presentem et futuram, laboriosam et quietam, aerumnosam et beatam, temporatem et aeternam.

42/1. **What are thes**, &c.: Latin, Quid est Domini mei. Cumque Domini circumstantes quaererent. The translator or transcriber misunderstood the passage. Julius F. II. 226 b has 'What is it, myn lordes?'

42/23. **ethiope**: see 47/27: The ethiope betokeneth the fende. In medieval allegorical literature an Ethiopian often represents a devil or some particular sin. It is described in Birgitta's Life how, during a period of fasting and asceticism, an Ethiopian, Castramargia, the devil of gluttony, sorely tempted Birgitta (S.R.S. iii, p. 201). Palladius (*Paladii Helenopolitani episcopi Historia Lausiaca*, ed. J. Meursius, iii, p. 427) narrates a vision of Saint Antonius which is probably the earliest medieval vision in which the judgement of souls is seen by an onlooker (*Die lateinischen Visionen des Mittelalters bis zur Mitte des 12. Jahrhundrets*, C. Fritzsche, *Romanische Forschungen*, iii, p. 264). Antonius, while praying to God, sees two souls, the one of a just and the other of a wicked man, stand before a black giant. The soul of the just man flies upward and becomes an angel, but that of the wicked man is struck down by the black giant into the sea (hell). Rabanus Maurus, archbishop of Mainz (*Allegoriae in universam sacram scripturam*, Migne, *Patrologia Latina*, cxii, col. 918), gives the following definition: Ethiopes sunt peccatores. Original as Birgitta is in her numerous descriptions of hell and purgatory, she undoubtedly owes much to the rich store of such visions which were so popular in the Middle Ages.

44/9. **lie**, MS. **be**: Latin, Scriptura dicit, quae mentiri non potest. *lie* and *be* are written very much alike; the scribe probably read incorrectly.

44/24. **mych lasse**, &c.; i. e. they are of much less avail in doing away his sins.

45/1-3. **hauynge ... with-oute þe**. A difficult passage: Latin, nihil habens diminutum in te, nec transmutabile, sicut decet Deum, extra te nihil absque te, quod gaudium habeat.

48/2. **limbus**. Cf. Durantus i, p. 324, note 5: subtus terram esse quattuor sinus, siue vnum in quattuor partes divisum, quorum omnium in praesenti Capite mentio sit: primus quidem & infimus Infernus dicitur, & locus est pro damnatis constitutus; secundus est Limbus puerorum, ad

Notes 127

quem decedentes sine Baptismo paruuli cum solo originali peccato eunt, ibique morantur ; tertius Purgatorium vocatur, in quo tandiu manent animae quamdiu pro commissis culpis diuinae iustitiae satisfecerint, & postmodum ad Dei visionem assumuntur; quartus locus dicitur Limbus Patrum, seu Abrahae sinus, qui erat constitus pro iustis, qui ante Christi Domini Passionem moriebantur.

50/3-4. The English translation incorporates in its chapter heading part of the revelation itself. The Latin text begins : Item loquitur Angelus, dicens.

50/22. moste = especially : Latin, maxime.

50/28. after this. . . . In the Latin text, Bk. IV. 9 begins here.

51/17. There is no break in the Latin text at this point ; the chapter heading and the following chapter of the English translation form the remaining part of Bk. IV. 9.

59/1. my frende, thy fader : Father Matthias, Birgitta's confessor and adviser (Durantus i, p. 115, note 2). Birger died in 1328 (S.R.S. iii, p. 188, note e), long before this was written.

60/9. the mynde on his werkes : Latin, recordatio operum eius.

60/25. fullfylly[ng] : praeter eius expletionem. According to N.E.D., *fulfilment* does not occur until 1775, nor does the form *fullfylly* occur ; the form *fulfyllyng* is common in the 15th cent. (cf. 60/13).

63/11. the yate of hell. The Latin adds : & eripuit amicos suos. Aperuit & Coelum laetificans Angelos, introduxit in eum ereptos de Inferno.

65/3. and of ane one he makyth a secunde : Latin, & de inimico facit amicum.

66/8. they : Latin, prothoplasti, the first created beings.

71/18. of the realme. The Latin adds : Si ergo talis homo sustineatur, & toleretur, damnabitur respublica, invalescet discordia, & intestina mala adaugebuntur in Regno.

73/1. for þer is not, &c. The translation is not clear ; Latin, nec est aliquis, qui non visitatur a Deo quamdiu viuit.

76/20. for this sowle hath l[o]ved þat is voyde : Latin, Quia ista illud quod vacuum est dilexit.

90/30. verteu, trowth, & rightwysnes. There is an influence here of the widely spread allegory of the Four Daughters of God, Misericordia, Veritas, Justitia, and Pax (Hope Traver, *The Four Daughters of God*, Bryn Mawr, 1907 ; and an article with the same title, P.M.L.A., 1925, xl, pp. 44-92). The *virgyn* here represents Misericordia (180. 16) ; *verteu* takes the place of Pax. The allegory usually concerns itself with the redemption of mankind, which is discussed by God, the Four Daughters, and sometimes by the Virgin Mary and the devil. An interesting variation of this theme is found in a story by Cesarius of Heisterbach : *Exemplum de quodam homine per multa mala opera a diabolo ducto ad iudicium dei, quem sancta Maria, Veritas, et Justitia a diabolo acceperunt.* A man burdened with sins is carried in a vision before the judgement throne of God, where the devil demands the surrender of the soul to him. Through the active aid of the Blessed Virgin Mary, whose assistance is implored by Veritas and Justitia, the soul is saved. The general similarity of this story to the revelation of

Birgitta is apparent ; but the two differ entirely in detail. The influence
of the allegory on Birgitta is not close, and possibly she was not conscious
of her indebtedness.

98/12. þat was brighter : Latin, quae erat. Refers to the Virgin.

100/10. kyng Saules doughter. Birgitta's memory of the Bible here
plays her false. Saul's daughter, Michal, was not a widow when David
married her (1 Samuel xviii. 27, xxv. 44).

107/23. doughteris doughter. The Latin has only *neptis* ; evidently
the scribe felt that *nyfte* required explanation. Cf. also 112/26 and
Glossary.

111/6. naughtfull : Latin, accidiosa, which Du Cange glosses molestus,
tristis, taediosus.

116/29. balaunces. In medieval depictions of the last judgement the
sins and good deeds of the soul are often weighed in a pair of scales. An
example of this is in the trance of Piers Toller (*North-English Homily
Collection*, G. H. Gerould, 1902, p. 56).

The devil often attempts to make false accusations against the soul,
either bringing up sins which he has expiated or fabricating sins which he
has not committed. See 119/3 ff. and Book VII, ch. 13 (Durantus ii,
p. 214) : Respondit Diabolus, Nam si ego possem aliquid ad eius imper-
fectionem fabricare, hoc libenter facerem. A. Maury (*Recherches sur
l'origine des représentations figurées de la Psychostacie ou Pèsement des âmes et sur
les croyances qui s'y rattachaient* in *Revue Archéologique*, 1844, vol. i, pp. 235-49,
291-317) makes a study of the origin and widespread use of the scales
motive. He assembles a number of very interesting illustrations in art
and literature of the belief in psychostacy and describes the various
trickeries to which the devil resorts, only to be defeated in his purpose of
capturing the soul by the Blessed Virgin Mary or some saint.

116/27-117/2. Birgitta often told anxious inquirers the condition of
their friends or relatives in purgatory, and what means would lighten
their punishment. ' Nam sepissime accidit, quod alique persone rogabant
eam cum deuocione et caritate, ut ipsa oraret deum pro ceteris animabus
aliquorum suorum defunctorum, et si ei videretur, quod essent in purga-
torio et loco quo egerunt suffragiis, quod ipsa eisdem viuentibus hoc
interrogantibus diceret et notificaret, per quas elimosinas et sacrificia aut
per qualia viuorum suffragia ab illis penis poterant liberari ' (S.R.S. iii,
196-7).

117/24. The chapter heading in the Latin (Durantus ii, p. 210) is of
interest : Haec sequens revelatio facta Dominae Brigittae sponsae Christi
incoepit in Neapoli statim post mortem Domini Caroli militis filii sui, &
continuebatur visio ista per viagium Hierosolymitanum interpolatim,
donec accessit ad Hierusalem, & ibi fuit finita in Ecclesia Sancti Sepulchri
Domini. . . . (A summary of contents similar to that in the Garrett MS.
follows.)

117/37-118/1. flesshly loue. Margaret Clausdotter, abbess of Vadstena
(*Chronicon de genere et nepobibus sanctae Birgittae*, S.R.S. iii, p. 212) tells of the
circumstances preceding the death of Charles. Birgitta, accompanied by
Birger and Charles, her sons, Catherine, her daughter, and other devoted
friends, stopped at Naples in February of 1372 on their way to Jerusalem.

Notes

Joanna, the beautiful and licentious queen of Naples, received the aged Birgitta and her band at her court. Birger paid the customary ceremonious homage before the queen's throne. When Charles's turn came he also knelt before her; but then, impressed by the queen's beauty, he rose from his knees and kissed her soundly on the lips. Instead of being offended, Joanna immediately became enamoured of the reckless young knight; within a few days she proposed marriage to him. Birgitta was highly indignant, not only because Charles was already married, but because of Joanna's very worldly life. She implored the assistance of heaven with fervent prayers; her request was granted, for Charles suddenly became sick and died after an illness of two weeks. Birgitta had a number of revelations after this, in which she denounced Joanna in no uncertain terms (Bk. VII, ch. 11).

120/28. **wordly pryde.** Margaret Clausdotter (*op. cit.*, S.R.S. iii, p. 211) says that Birgitta presented her two sons to Pope Urban V. Birger was dressed modestly in a long gown; Charles was attired in the costume of a knight, wearing an ermine cloak, skins of animals, and a heavy silver belt. The Pope, looking on them, said to Birger, 'Thou art thy mother's son'. Turning to Charles, he said, 'Thou art a son of the world'. Then Birgitta fell on her knees before the Pope and implored the remission of their sins. The Pope lifted the belt which Charles wore and said, 'It must be sufficient penance for him to wear this great weight'. Birgitta replied quickly, 'O Holy Father, take from him his sins, and I shall take away the belt'.

124/24. **And.** The following leaf, the eighth leaf of the last gathering, has been cut off with some sharp instrument. Since *And*, at the bottom of fol. 77 b, is the beginning of a sentence, and since the remaining part of the revelation could easily have been finished on the next leaf (Durantus ii, p. 214), the revelation was in all probability completed by the scribe. The translation of the remainder of the chapter in Julius F. II, which somewhat abbreviates the Latin, is given in the text.

GLOSSARY

(The glossary is selective, and includes only unusual words and abnormal forms of words. Where the word is common or the derivation clear, no etymology is given. The equivalent, *as it appears in the Latin text of the Revelations*, is given when it clarifies the meaning or form of the word. When the designations of mood and tense are omitted, supply pres. ind.; when the mood only, supply ind.)

A

Abhorable, *adj.*, detestable : 60/31. First example in N.E.D., 1633.
Ablat, *p.*, ablated, taken away : 123/36. First example in N.E.D., 1542.
Accendid, *p. p.*, set on fire, kindled : 116/13.
Accion, *n.*, legal process, the taking of legal steps to obtain judicial remedy : 89/25. Lat. *actori*.
Aggrege, *inf.*, aggrieve : 76/12, 85/6 ; *p. p.*, **aggreged**, 84/11. O.F. *agregier* ; Lat. *aggrauare*.
Alther, *adj.*, of all, gen. pl. ; 58/35 ; **althir**, 104/31.
Alto, *adv.*, wholly, completely : 108/12 ; **allto**, 115/29. See N.E.D. under All, C. 14, 15.
Alyene, *v.*, alienate, estrange, transfer (property or ownership) : 91/37 ; *p. p.*, **alyende**, 2/21.
Anenste, *prep.*, before, regarding, against : 28/33, 51/27, 79/1 ; **anempst**, 103/35, 104/4, 7, 8, 10, 119/33. O.E. *on efen* ; Lat. *coram*.
Arted, 3 *pl. pret.*, restrained, pressed : 115/32. Lat. *arctarent*.
Ascapeth, 3 *s. pres.*, escapeth : 70/2.
Assissours, *n.*, assizers, sworn recognitors : 8/23.
At, *conj.*, that : 26/10, 49/18, 65/27. O.E. *þæt*; a worn-down form, perhaps from O.N. *at*, used in same senses, or perhaps independently developed in No. dialects (N.E.D.). Lat. *quod, quae*.
Auovterer, *n.*, adulterer : 42/24. O.F. *avoutre*.
Auter, *n.*, altar : 14/2; **awter**, 36/36, 94/26. O.F. *auter* ; Lat. *altar*.
Ayane-byer, *n.*, saviour, redeemer : 3/13 ; **ayane-byar**, 78/2; **ayaynebyer**, 16/37, 83/9. Lat. *Redemptor*.

B

Baptem, *n.*, baptism : 36/17, 76/36.
Bedell, *n.*, beadle : 94/7. O.E. *bydel*.
Beld, *p. p.*, built : 9/10 ; **beldyng**, *pres. p.*, 9/10 ; **byld**, *inf.*, 67/36. Lat. *aedificare*.
Beldame, *n.*, grandmother : 112/27. Lat. *auiae*.
Besyly, *adv.*, attentively, carefully : 121/5 ; **besily**, 101/18 ; **bysely**, 22/27.
Blesful, *adj.*, full of blessing : 104/35. Lat. *benedictus*.
Bode, *p. p.*, commanded, proclaimed : 3/35, 97/28, 30. O.E. *bēodan*.
Bodely, *adv.*, boldly : 51/9. Lat. *audacter*.
Borione, *inf.*, bud or sprout : 22/9. O.F. v. from *borjon*, a bud ; cf. F. *bourgeonner*. Lat. *germinare*.
Bosn, *n.*, bosom : 72/29, 79/18. O.E. *bōsm*.
Brede, *n.*, breadth : 74/35, 83/33, 85/29. O.E. *brǣdu* ; Lat. *latitudinem*.
Brille, 2 *pl. imper.*, pour out : 105/19. O.E. *byrlian*.
Byshede, *p. p.*, drenched, moistened : 47/6. M.E. from *be +shed* ; Lat. *circumfusa*.

C

Caryth, *v.*, carrieth : 3 *pl.*, 22/30; 3 *s.*, 22/31. Lat. *promoveant*.
Cheker, *n.*, ex-chequer : 91/29 ; **escheker**, 72/10. O.F. *eschekier* ; Lat. *Fiscalium*.
Choweth, 3 *s. pres.*, **cheweth** : 59/26.
Chynes, *n.*, chines, backbones : 108/2.
Clobbed, *p. p.*, knotted, pressed into a confused mass : 76/29. Lat. *conglobata*.
Coluer, *n.*, dove : 8/16. O.E. *culfre*.

132   Glossary

Compuncte, *p.p.*, affected with compunction or remorse : 67/28, 74/19.
Comynte, *n.*, commonalty, commonwealth : 91/15; coméntye, 93/35. O.F. *comunalte*; Lat. *communitatis.*
Correkke, *inf.*, correct : 91/33.
Cur, *n.*, care : 85/8. MS. *toke kepe and cur*; Lat. *curabit.*

D

Delices, *n.*, pleasures: 19/22. Lat. *delectabilitate.*
Dempte, *p.p.*, judged : 116/21.
Disperplyng, *pres. p.*, dividing, dispersing : 102/22. O.F. *desparpelier*; Lat. *distendentens.*
Dispocion, *n.*, abbreviated form of disposition : 50/5, 50/27, 52/33. Lat. *dispositio.*
Distrowble, *inf.*, disturb, trouble greatly : 71/17; 3 *s.*, distrowbleth, 18/11. O.F. *destrobler*; Lat. *persecutor, distendit.*
Dolly, *adv.*, sluggishly, slowly : 35/35. The first example in N.E.D., 1591. O.E. *dol*; Lat. *remisse.*
Dredeful, *adj.*, fearful, full of dread : 50/14. Lat. *timorosa.*
Dysperpeler, *n.*, disperser : 5/29. See disperplying; Lat. *dispersor.*

E

Elke, *pron.*, each : 21/28, 29. See N.E.D. ilk, a^2.
Endeles, *n.*, endlessness : 86/18. Only citation in N.E.D. is *endlesse*, used by Trevisa in 1398 as a quasi-substantive meaning arithmetical infinity. Lat. *aeternitatem.*
Enherite, *v.*, to make heir : 106/14.
Enmye, *n.*, enemy : 50/20 ; *pl.*, enmyse, 50/19 ; Enmyes, 99/16, 20. Lat. *inimicus.*
Entriked, *p.p.*, deceived, entangled : 84/26. O.F. *entriquer*; Lat. *implicati.*
Evyn cristen, *n.*, fellow Christian : 28/35 ; evyn crysten, 36/4 ; euyn cristen, 29/6; eyn cristen, 28/12, 28.

F

Farrer, *comp. adj.*, fairer : 22/36. Lat. *pulchrius.*
Fawtoures, *n.*, adherents : 9/6. O.F. *fauteur.*
Felde, *p.p.*, felt : 42/19. Lat. *expertus.*
Fered, *p.p.*, inspired with fear, terrified : 97/10.
Flayn, *p.p.*, flayed, skinned : 76/28. Lat. *decoriatum.*
Fonned, *p.p.*, to be foolish, infatuated : 56/26. M.E. *fonnen*; Lat. *infatuatus.*
Frelte, *n.*, frailty : 18/26 ; freltee, 21/2 ; freelte, 18/34.
(F)rosses, *n.*, frogs : 82/18. For MS. *throsses*, see article on frosh in N.E.D. No example of *throsses* for thrushes is given in N.E.D. Lat. *ranae.*
Fruyte, *v.*, bear fruit, fructify: 22/19.

G

Gameful, *adj.*, jesting, sportive : 111/6.
Glorifie, *n.*, glory : 55/35. Not in N.E.D. Lat. *Benedictum sit.*
Good, *n.*, God : 38/14 ; Gode, 50/33; Godd, 61/32, 64/29.
Goodely, *adj.*, Godly : 24/25 ; gudely, 24/36. Lat. *divinus.*
Goodhed, *n.*, Godhead : 86/23 ; godhod, 55/35.
Grinted,3 *pl.pret.*, ground or gnashed the teeth : 107/28; 3 *pl.*, grintith, 111/8. Lat. *collidebatur.*
Gurched, *p.p.*, murmured, grumbled : 28/16; *pres. p.*, gurching, 42/26; grucchyng, 110/3. O.F. *grouchier*; Lat. *murmurare.*
Gurcher, *n.*, grumbler : 33/8.

H

Happes, *pl. n.*, hap, fortune : in happes, perchance : 67/28, 102/7. O.N. *happ*; Lat. *forte.*
Heleth, *n.*, health : 76/10.
Helen, *inf.*, conceal, cover : 18/18 ; 3 *s.*, heleth, 17/37. O.E. *helian*; Lat. *restiant.*
Hely, *n.*, Elijah ; his translation is described in 4 Kings ii. 1-11 : 56/14, 19. Lat. *Helias, Elias.*
Hetee, *n.*, heat : 15/12.
Hevy, *v.*, make heavy, trouble ;

Glossary

3 pl., 28/22. O.E. *hæfigian*; Lat. *molestantibus*.

Hooles, n., holes : 65/11 ; howles, 65/9.

Horred, 3 pl. pret., trembled, quaked : 95/2. 'To abhor' is the only definition given in N.E.D., which has three quotations. Lat. *horrebant*.

Hossebond, n., husband : 1/22 ; hosbounde, 4/11.

Hungorie, n., 49/14.

Hylle, *inf.*, cover, conceal : 19/9 ; hille, 113/15 ; 3 s., hilleth, 53/18. M.E. *hulen*.

Hyued, p.p., raised, exalted : 87/14 ; heved, 58/2.

I

I-now, *adj.*, enough : 25/24 ; I-noght, 27/14 ; I-neught, 71/1.

Irn, n., iron : 43/2, 47/1, 79/31 ; irne, 72/1, 30, 79/11, 107/35 ; iren, 111/4 ; yren, 110/39.

J

Iaper, n., jester : 93/12. Lat. *ioculatori*.

K

Kitte, v., cut ; 3 s., kitte, 22/16 ; kitteth, 112/13 ; pres. p., kittyng, 107/35 ; p.p., kytt, 79/35, 80/2 ; kutte, 112/17 ; cutte, 111/5. Lat. *abscindere*.

Knawe, *imper. s.*, know : 117/17.

L

Lake, n., lack : 48/7. Lat. *defectus*.

Lefte, 3 s. pret., neglected or omitted to perform (some action, duty, &c.) : 104/1.

Lepe, n., hamper, basket : 27/29. O.E. *leap*; Lat. *sporta*.

Lett, *inf.*, impede : 32/30.

Lettruer, n., literature : 7/24 ; letruer, 15/32 ; lettrur, 16/16. O.F. *lettreure*.

Leuennyng, pres. p., levining, lightning : 115/23. Lat. *fulminans*.

Leving, pres. p., living : 115/31.

Love-drede, n., the fear that proceeds from love : 24/28.

Lowsed, p.p., loosed : 49/23. O.E. *losian*; Lat. *solui*.

Lyvelod, n., means of living :

66/27 ; lyfelod (Lat. *obventio*, revenue), 91/29. Lat. *victus*.

M

Maly[t]e, n., stomach : 77/28. MS. *malyce* ; see Godefroy, mailleite, mulete, *estomac*. Not listed in N.E.D. Lat. *visceribus*.

Maughtes, n., moths : 82/15.

Medeled, p.p., mixed, mingled in conflict : 86/17. Lat. *confusum*.

Merowth, n., marrow : 83/33. O.E. *mearh* ; Lat. *medulla*.

Morede, p.p., increased : 30/35.

Morentyde, n., morning time, dawn : 53/32 ; mornetyde, 49/36. O.E. *morgentīd* ; Lat. *aurora*.

Mowe, *inf.*, be able : 49/27, 74/25, 115/6 ; *inf.*, mow, 59/17, 115/5 ; 3 pl., mowe, 104/2 ; mowen, 105/11. Lat. *posse*.

N

Naughtfull, *adj.*, possessed of no value, useless : 111/6. Lat. *pigra*.

Negh, v., approach, come near to : *inf.*, negh, 4/2, 57/29 ; 3 s., neghe, 99/2 ; neght, 4/3 ; neghis, 89/1 ; 3 s. pret., neyght, 57/24 ; p.p., neghed, 88/36. From O.E. adv. *nēah*.

Neghtburr, n., neighbour : 14/35 ; neighburgh, 102/1.

Norsshyng, pres. p., nourishing : 106/18.

Nowe, n., that which is new : of nowe, with some change or alteration : 32/37.

Noyous, *adj.*, troublesome, injurious : 102/27. See nye.

Nye, *inf.*, annoy, injure : 89/7, 90/18, 92/15 ; 3 s., noyse, 14/20. O.F. *annoier, ennuier* ; Lat. *nocere*.

Nyfte, n., granddaughter : 107/22, 112/26. 'A niece' is the only definition given by the N.E.D. ; but here nyfte = *doughtres doughter* : 107/23, 112/26. O.E. *nift* ; Lat. *neptis*.

O

Oned, n., onehead, unity : 86/13. See onehead in N.E.D. Lat. *vnitatem*.

Oost, n., host : 65/34.

Or, *conj.* and *adv.*, ere, before : 14/33, 87/24. O.N. *ār*.

Ordinate, *adj.*, well-ordered : 26/26.
Orelege, *n.*, sun-dial : 69/1. Lat. *horologio*.
Owch, *n.*, necklace : 62/22. O.F. *nouche*.
Ower, *n.*, owner, possessor : 48/23. Lat. *possessori*.

P
Peronell, *n.*, St. Petronilla : 41/29. There is a M.E. *Legende of St. Petronilla* (*Lydgate Canon*, E.E.T.S., E.S., cvii, p. 266 ff.) in which the forms *Parnell* (l. 130) and *Pernell* (l. 157) occur.
Picke, *n.*, pitch : 111/28, 36, 112/4.
Poynte, *n.*, an instant of time : **in a poynte**, in a moment : 84/20. Lat. *in vnico puncto*.
Precypitacion, *n.*, action of hurling down : 65/33. Earliest definite example given in N.E.D., 1502 (1477 example questionable); earliest recorded use in this sense, 1607.
Pyght, *n.*, pith : 73/16. O.E. *piþa*. Lat. *medulla*.

Q
Queres, *n.*, choir : 56/17 ; **quers**, 56/33 ; **quores**, 56/7. Lat. *choros*.
Quyke, *adj.*, living : 20/21 ; **whykke**, 20/22 ; **qwhik**, 68/28 ; **whyke**, 77/1. O.E. *cwic* ; Lat. *viva*.

R
Reicetter, *n.*, resetter, harbourer of thieves : 5/29. O.F. *recetour*, derived from Lat. *receptorem*. Lat. *lacerator*.
Releefs, *n.*, leavings, remains of a meal : 114/4, 10. O.F. *relief*. Lat. *reliquas*.
Reperell, *inf.*, repair : 22/22. O.F. *repareiller* ; Lat. *repararet*.
Reynyng, *pres. p.*, running : 10/21. Lat. *currens*.
Roten, *p. p.*, root : 58/4 ; **roted**, 58/12. O.N. *rōta*; Lat. *radicor*.
Rowned, *v.*, whispered : 3 *pl. pret.*, 89/34. O.E. *rūnian* ; Lat. *sibilaverunt*.

S
Sacrede, *p. p.*, consecrated : 78/29. O.F. *sacrer* ; Lat. *consecratus*.
Saffren, *n.*, saffron ; used as an aromatic, pungent drug and spice in the Middle Ages : 39/5. Lat. *insipidus*.
Sake, *n.*, sack : 10/20.
Seriously, *adv.*, in order, in a series : 84/19. Lat. *seriatim*.
Seth, *conj.*, seeing that : 20/2.
Sewed, 3 *s. pret.*, petitioned, sued, made application before a court for some grant : 67/1. Lat. *insonuit*.
Singlarte, *n.*, singleness : 33/1. Lat. *singularitatem*.
Skyll, *n.*, skill, reason : 29/3ɟ. Lat. *ratione*.
Sleuth, *adj.*, slothful, slow : 91/17. Earliest example given in N.E.D., 1567. Lat. *remissior*.
Sliper, *adj.*, slippery : 68/3 ; **sleper**, 114/20. O.E. *slipur* ; Lat. *labilis*.
Slouthe, *n.*, sloth : 121/31 ; **slewth**, 16/12 ; **sloup̄e**, 121/30 ; **s[l]awth**, 27/37 ; **slewth**, from O.E. *slǣwþ* ; slouthe and **slawth** from M.E. *slāwþ*, from O.E. *slāw*. Lat. *segnities*.
Sowlle, *n.*, food, any kind of food eaten with bread : 13/21, 28 ; **sowle**, 16/1. O.E. *sufol* ; Lat. *edulium*.
Sparr, *inf.*, close, bar : 5/25, 24/35 : 3 *s.*, **speryth**, 25/1 ; *p. p.*, **sperede**, 24/12 ; **sperde**, 101/24 ; **sperd**, 112/9 ; **spered**, 114/14. O.E. *sparrian* ; Lat. *claudere*.
Sprenkle, *n.*, sprinkler, especially one for sprinkling holy water : 106/38.
Styede, 3 *s. pret.*, rose, ascended : 1/18. O.E. *stīgan*.
Sueth, 3 *s.*, followeth : 106/23. O.F. *suer* ; Lat. *sequitur*.
Superflew, *adj.*, superfluous : 34/37.
Swaged, *p. p.*, appeased : 52/13. O.F. *suager*.
Sweth, *n.*, Sweden : 86/36. Lat. *Suetiae*.

T
Thiresty, *adj.*, thirsty : 50/15 ; **thiristy**, 49/15.
Thrilled, *p. p.*, pierced, penetrated : 79/10.
Thruste, *n.*, thirst : 63/1.
Trauelowse, *adj.*, laborious : 22/24.
Tremeleth, *v.*, trembleth : 50/13 ; **tremlith**, 111/12 ; *pres. p.*, **tremelyng**, 111/8 ; *past ind.*, **tremeled**, 107/27.

Glossary 135

Tristyng, *pres. p.*, confiding : 4/11.
Troblesse, *adj.*, troubled, disturbed: 20/31. First example in N.E.D., c. 1. 449. Lat. *turbidam*.
Trusty, *adj.*, trustworthy : 4/14.
Trystely, *adv.*, confidently : 3/9.
Tyll man, *n.*, farmer, ploughman : 22/7; tylle man, 22/21. Lat. *excolentis, rustici*.

U

Vnlikely, *adj.*, dissimilar : 60/16. Not listed in this sense in N.E.D. Lat. *incomparabilis*.
Vnneth, *adv.*, with difficulty, scarcely : 11/4 ; vneth, 15/31. O.E. *uneāpe* ; Lat. *vix*.
Vnspectable, *adj.*, not able to be regarded, incomprehensible : 43/13, 45/8. Lat. *incomprehensibilem*.
Vsshe, *n.*, issue : 30/25; yshew, 31/13.

V

Venym, *n.*, venom : 72/25, 80/6, 80/8, 105/10 ; venem, 72/22 ; venum, 38/8.
Veyleable, *adj.*, beneficial, advantageous, efficacious : 14/31. Lat. *bona*.
Vowterer, *n.*, 4/11 ; *see* auovterer.
Vyce, *n.*, voice : 44/34. Lat. *voce*.
Vykked, *n.*, wicked : 21/25.

W

Wakernesse, *n.*, watchfulness : 25/8. Not in N.E.D. ; formed from the adjective *waker*. Lat. *vigilantiam*.

Warnes, *n.*, cautiousness, vigilance : 117/15. O.E. *wœrnes*.
Warr, *adj.*, cautious, ware : 27/13 ; war, 28/21, 32/21 ; whar, 23/12. O.E. *wœr*.
Wery, *adv.*, very : 98/4.
Wessell, *n.*, vessel : 72/24.
Weyte, *p. p.*, wet, moistened : 80/17. O.E. *wǣtan*; Lat. *intinxisset*.
Whele, *n.*, wheel : 70/10, 80/30 ; wheel, 108/8. Lat. *rota*.
Whenched, *p. p.*, quenched : 8/24.
Whiter, *n.*, quitter, pus ; 47/8. Lat. *sanies*.
Whykke, *see* quyke.
Whyt, *prep.*, with : 58/12.
Worde, *n.*, world : 28/33.
Wordely, *adj.*, worldly : 18/7, 23/20, 47/19 ; wordly, 101/21, 102/33, 120/28.
Worschip, *n.*, worship : 106/21 ; wyrshuppe, 7/34.
Woyce, *n.*, voice : 62/30.
Wratthe, *n.*, wrath : 113/12 ; wreth, 37/28.
Wroth, *adj.*, angry : 89/29.
Wrayste, *v.*, wrest, deflect from the normal state : 95/28.
Wyrschoped, *p. p.*, worshipped : 98/14.
Wyssemen, *n.*, wise men : 3/36. Lat. *sapientibus*.

Y

Yate, *n.*, gate : 63/11, 123/7.
Ympnes, *n.*, hymns : 43/22.
Ysache, *n.*, Hezekiah ; cf. Isaiah, chap. 39 ; the name of the king is in neither Durantus' Latin nor Klemming's Swedish text : 64/15.

The manufacturer's authorised representative in the EU for product safety is Oxford University Press España S.A. of El Parque Empresarial San Fernando de Henares, Avenida de Castilla, 2 - 28830 Madrid (www.oup.es/en or product.safety@oup.com). OUP España S.A. also acts as importer into Spain of products made by the manufacturer.
Printed and bound by CPI Group (UK) Ltd, Croydon, CR0 4YY

22/04/2026

02094916-0010